D1833250

MANY A HARD NUT

MANY A HARD NUT

Key Social Issues and Remedies

S. Ganesan M.A.

GYAN

Many A Hard Nut

Key Social Issues and Remedies

S.Ganesan M.A.

ISBN: 978-81-212-1097-3

All rights reserved. No part of this book may be reproduced in any manner without written permission.

Published in 2011 in India by
Gyan Publishing House
23, Main Ansari Road, Daryaganj,
New Delhi-110002
Phones : 23282060, 23261060
Fax : (011) 23285914
E-mail : books@gyanbooks.com
Website : gyanbooks.com

Laser Typesetting : Lucky Graphic, Delhi
Printed at : Chawla Offset Press, Delhi

CONTENTS

PREFACE

This book is a blend of fiction, facts, realities, incidents and information from various sources, including the media. The book focuses on some of the serious challenges, mankind is facing today. It consists of 15 chapters on diverse topics and is intended to impart moderate knowledge of several key issues at one go. Each chapter deals with a topic of crucial importance for safe and pleasant human life. Every subject has a social concern and background, and therefore, the matters conveyed have an impact on the lives of people at large. I have taken up among other things, the topics of food security, energy security, terrorism, global warming, racism, religious intolerance, human rights violations and crimes that torment society. I have also focused on corruption and scandals that are reigning and plaguing Indian democracy. Everyone has to learn from others' mistakes. We have to act and do things by knowing how we should not act and what we should not do. From this angle, I hope that the narration of adversities could phase out the flaws in offenders and pave the way for rectification of their misdeeds and reformation of society. Since it will be a Herculean task to retrieve the situation prevailing among those who are already steeped in vices and foibles, this book targets the younger generation, especially students to groom them as honourable citizens. The contents aim to edify them to cherish virtues and human values. The topics have been presented in the form of discussions between the protagonist and some experts in their respective fields. While analysing the problems of people, certain possible solutions to them have also been propounded. Some topics lay emphasis on social and administrative reforms, and evolution of good characters among people. Every chapter concludes with an element of comedy to keep the readers relaxed. I think that the matters dealt with, may enhance the general knowledge of the readers about most of the burning problems of these days. Besides, in the conext of globalisation, students need to hone their skills in English. Dr. Samuel Johnson has said, "If you can become a master of prepositions, you will be a master of English". Apart from an advice, the pioneer of English Dictionary has implied that correct use of prepositions require diligent study. Bearing this in mind, I have adopted written style of language in dialogue form too. The book could enable development of grammar and vocabulary. So, I hope this book will be beneficial to readers, especially those interested in matters of social concern and students pursuing their collegiate education.

Author

1

RELIGION AND CASTE SYSTEM

Ding-dong.................ding-dong......................ding-dong............

The peal emanating from the Government Higher Secondary School announces the time as 9.45 a.m. The sound's producer is akin to a chapel bell for the people of Madapuri, a large village on the threshold of upgradation into a town.

The students, teachers and staff assemble in the yard for traditional prayer. As two girl students sing the hymn, all others reverberate. Then the headmaster-incharge addresses the gathering:

"Dear colleagues and students!

I am delighted to introduce our new headmaster Mr. Mohan Das who has joined duty today. On your behalf, I am glad to welcome him and hope that he will lead our school to greater heights."

All the students, teachers and staff greet the new incumbent with acclamation. Mr. Mohan Das responds to them saying, "Thank you for your kindness and affection. Like all of you, I am also eager to make our school distinct. In order to achieve this goal, I seek sincerity and co-operation of everyone in this school. Most of the students aim to be present here on time. Unexpected hitches result in your late arrival which amounts to indiscipline. I therefore, like to advise you to be present here in time for the prayer and not on time. It is definitely possible if you start from your home a few minutes earlier. Such habit can avert your hurry and panic that might affect your health. If you have any grievance, please bring it to my notice during intervals. You may consider me as affable. Thank you all." The assembly disperses and all the students and teachers are heading for their respective classrooms.

The headmaster Mr. Mohan Das enters the classroom for + 2

(XII std.) students. All the students get up and stand in obeisance. They utter in one voice, "we are pleased to welcome you sir".

Headmaster : "That's very kind of you. I too feel rapture to be in your midst. Please sit down. You may be aware of my role as your class teacher. However, I shall teach only English for you and XI std. students, apart from my duties as headmaster of this school. I have ascertained that we have only one section in +2 consisting of 20 boys and 15 girls. Now, I wish you to introduce yourself one by one, stating your name and the place you are hailing from".

Beginning from the front row, every student makes a self-introduction. Then the headmaster continues :

"Let me take up the lessons from tomorrow onwards.Today we shall discuss some general matters.To be a successful learner, you must carefully listen to various teachings and get rid of your doubts then and there. Just consider learning as a way of spending your time. Studies are not a burden if you practise to relish and enjoy them. Profound concentration devoid of any distraction is a must while listening and reading. It will simplify the learning process and enable you score high marks in the examinations. Periodical revisions of the subject could sustain your memory. Regarding the strategies to face the examinations, I shall illuminate you at an appropriate moment. If you adopt these techniques, you can save time and need not be a bookworm always. In fact, I never like to be a pedant. Because syllabi-oriented education contributes only partly to the evolution of human personality, whereas worldly experiences complement this education and mould the learner into a matured humanbeing who can tackle the challenges of life. The preachments of preceptors and sages are vital to edify people in general and adolescents in particular, especially in the context of a threat of extinction to human virtues and values in today's world, which will have a disastrous bearing on future generations. To possess these traits, all the students should have wide exposure to the world swayed by dynamic advancements, mainly through the media. You must discuss global affairs and exchange views among yourselves and external friends. I hope you will agree with my stance on the matters that I have related."

Vijay : Your views are indeed plausible, sir.

Others : We will strive to follow your guidance, sir.

H.M.: That's good; thank you. Now, I shall put a question in

English grammar and another relating to general knowledge to each of the students. It is just to assess your standards. So, try to answer them.

Students : Okay, sir. We are ready to answer.

The headmaster puts two questions to every student and gets the answers. At the end of the exercise, he comments, "Your abilities in grammar which provides a solid foundation to brush up on linguistic skills, are commendable. But then again you are all lacking in general knowledge."

Margaret : Hitherto we haven't focussed upon that realm.

H.M.: Your candid statement and syntax deserve praise. You need not worry about your shortfall in general knowledge since there are several sources to hone that skill. Apart from mental faculties, physical stamina is also equally important. You must therefore, evince interest in sports and games. With this, I shall take leave of you today as the period is nearing end and your next teacher is due to arrive in shortly.

Vijay: Excuse me, sir. As the class pupil leader, I desire to put forth a plea on behalf of all the students of + 2.

H.M.: Oh, yes. You are welcomed to reveal your thoughts.

Vijay: We are all anxious to accord a reception to our new class teacher. We request you to kindly agree to our wish and attend the event.

H.M.: I respect your love for me and so feel no hesitation to attend it. When do you propose to arrange for it?

Vijay: If you have no inconvenience, we can arrange for it around 6 p.m. today. We shall request all other teachers to be special guests.

H.M.: It's nice. I shall stay here in the evening. I request you to make it a low-key affair and not a high-profile function. Be simple and not lavish in all your activities.

Students: Thank you, sir.

H.M.: Thank you, bye.

In the same evening, all the students of +2 assemble in the entertainment hall of the school. They have arranged to provide sweet, snacks, fruits, ice cream and coffee. All the teachers and staff join them by 5.45 p.m. The headmaster-cum-chief guest arrives sharply at 6 o'clock, and is applauded by all the students. A few boys and girls serve the dishes and the party moves at a snail's pace lasting about 45 minutes. Then Vijay, the class pupil leader, approaches the podium.

Vijay: On your behalf I adorn our headmaster-cum-class teacher with this garland. (He garlands the headmaster and all the students clap.) We all welcome him to be our foremost guide during this crucial period of our educational career. We wish him possess good health and success in all his endeavours.

H.M.: Thank you very much for your treat. Your overwhelming affection for me is heart-warming. You expect me to be your guide. You are all in the final year of studies in this school. My situation is analogous to yours because I too will be leaving this school next year. The only difference is that our destinations will not be alike. While you will pursue higher studies, I will be relieved on retirement. I have been transferred from other district and posted here on preferment given at the tail end of my service. So, as long as I am here, I will be not only your guide but also a senior friend. Usually my social sphere is not confined to, but transcends the academic compass. My reforming zeal inclines me to share others' views on national and global issues. I am also ardent to share the problems of those known to me. You may therefore, regard me as one among your family members. Thank you all once again.

The party formally comes to an end. However, the guests and hosts are yet to disperse. Some informal talks are going on among them.

Akash: Where are you residing, sir?

H.M.: After reaching here yesterday, I called on the Panchayat Board President. For the time being, I am keeping my paraphernalia in his office.

Vijay: Shall we try to secure a house for you, sir?

H.M.: No, thanks. The President himself has arranged an accommodation for me. After cleaning and white wash, it will be provided to me in a day or two.

Emili: When will you bring your family, sir?

A shock flickered across the headmaster's face, followed by a smile feigning pleasure and no words. Emili felt embarrassed. There was a lull in the interaction.

Abhinaya : (Breaking the silence) Sorry, sir. Is her question wrong?

H.M.: No; She is right in her thought while the lapse is on my part.

Vivek: Your statement is enigmatic, sir.

H.M.: Is it so? Playing it straight, I am a bachelor and my parents passed away many years ago.

Vijay: Alas! Do you manage with hotel food, sir?

H.M.: No; I have a boy with me. He would cook and render necessary assistance to me.

Vijay: Will he come here ere long, sir?

H.M.: He has come along with me. He is now staying in the Panchayat Office.

Vijay: Oh, God! As we had no inkling of his stay there, we have missed him for the party. Hello, Vivek........ Please remember to send a packet of tiffin for him. (Vivek nods) By the way, are you a confirmed bachelor, sir?

H.M.: It is not so. It was a dismal affair at an early age, in which I became a hapless victim of treachery.

Vijay : Were you jilted by someone, sir?

H.M: Not that; all that happened was a heart-rending episode.

Anand: We are avid for the details of what happened, provided it is not a covert matter.

H.M.: I am always explicit in all matters without any inhibition. So, I am not reluctant to divulge my personal affairs.

Vijay: Thank you, Sir.

H.M.: I was born and brought up in an agricultural family at a village near Chennai. I studied in the local school and then joined a College of Arts and Science in the city. After obtaining degree in English Literature, I pursued my studies in a College of Education and qualified for the post of graduate teacher. I registered in an Employment Exchange but there was no scope for early appointment. I desired to join postgraduate course but by that time, my sister's premature death plunged our family in grief and derailed my aspiration. After the lapse of a mournful period of six months, I got a job in a private school where I taught English for nine months. As I was on a paltry salary, my father asked me to quit my job. I acted accordingly and began to help him in our agricultural operations. Besides, I was studying to get postgraduate degree under Distance Education Programme.

As I frequented our land, I could see a girl–an agricultural labourer working along with her mother, very often. I came to know that her name was 'Chitra' when others called her. She was a handsome teenager but I was neither stirred nor had any inclination to date her. One day, there was no work in our land. However, I had asked Chitra and her mother to come for drying harvested groundnuts. But Chitra came alone at 9 a.m. and told me that her mother was indisposed. We both carried the bags of groundnuts out of our barn and spread the nuts sparsely over the threshing floor in our land. That scorching hot day was a boon to us but made me weary, especially because of missing my breakfast. Around noon, while rotating the groundnuts, I felt giddy and fainted on the threshing floor. When I regained consciousness after a few minutes, I found myself in the shade of a nearby tree. It was apparent that Chitra had sprinkled water onto my face, carried me by her arms, and laid me underneath the tree on her outer garment spread on the ground. She asked me whether I had my breakfast. As I replied in the negative, she said, "You swooned out of starvation and heat. I was startled by your sudden fall. I was at sea for a minute." Then I told her, "You are a strange doctor who first treated me in trance and took up the aetiology after I awoke. Usually aetiology precedes treatment but yours is a weird somersault." She questioned, "What treatment have I rendered?" I answered, "The super hydrotherapy, physio (physical) therapy and finally nature's (shade) therapy." Then she objected saying, "No; the final therapy is yet to be given on the basis of diagnosis." I reacted, "Have you got the drug for it? Why do you waste time?" Then her countenance blanched for a little while. After a pause, she replied, "I have the specific remedy, rather a panacea for you but I can't give it to you since I am not qualified to do so". Then I asked her to solve the mystery and show her panacea. She ran into the motor room, returned with her tiffin box and placed it before me. She said, "I am curious to provide this food for you but my hands are tied and you are also forbidden from having it”. As I asked her to give the reason for her contention, she retorted, “Have you no reason? Are you not aware of my wretched caste and untouchability?” Her questions resurrected Rabindra Nath Tagore’s ‘Prakriti’. But I was not a Buddhist monk like Ananda to whom Prakriti cited her low birth and initially declined to give water to slake his thirst. To illuminate Chitra, I expounded on egalitarian creed. After my persuasion, she cut a piece of plantain leaf and served food for me. My thoughts likened her act to Prakriti’s pouring of water into Ananda’s cupped hands after listening to his philosophy of human parity. After having lunch hosted by chitra and taking a short siesta on her outer garment itself, she suggested that I could return home. I agreed and left our land at 3 p.m., telling her that I would send my father to gather up and store the groundnuts with her assistance. When I reached home, my mother chided me for my late return to lunch. As I told her that I had had my lunch from Chitra, she was bellowing. Her stentorian outburst drew the attention of our neighbours and they were peeping at us through their windows. I felt embarrassed and remained sullen. She further warned me to keep ‘untouchables’ at a distance. She frowned at me as a disgraceful creature. At that moment, the great Tamil poet Subramaniya Bharati who faced discrimination at his own home for his close association with non-Brahmins came to my mind. The fact that she berated me with communal mindset triggered my contemplation of social evils. As the night closed in, my thoughts drifted into an obsession with the events of that day in the company of Chitra. She was reminiscent of Thomas De Quincey’s ‘Ann’ the miserable street girl of sixteen, on whose arms he himself fainted one night due to prolonged starvation at the age of seventeen, and who after gently laying him down, ran to get a glass of portwine and spices which revived his spirits. That sleepless night brought her closer to me. Since then I was enthralled by her leading to an inclination to meet her time and again in her solitude, which I either waited for or tried to create. My efforts came to fruition on several occasions and our meetings blossomed into love. Though I was ecstatic, Chitra was apprehensive of dire consequences. As days passed on, she turned tenacious to unite with me. with our close relationship, we began to ponder on our future course of action. I assured her to take her with me at any cost after securing a job for me preferably at a distant place. When our romantic relationship had passed six months, our link was brought to the knowledge of both the families by a busybody. Chitra’s parents had smacked her and stopped her work in our land. My father initially scolded me for my love affair and later advised me to avoid it citing social barriers. My conservative mother was whining persistently that my act was egregious. My maternal uncle who visited our home three days later, woke up to my love affair. He patiently paid heed to my desire to marry Chitra. As his response was hopeful to me, I requested him to help me in this matter. He assured me that he would support me to fulfil my wish and asked me to wait for three months and avoid meeting the girl. His words built up hope in my mind and I trusted him. He later got into a huddle with my mother in our backyard for a long time which I didn't eavesdrop. I thought that he was convincing her in my favour. He left for his native place the next day. Since my love affair triggered a shambles in our home, Since my love affair triggered a shambles in our home, I kept myself confined to home but having no words with my parents. My younger brother Ram, studying X std. then, served food to me in my room. After a week, I spoke to my father in a resolute mood asserting my firm desire to marry Chitra. Although he did not relish it, he capitulated to my will but floundered to tackle my mother. In the evening, he strove for coaxing my mother into giving her consent to my proposal by presenting his plausible exposition. Though he interceded with her on behalf of me, she was indifferent with grim countenance but was not infuriated. The change in her attitude raised my hope to succeed in my endeavour. Next day, she went to her brother's home and returned in the evening. At that time, I had no inkling of the motive for her trip in the context of my uncle's recent visit to our home. A week later, I received the call letter to attend an interview for the post of graduate teacher at a private High School in Bangalore, which I had applied for. The same day, I was walking towards our land after a gap of a fortnight. On my way, I had a hap to meet Chitra inadvertently while she was going alone to fetch water. She was astounded by our meeting. She hugged me and began to sob. I comforted and consoled her with an assurance that I would take her to Bangalore, exuding confidence to get my job there. Having no scope to lurk in that place, we diverged within five minutes. I left for Bangalore on the eve of my D-Day. After the interview, a member of the selection panel implied that I was chosen for the post. I was exhilarated because five other candidates had aimed for one post of 'English teacher'. The authorities generally told that the selected person would be informed soon. Mulling my conjugal life over in Bangalore, I travelled back home. When I alighted from the bus at my village, I felt exalted but ironically, the worst trauma awaited me. At the bus-stop, Gopal, a bosom friend of mine, related the whole episode to me thus:

"I am very sorry to tell this Mohan Das. After your departure day before yesterday, your uncle came here with a band of mercenaries. At his behest, those crooks stripped Chitra, paraded her along the street and she was also flogged. All the villagers remained mute spectators. Her parents who came to her rescue were also beaten. When I questioned them why they were behaving so savagely, they branded her a whore. When I asked your uncle to be scrupulous, he retorted that a Dalit girl had deprived his daughter of her right to marry you. Finally they led Chitra who was actually trembling with fear, to her home and intimidated her parents into vacating the village before dawn. Since she had suffered the humiliation of being divested of her attire, Chitra committed self-immolation that night itself. Knowing this tragedy, the wicked set her house ablaze while her parents were wailing beside her charred corpse, to project their twin crimes as a fire mishap. After burying Chitra's body in haste, her parents fled last night itself. The police formally visited our village, held an enquiry and recorded it as a fire accident. Your triumphant uncle and his confederates left by noon today. I have briefly informed Chitra's only brother now in Dubai, about the dismal incidents. I am really upset about your lover's fate. Please don't be heartbroken. I wish you to sustain your courage to face any challenge in life. Now, let us go to your home."

After hearing about the ghastly crimes that cost me my beloved's life, I felt completely shell-shocked. I was in the grip of an absolute mayhem. But two factors were clear to my mind. My mother had gone to meet her brother to devise an intrigue. Besides, my uncle from whom I expected support following his assurance, became a traitor to me because of his selfish aim to make me his son-in-law. With mental fatigue, I reached my home along with my friend Gopal. I decried my mother for having connived with my uncle to commit barbarous acts. I rebuked my father for turning a blind eye to the atrocious crimes. I was annoyed as he turned a deaf ear to my outburst. My outpouring of detestation of his reverse stance on my love affair and collusion with my mother to let my uncle carry out his sinister designs, evoked parental passion. Both my father and mother tried to defend their actions and mollify me. But I was on the brink of insanity. Chitra's cruel death on fire left everything blank and empty for me. I couldn't stay at our home anymore. As I began to pack my clothes and other things, my parents were bidding to prevent me from moving out. But I was in no mood for being yielding. Holding my suitcase in hand, I said to my parents, “I feel ashamed to be your son. Your duties are not confined to feeding and educating children. Parents must understand and recognize the feelings, aspirations and legitimate wishes of their children besides watching them to prevent from going astray. Those who conspire against the lawful desires of their children can’t have any parental privilege. You therefore, cannot claim to be my true parents just because I was born to you. Now, I vow never to see you again in my life. Henceforth I cease to be your legal heir. So, I am not entitled to anything in your possession. Don’t try to pursue me. Goodbye!”

I left home in a huff with my suitcase and Gopal accompanied me to the bus stop. On our way, he told me that he had remained silent because he didn’t like me to stay in our village for a few months. He spoke philosophically to assuage my feelings and encouraged me to secure my employment and prosper in my life. As he asked about my destination, I promised him to send my address on condition that he should not give it to anybody else. I took leave of him and proceeded to Bangalore. I booked a room in a lodge for three days and informed the school where I had attended an interview, about my stay in Bangalore. Next day itself, the management called me and handedover the appointment order. I joined duty immediately. It was a red-letter day for me. After two days, I occupied a room on monthly rent and dropped Gopal a line, giving him my new address. He was a permanent resident of our village having his own shop. He rarely wrote letters to me and I too sent him replies.After two years, he sent a telegram to me, informing my father’s death. I reached my village in a hurry and attended the funeral. As Ram was studying +2, I advised him to score high marks. Having no word with my mother, I returned to Bangalore at once and didn’t turn up for further rites. Eight months after my father’s death, my mother too died suddenly and I got the information from Gopal. I went to my village and arranged for cremation. I stayed there for twenty days and leased out our land to a tenant. Just then my brother Ram had completed + 2. Having nobody else in our family, I took him along with me to Bangalore. After publication of the exam. results, he got admission to an Engineering college with hostel facility in Bangalore. Thenceforth I used to visit our village once in a year to collect the rent for land. When I had completed 4 years of service in the private school, I got government appointment through Employment Exchange office. I was posted to a high school in Salem district and it was convenient for me to visit my brother often. So, I left the private school and joined the new post. After Ram got his B.E. degree, I arranged for his employment at a company in Bangalore itself. When I proposed for his wedding, he declined and insisted that I should marry first. But I was averse to marry any girl after having lost Chitra. A philosopher has said, "You may fall from a tree but not from love". Nobody can come to terms with the failure of love, if it is true. Shakespeare, while defining the qualities of love in his 116th sonnet, says that love is something unique which does not change in any circumstances. He adds that true love bears all travails and heads through struggles even upto ruins. In fact, the great dramatist-cum-poet refers to his love for his friend. If it is so strong, how potent should the true love for a girl be? The grievous injury inflicted on the heart by failure of love may be healed by the passing years, but the scar remains indelible until the last breath of the victim.It could be felt only by those who experienced such failure. So, I was obstinate to avoid my marriage. I therefore, persuaded Ram into marrying any girl of his choice. Finally he agreed and asked me to arrange for his marriage. I acted accordingly and his family was settled in Bangalore. I served in Salem district for three decades facing only a few local transfers. As I already told you, this is my first district transfer on promotion. Thank you for so patiently hearing about my personal life."

Vijay: Your ingenuous character is heart-warming but the heart-rending revelations have plunged us into sorrow. Obviously, caste is the factor that made your life tragic. Is caste a creation of religion?

H.M.: It is a complex subject. The pernicious scourge of 'caste' wrought havoc in various forms on the lives of crores of people in India. I am just one among them. Caste is not a product of religion barring Hinduism. Though there are some divisions in Christianity, they are not on the lines of caste. The caste divisions in Islam and Sikhism are latent and obscure. If we question any member of those religions about his caste, he identifies himself only in the name of his respective religion, and we are satisfied with his reply stating, "I am a Christian/Muslim/Sikh, etc." We are not inclined to probe into his caste because in these religions, caste has no importance and it does not create disparity among the people. But in Hinduism, nobody says "I am a Hindu", if asked about his caste and such reply does not satisfy anyone because caste is important and conspicuous in Hinduism.

Vijay: Do you mean that Hinduism is defective?

H.M.: Yes, of course. Hinduism has been safeguarding the caste system – a lethal social set-up for thousands of years, by means of doctrines, scriptures, religious practices and customs. For this, the Hindu Law is a strong defensive mechanism. In this regard, I would like to reflect some of the views of Dr. B.R. Ambedgar, a saviour of the downtrodden people and the chief architect of the Indian Constitution. He has said: "Religious principles are the basis for caste discrimination. The people following caste practices are not the offenders but only the religion which evoked the passion that 'caste is holy' is the offender. Hinduism has no general principles that are beneficial to all castes and all countries at all times. Hindus consider only the rules of Vedas or the morals viewed as rules, as religion. The people have no will to lead a moral life of their own spontaneity with freedom. Hinduism dogmatizes the people to abide by its laws and lead a life of slaves of the laws that are discriminatory to different castes. The people must be made to realize that it is not a religion at all but only biased laws framed with vested interests. Unless this is done, reforms towards a casteless society are not possible. A cruel and subtle device to rein back people and enslave them is called 'Hindu Civilization'. What else could be said about a civilization that has created a class of people and preached commission of crimes as their communal occupation for livelihood? By what other name could we call the Hindu civilization in which a group of people steeping in primitive savagery even in the midst of developing civilizations, has segregated another group of people in such a manner that they can't have rapport with the human society, and branded them 'untouchables'? Any activist of Hinduism does not seem to view the existence of such divisions as a matter of concern or shame. We desire Hindus to realize that this is a matter to be ashamed of and not to be proud of. The preachers of Hinduism having weird mentality are the cause of the religious emphasis that people should regard false beliefs as their qualifications, holiness and principal character. The possession of ability and status by Brahmins must be ascribed to Hinduism which treats them as upper class people. The same Hinduism portrays others as mean people. Brahminism is the poison that botched up Hinduism. You can protect Hinduism only if you destroy Brahminism".

Sudha: Is religious conversion a remedy to this problem?

H.M.: It is a wise question. Religious conversion is everyone's fundamental right. Honourable E.V. Ramasamy, popularly and affectionately called 'Thanthai Periyar' (father-great personality) a rationalist, social reformer, writer, orator, iconoclast and the greatest radical thinker of south India dubbed Hinduism 'a sewage' because it thrust a stigma of untouchability upon a class of people. He counselled the oppressed to quit Hinduism and embrace Islam or Christianity, and carried out thousands of conversions about eight decades ago. Periyar told that no religious people in the world would take exception to the idea of uniting the whole mankind into one group save Brahmin-dominated Hinduism. He aired his notion that religion was made of wiles intrigued by Brahmins to make other people, their perpetual slaves using the title 'Shudra', and to preserve this, Brahmins had created temples and gods.

Ravindran: Was Periyar averse to religion?

H.M.: Periyar said, "Nature has gifted man wisdom, benefits of five senses and scope to gain experience, which are quite enough for sensible life. Brushing aside these factors, contradictory religion is not necessary".

Anand: We are not the only people following religion. It is practised in the Western countries also.

H.M.: Regarding this, Periyar said, "Most of the Western scholars neither mingle religion with nor exercise religious beliefs in their scholarship."

Vivek: Was there any sage abroad who had an identical view on religion?

H.M.: It is an intelligent thought. Robert Green Ingersol (1833-1899) said, "Religion never enabled man to possess morality, humanitarianism, diligence and ability. All religions and doctrines across the world evolved from innocence, fear and subtlety. Throw away the religions, their policies, doctrines, books, icons and the laws that defend them, which efface from the human heart, the desire for rights and sense of reason. If the motto-'Don't think! Have faith' comes before you from any corner of the world and in any form, smite and crush it."

Akash: Is there any decline in the practice of religion in advanced countries?

H.M.: The American Religious Identification Survey has unveiled certain datas on devotees and heretics in that country. As per the revelations, of the U.S. adults, Christians comprised about 86 per cent in 1990, 77 per cent in 2001 and 76 per cent in 2008. The survey found decadence in the role of traditional organized religion. Thirty percent of married couples did not have a religious wedding ceremony and 27 per cent of respondents were averse to religious funeral. The number of Americans with no religion rose in every State. The percentage of respondents clinging to heresy was 8.2 in 1990, 14.2 in 2001 and 15 in 2008. The gradual rise of disbelievers is quite apparent.

Sanjay: Could you please reveal your own opinion on the need for religion?

H.M.: I always uphold the views of Periyar and Ingersol about religion. Moreover, religions do not conform to science because they did not emerge from rationality. Different religions have enjoined diverse dogmas which are not based on reason. They curb basic human rights and act against secular values. Although all religions preach love and compassion towards others, they are not truly followed by people and they practise only discrimination. If fact, religions have divided the mankind into different sects and groups. Just imagine how the human race would have been if no religion had emerged in this world. Had the religions not emerged, the entire mankind could have existed under one roof without any divisions. However, religious leaders claim that religions came into existence to edify people and unify society. But the results are ironical.

Vijay: The widespread belief is that religions are the guides for people to lead their lives happily. If religions become extinct what is the alternative?

H.M.: This belief has to be erased from the minds of people. They could find a plethora of books containing beneficial precepts in all the languages. For example, 'Thirukkural' in Tamil is a comprehensive guide for virtuous and ecstatic life. It is far beyond caste, religion and God with no trace of superstition. It delineates morality, wisdom, love and noble characters as God and religion. Shakespeare's plays and poems display an in-depth study of life. People can choose the best books and study them to make their lives successful by tackling various challenges at different stages. For this, they must cultivate reading habit. Besides, illiteracy must be eradicated from the developing and the undeveloped countries so that literate people could read the books in the vernacular.

Emili: Is it possible to eliminate the religions from the world?

H.M.: It can't be done overnight. The conservative people will reject such ideas. Therefore, radicals must inculcate scientific thinking and approach in the present and future young generations. People must be coaxed to realize the realities and reject myths. Indomitable and enduring efforts are vital for success in this endeavour. Persons supporting this notion must become activists. They must be integrated in every country initially and organizations formed to take up compaigns. The intelligentsia and the media must be actively involved in the reformist movement for elimination of religions. The activists of the movement must leave no stone unturned in their march towards their goal. After some progress, the national level organizations could be linked globally to intensify their efforts and hold conferences. Strategies and programmes may be formulated and executed. If the efforts are consistent and do not sag, they could usher in a change in the mindset of religious believers, though it may take a long period of time.

Sudha: Is there anything possible to do for early results in the present religious set-up?

H.M.: Looking at the issue from this angle is wise because it will be a Herculean task to eliminate the deep-rooted religions in the near future. While taking steps for elimination of religions on the one hand, religious reforms must be brought about on the other. Reformation of Hinduism in particular is imperative. It will pave the way for early results.

Kumar: How should be the nature of reforms?

H.M.: The reforms must be based on new ideals. Hinduism must embody equality, brotherhood, love, helping disposition, verity, freedom and democratic principles. It must favour egalitarian society with no discrimination by birth.

Vijay: What are the views of Periyar about caste?

H.M.: Periyar began his social revolution at an early age and served the people up to his age of 95. He took up extensive travels to every nook and cranny of Tamil Nadu State and several parts of other States in South India and addressed the people to disillusion them. He expressed his views on all social issues very extensively during his public meetings, functions and in many books. It is not feasible to reiterate all of them here. However, I shall give you a few excerpts from them:

"Hinduism and its caste divisions were created to stabilize the 'master-servant' concept. There are no 'Parayan' (a class of untouchables), 'Brahmin,' or 'Shudra' in England. Caste and fate do not exist in Russia. I am a foe of not any Brahmin but of Brahminism. I always say that only Brahminism should be ruined and not Brahmins. There is no enough evidence to show that any of the Tamil Kings possessed self-respect. There is also no proof to know whether any of the Tamil Kings had thought why he was dubbed 'Shudra'. Temples were opened for people classified as 'untouchables' only after we called for blasting with dynamite, the temples which denied entry for them. Caste discrimination in Railway canteens was put to an end only after we called for erasing with tar, the names of castes written there. Who did strive for the use of public wells, drinking water tanks and entry into temples, coffee shops and government jobs by the people of the scheduled castes? Can the Congress Party in India claim to have served for this cause? It is only the Justice Party and Dravidar Kazhagam which took pains for it. (Periyar was in the Justice Party prior to his founding the Dravidar Kazhagam). We never flinched from our struggle for any purpose. I launched a struggle for the so-called 'untouchables' to move about in a street at Vaikkom in Kerala State. Finally I achieved their entry into temple. I have no conceit in telling this. It was possible because of the people's support, truth in principle and experience in struggles. No one is inferior to me. Likewise, no one is superior to me. It means every person must live with freedom and equality. But caste system creates inequality among the people. Those who go for intercaste marriage or eat food in a home of the oppressed are treated as outcasts by other people. Just think of the morality and probity of these people. So, the caste system must be destroyed. The harassment that we are subjected to, will not fade unless and until the caste-structure framed to accord comfort and pleasure to a few and torment all others is eliminated from this country. Even if Brahmins yield to us in the matter of caste, it will not become extinct until Krishna (a god in Hinduism) and Baghavat Gita (a scripture in Sanskrit) continue to be hailed by the people of India. We can get the real freedom of our country only when our people, especially those in villages come forward to eradicate superstitious habits and beliefs, infatuation for caste and religion and absurd godly traits."

Subash.: What is the origin of caste, sir?

H.M.: Justice Markandey Katju, a judge of the Supreme Court of India has analysed this issue in his article published in January 2009. He says, "The origin of the caste system was in all probability racial. It is said that caste originated when a white race, the 'Aryans' who came from the north-western direction conquered the dark coloured races inhabiting India at that time, probably 5000 or so years ago. Some people deny that 'Aryans' came from outside India and assert that India was their original home (Aryavarta) from where a section of them migrated to Europe. It is difficult to accept this view because people migrate from uncomfortable areas to comfortable areas. Why should anyone have migrated from a comfortable country like India which had level and fertile land ideal for agriculture, to a place like Afghanistan or Russia which was cold and mountainous and therefore uncomfortable? Indian history bears out the view that almost all invasions and immigrations were from outside India, mainly from the north-western direction and to a lesser extent from the north-eastern direction, into India. The caste system is called 'Varna Vyavastha', and the word 'Varna' in Sanskrit means colour (of the skin). This also points to the racial origin of the caste system. While the caste system thus appears to have racial origins, it subsequently developed an altogether different basis in tune with the needs of the feudal society. In other words, the caste system, though it originated in race, subsequently developed into the feudal, occupational divison of labour in society."

When the 'racial origin' is pointed out, we must be conscious that 'Aryans', later called 'Brahmins', kept themselves as a separate race and segregated the aborigines. For their own comfort and pleasure they created Hinduism and absurd 'Sastras' (doctrines) including 'Chadurvarneeyam' which laid down four divisions of people, namely Brahmin, Kshatriya, Vaishya and Shudra as traditional castes. Subsequently, hundreds of castes were created by thrusting hereditary occupations.

Abhinaya: How does caste plague the society?

H.M.: The caste system is one of the greatest social evils in India. It imposed several restrictions on the people. Brahmin alone should possess education and develop wisdom. Kshatriya should render military service. Vaishya must be engaged in agriculture and trade. Shudra should do slavery jobs. How ridiculous it is! Moreover, according to the doctrines, Brahmin alone is competent to be the master for the other three classes. No one else should be accepted as master just because of his scholarship. It shows how cynical the Brahmins were! The caste system is contrary to rationality. A Hindu has no freedom to act according to his logical faculty. The caste system is a traditional arrangement to cause inequalities among workers though it is claimed to be an occupational set-up by its supporters. Everybody should have the freedom to choose his occupation. Then only he would carry out his job efficiently and the country could prosper. But in the caste system, occupations were predetermined for individuals regardless of their liking. But now, this odious scenario has almost changed. As Hindus consider many occupations as base, the concerned workers detest their jobs. Without enthusiasm, they cannot be talented workers. Hinduism is a blend of many castes. The divided castes are graded with ranks from low to high position. Each caste feels and boasts of its position. Every caste regards itself as a separate society. So, every caste keenly considers protection of its own interest as its object. There is no harmony among Hindus. They have no common passion that they are all Hindus. Only caste feeling is paramount in their minds and hearts. Since every caste is struggling to protect its own welfare, Hindu society may be viewed as a group of selfish lot. The people of one caste speak ill of others and develop hatred. Caste is the cause for lack of affinity among the people. The culture of depicting one caste as superior and the other as inferior is abundant in the literatures of Hinduism. Only upper class people have a place in the sun. The people of some castes remain uncivilized even now because of continuous oppression. Hindus' character is not to consider a person's good qualities unmindful or his caste. They have a tendency to support or hail the actions of their communal brethren without pondering over them. Such attitude is against human virtue. Caste system is a biased divisive force which is very powerful to destroy reason and justice.

Caste feelings often trigger violence between different castes. Forty four Dalits of keezhvenmani village in Nagapattinam district of Tamil Nadu were burnt to death on 25th December 1968 after a protracted agitation for higher wages for agricultural labour. At a night in the year 1997, 58 Dalit labourers were taken to a land of an upper caste landlord for harvest under moonlight. Suddenly all of them were shot dead. The carnage happened in Bihar State. There was a brutal attack on some persons of scheduled caste at Melavalavu village near Madurai in Tamil Nadu in June 1997. A group of persons attacked the Panchayat President Mr. Murugesan, Vice-President Mr. Mookkan and some others with deadly weapons, resulting in the death of six persons and injuries to many others. The incident was attributed to the enmity between two communities caused by the reclassification of the general panchayat constituency as a reserved (for S.C.) constituency in 1996. The trial court convicted 17 persons of the 40 accused and awarded life imprisonment. On appeal, the High Court confirmed the trial court's order on 19th April 2006. On 21st October 2009, the Supreme Court upheld the life sentence awarded to 17 persons in this case.

In 2008, the Dalits of Uthapuram village in Madurai district of Tamil Nadu protested against the wall separating them from caste Hindus. The State Government ordered partial demolition of the wall, making a public pathway. Even after that, the Dalits faced several problems including inability to use the pathway. They alleged harassment by the police. The Madras High Court Bench ordered for an enquiry by a two-member commission into the alleged police excesses on 2nd October 2008 that allegedly took place after a wordy altercation between the Dalits and caste Hindus over painting the temple wall, escalated into large-scale violence the previous day. The commission confirmed gross violation of human rights. The enquiry report stated that 5 women had undergone termination of pregnancy while another woman's child had died immediately after delivery. Two others had sustained injuries to their genital parts and 26 women had been attacked along with their children. The victims included 43 persons aged between 50 and 70 years. The report also said, "There were also certain cases of illegal detention too. Women had undoubtedly suffered great humiliation, physical assault, infringement of fundamental rights and mental agony. We were able to see a sense of insecurity in the minds of the Dalit victims." The commission recommended a total compensation of Rs. 15,20,900 along with a break up for each of the 193 victims who sustained physical injuries and underwent mental agony besides material damage. The All India Democratic Women's Association (AIDWA) filed a Public Interest Litigation (PIL) petition in the Madurai Bench of the Madras High Court seeking compensation for the Dalit residents of Uthapuram who had suffered injuries, mental agony and material damage. Passing interim orders on the PIL petition, a Division Bench directed the State Government on 4th August 2009 to pay a compensation of Rs. 15.2 lakh to 193 affected Dalits including 43 aged people and 26 women as recommended by the commission.

A violent clash erupted between students of two different castes within the Government Law College campus in Chennai on 12th November 2008, resulting in severe injuries to many students. The fact that many police personnel deployed following prior intelligence information, stood as mute spectators of the brutal attacks, drew flak from all sections of the society. The Director General of Police himself has admitted the failure of his force to intervene and prevent the crime. There was a dispute between the Dalits and caste Hindus over celebrating a temple festival at Senthatti village in Tirunelveli district of Tamil Nadu. As a petition to the collector and peace meetings turned futile, no amicable solution could be found to the problem. As the Dalits were prevented from going ahead with their celebrations, the row intensified. It resulted in the murder of two Dalits on 7th March 2009 allegedly committed by caste Hindus.

A youth Ved Pal Maun was murdered in Singhwal village in Jind district of Haryana State for marrying a girl within the sub-caste reportedly on the directions of caste panchayat (judgment committee) in July 2009. Similarly, after a few weeks, a caste panchayat in Jhajjar district of the same State issued a 'fatwa' (an order to kill) against another young couple Shilpa and Ravinder, citing the same reason though they got married in April 2009 as arranged by their families. The couple living in Delhi, contested the viewpoint of the panchayat and alleged that their stand was not heard of. They said that the police had not taken any action on their complaint that 22 persons were threatening and hounding them. The AIDWA condemned such caste domination violating constitutional rights, and demanded arrest of the accused. Twenty-five-year-old Murugan, a lone graduate from a Dalit community at Vadivelkarai village in Madurai district was opposing restrictions imposed upon the community by caste Hindus. He was also conducting free classes for children belonging to the Dalit community. On 13th August 2009, he was beaten up for riding a bicycle before caste Hindus. He sustained a head injury and was admitted to the Government Rajaji Hospital in Madurai. His brother was also attacked for the same reason in 2007. Dalit residents had reportedly alleged that the two-tumbler system was existing in that village.

A group of Dalits led by Revenue Divisional Officer (RDO) Mr. Rajendran on 14th October 2009 was stopped on the road leading to Ekambareshwarar temple at Chettipulam near Vedaranyam in Tamil Nadu by about 300 people protesting against their entry into the temple. Even while the RDO was holding talks with the protesters, the mob turned violent. He was manhandled and stones, logs, bottles and iron rods were reportedly flung. The RDO, his driver and two policemen suffered injuries and three government vehicles were damaged. About

19 persons were arrested under the Protection of Civil Rights Act, 1955. A four-member team of 'Evidence,' a Madurai-based human rights organization, visited Chettipulam. Their findings pointed to latent prevalence of discrimination against Dalits. An agreement was reached later at peace talks between the Dalits and caste Hindus. Accordingly, the Dalits were led by the District Collector and the District Revenue Officer (DRO) into the temple on 27th October to offer prayers amid enough police security.

An anganwadi (Kindergarten) at Ammapatti village in Theni district of Tamil Nadu was allegedly serving food to children of Dalit and caste Hindus separately. It was making the Dalit children bring their own utensils while providing them to caste Hindu children. The caretakers allegedly instructed the Dalit children not to mingle or play with the caste Hindu children. Following shifting of the anganwadi to a new building in the caste Hindu area, the Dalit children were 'ordered' not to wear chappals and enter caste Hindu areas. The same restrictions were imposed on their parents too. The Dalits in the village stopped sending their children to the anganwadi. They complained about the discrimination to the Superintendent of Police during his visit on 14th October 2009 for a grievance redress meeting. A fact finding team of 'Evidence'- the Madurai-based organization carried out an investigation on 20th October and recorded testimonies, and obtained written statements from 39 Dalits in the village. Mr. A. Kathir, Executive Director of the organization reportedly expressed sorrow at the discrimination of Dalit children at a tender age and demanded action against the erring workers under the relevant Act.

Mr. Tabish Ahmed Khan, Member of Legislative Assembly (MLA) from Khesraha in Uttar Pradesh, his brother and their supporters razed to the ground, the thatched house of Mr. Ram Lakhan, a Dalit in Rajedeeha village and allegedly grabbed a piece of land in the last week of October 2009. A First Information Report (FIR) was lodged against the MLA and others. A Dalit woman Bhagyalakshmi went to draw water from a hand pump at Thenpalanji village near Tirunagar in Madurai. A few upper caste women stopped and scolded her. Her mother-in-law Andichhi filed a complaint with the Tirunagar police, who arranged a peace meeting and settled the issue. But a group of caste Hindus assaulted and humiliated Andichhi on 19th November 2009. A Dalit man and his daughter were burnt alive at Mirchpur in Hissar distriet of Haryana on 21st April 2010. These are only a few examples. Killing, torture and harassment of lower caste people have been reported often from many parts of India. Such persecution is likely to continue in the future also.

Caste stands in lovers' way. Love and marriage with a bride or bridegroom of one's choice is difficult because marriages are usually performed within the same caste. Sometimes this practice leads to suicides committed by lovers. Caste system is robust to sway politics. That leaders of political parties select their candidates for all the constituencies mainly on the basis of the contestants' respective caste vote banks, is a testimony to the power of caste. Certain constituencies are reserved for the candidates from scheduled castes because they can't win if the contest is common to all castes. Most of the people vote for the candidates of their own castes. We find the same situation in the elections to the posts of various associations. Even educated persons adopt caste mentality in their actions. In bureaucracy, there is clandestine favouritism at all levels towards related employees which amounts to discrimination against others. Though castes exist in Islam, Christianity and Sikhism, they are not conspicuous, active or discriminatory despite some rare instances in the world like the rift between Shia and Sunni Muslims in Iraq. However, the people of those religions look at caste for matrimony, election of clerics, etc.

Rahul: I have heard that Dr. B.R. Ambedkar was seated separately at school. Could you please elaborate on his experience?

H.M.: The period of his life was egregious in making the lower class people wretched. The genius suffered ill-treatment in his boyhood. The children of lower castes including himself were segregated from others. Dalit children were treated as 'untouchables' and not allowed to get water from the common pot. Many painful experiences and the anguish he suffered in his younger days evolved him a thinker. As a matured sage, he has authored several books focussing upon caste, religion, social reforms, etc. He has written, "Under Beshwa rule, 'untouchable' should not walk in the public streets of Maharashtra because their shadows would make stain on caste Hindus. To avert any accidental contact with shadow, Beshwa had ordered 'untouchables' to fasten a black rope around their necks or wrists. In 'Pune', the capital of Beshwa rule, there was an arrangement that an 'untouchable' while walking in public streets, should keep a broom hanging from the back of his waist to prevent the dust raised by his feet from staining caste Hindus. In Pune, 'untouchables' were obliged by law to hang a spittoon from the neck to prevent staining by their spitting in public streets.

In November 1935, many ladies of untouchable caste fetched water in brass pots in 'Janu' village of Ahmedabad district. Viewing it as contempt for Hindus, a few caste Hindus smote those women. In April 1936, a few 'untouchables' of 'Chakvarak' village in Jaipur Dukedom (now Rajasthan) arranged a feast on return from a fete for the people of their caste. Ghee was served in that feast. Knowing this, Hindus thought that they only had the privilege to use ghee, and the use of this product to cater for untouchables was a disgrace to the status of Hindus. The Hindus therefore, gathered themselves, flung to the place of the feast, bashed the people eating there and drove them away.

The 'Social Reforms Party' consisted of mainly educated upper class Hindus. So, they devoted themselves to Hindu family reforms only. Their struggle for reforms influenced only family reforms. They did not realize the need to launch vigorous stir to eradicate caste. So, their struggle had no impact on reforms for elimination of caste. Because of that, their party failed to achieve any benefit. Rationality and morality are the important weapons for reformists. But the doctrines of Hinduism prevent Hindus from analysing whether caste is appropriate to rationality. So, the fort raised around caste cannot be demolished. It could be destroyed only if the religious doctrines and vedas which do not regard rationality or morality are destroyed."

Vijay: Why do people not resort to revolution for elimination of caste system?

H.M.: We can find answer to this question from Dr. B.R. Ambedkar's views expressed as follows:

"Karl Marx, while encouraging common people to launch 'The Economic Revolution', told them that by joining the revolution, they would not lose anything but their fetters of slavery. We can't tell our people as Marx did because the castes have been divided very subtly. The rights and privileges of a caste are proportionate to its status of superiority or inferiority in the society. If the caste system is destroyed, some castes will have to lose more rights and privileges than other castes. Because of the 'superior-inferior' factor, it is impossible to consolidate the people to eliminate the caste system. Unlike many world countries, social revolution did not take shape in India because the innocent people, weakened by the system of 'chadurvarneeyam' had no courage or valour to resort to revolution".

Mehala: Is there any contribution from world leaders to counter this social evil?

H.M.: We must not expect their role on this issue because it is an internal problem of our country. Most of our national leaders always lack alacrity on this malady. Only those who suffered something difficult or unpleasant due to the caste system can realize that abolition of the system is imperative. Others usually wink at the cruelties of caste and some of them often induce caste feelings for their personal gains. Some foreign leaders, while attending conferences, seminars and delivering memorial lectures, generally insist on the unity of people belonging to different sections of society in India. For example, Mr. Nelson Mandela who devoted himself to end apartheid in South Africa, has stressed the need for harmony among the people of various classes. Mr. Martin Luther King Jr. and Coretta Scott King paid a historic visit to India in 1959 and termed it as their pilgrimage to the land of Mahatma Gandhi. To commemorate the 50th anniversary of this visit, their son Martin Luther King III visited India in February 2009. He exhorted Indians to work assiduously to abolish the caste system. He added that the affected people should clamour for their rights and justice. He quoted his father as having said, "Injustice anywhere is a threat to justice everywhere".

Ravindran: What is the remedy you suggest to remove the evil of caste?

H.M.: Since it is a perennial problem, it requires manifold actions. The syllabi in the educational system must include chapters that can motivate students to reject this evil. It may be an enduring recipe for solution of this problem. Karl Marx said, " History is nothing but the class struggle that is persistent in the human race". So, history lessons must be designed to teach the lifestyles of people, the harassments they were subjected to, and their efforts and struggles to get rid of them. It could be more useful than the study of incidents in the lives of former rulers. The belief of the people that 'the religious doctrines are sacred' must be dispelled because the doctrines portray caste as divine. Therefore, the holiness and divinity attached to caste must be effaced first.

Disparity among the people will continue to exist unless a feeling of brotherhood emerges. Along with this feeling, a relationship is also possible by mixing of blood. Therefore, intercaste marriages could be an effective means of abolition of caste system. But they may entail problems in the present social set-up. For instance, 23-year-old V. Mahesh, a Dalit youth from Puthery village near Nagercoil in Tamil Nadu, married a caste Hindu girl out of love at a temple in Puthery on 8th October 2008 against the wishes of the girl's parents. Since then, they had been receiving threatening phone calls. Even after the local police negotiated a peace, the couple faced troubles. The girl's mother engaged a few persons who attacked Mahesh and his parents, and attempted to abduct her. Being unable to bear the harassment, the couple moved to Tiruchy city. But a gang waylaid Mahesh and abducted him in a car with an intention to kill him in Andhra Pradesh. With the sympathy of one of the gang, he escaped from the abductors. His complaint failed to push the police for action.Then he moved the Madras High Court Bench at Madurai alleging harassment by his in-laws. The Bench directed the police to provide protection to the intercaste couple. Such problems notwithstanding, intercaste marriages should be actively encouraged, aided, performed and protected by social organizations, Human Rights Commission, National Commission for Women, etc. The role of State and Central Governments is pivotal in this endeavour. The Governments must do everything within their powers to the wedded couples. Free registration of intercaste marriages, financial aid and preference in employment to the couples and free education to their kids are some of the measures for consideration. Concessions in train fare, interest on bank loans, income tax and medical expenses, etc. may be provided to the couples. A distinct 'Identity Card' may be issued to them to avail the special benefits with ease. Police protection against rowdy elements whenever necessary, and making amendments to the relevant laws to facilitate stringent action against those who harm them, are vital. These steps will be conducive to large-scale intercaste marriages.

Vivek : If the caste system comes to an end, what will be the fate of the reservation policy?

H.M.: Well; it is a wise perspective. 'Periyar' fought hard to secure and defend reservation for scheduled and backward classes in educational institutions and government jobs. He desired to uplift them with the same weapon, namely 'caste', due to which they became downtrodden. As a result, many persons of the lower classes got education and employment. A few of them reached high positions. But many decades have passed since reservation policy was introduced. However, over a long period of time, the fruits of reservation have reached only a fewer number of families vis-a-vis the number of families not benefited in every caste. It is so because the employed persons have guided and helped only their kith and kin to get education and employment. Politicians of lower castes also have followed suit. Officials woo all the innocent people of their respective castes for launching any agitation to clamour for concessions and neglect them afterwards as politicians do before and after elections. So, only a limited number of particular families belonging to each scheduled or backward class are basking in popularity and comforts while others are suffering abject poverty. Afew years ago, the Kerala High Court upheld a legislation to exclude the creamy layer (rich persons) from the ambit of the Reservation Act. The Government of India enacted a law in 2006 providing a 27 percent quota for Other Backward Classes (OBC) in higher educational institutions.That law was legally challenged. The Supreme Court of India, while upholding the law in April 2008, directed that creamy layer must be excluded from the quota. Therefore, the benefits of reservation have not widely covered the affected people. Besides, the people of all castes have their own associations. In recent years, every caste association has stepped up its efforts, rallies, agitations and struggles to derive maximum benefits from the Government. A few associations vie with each other for favours, and recriminations between themselves are also visible occasionally. This dismal trend is inimical to the harmony of society. Political leaders, always keeping an eye on their vote banks and under obligation to satisfy different sections of people, announce sub-quotas within the existing quotas of reservation. Many backward classes are demanding to reclassify them as either scheduled or most backward caste. For example, the Gujjar community people in Rajasthan State resorted to a violent stir for 27 days during May-June 2008 demanding scheduled tribe status. The stir spread to some parts of neighbouring States where the Gujjars live. The train services were disrupted for many days due to their blockade. During their unruly agitations, 18 persons were killed in police firing at Sikandra in Dausa district. The stir came to an end after reaching an agreement with the State Government. Time and again fake caste certificates have been used and many such cases were dealt with by courts. All these abominable developments can be attributed to the availability of reservation. Political leaders and authorities do not comprehend that reservation was expedient before our independence and now it needs to be repealed.

Sudha : Will the withdrawal of reservation not affect the lower classes?

H.M.: No. It will benefit all the people as a whole in the long run. However, some preparatory measures will be required. The Government could order a survey to collect comprehensive data showing the total number of persons and families benefited by reservation and those left out. This must be done within a time frame of six months. Based on the data, a list can be prepared castewise to include at least one boy or girl at the studying age from each family (excluding creamy layer) left out of reservation benefits. The enlisted boys and girls must be provided with training in various skills or higher education according to their merits. The Government may treat them as the targeted group and arrange for close watch on every individual. The deserving candidates may be specially trained to appear for competitive examinations on the same lines as the scheduled caste candidates are trained for All India Services Examinations at present. The families which could not avail the benefits of reservation for so long would be evidently poor. The Government therefore, must bear all the expenses of education, training, travel, etc. for the candidates from these families. The targeted group must be given priority in employment. An expert committee may be constituted to make an in-depth study of the issue, make necessary recommendations and propound a project which may be implemented after the Cabinet nod. The entire exercise must be completed within a specified time frame not exceeding ten years. Then the Government must wind down the project and scrap the 'Reservation Act.'

At this stage, the Government should strive to reach a political consensus on the need to dispense with the long-standing practice of entering the name of caste in all applications, school and the Government records. The Government must garner the support of people, various organizations, the media and intellectuals to tackle possible opposition from some quarters. Then necessary legislation should be passed in this regard. Strategic, sincere, systematic and relentless efforts of the Government, juxtaposed with social reforms could surely fulfil the ambition to annihilate the caste system and establish an egalitarian society in India. When it so happens, the beneficiaries of reservation who are likely to protest against reformist actions now, will welcome them because they too will be enjoying a new social status that remains inaccessible to the lower classes. Even the families that have enjoyed government jobs for three generations consecutively and amassed wealth cannot claim to possess social status. It is only because they belong to lower classes. Even in cities and towns, the tenants of lower classes hide their real castes because they may be denied accommodation. Houses are mostly rented out to tenants only after ascertaining their caste. In rural areas which comprise more than 80 percent of India, we can see penury and squalor among most of the lower class people. Untouchability is still prevalent in many villages and two-tumbler system (providing separate tumblers for the 'untouchables') is adopted. In the countryside, agriculture is the main occupation. Many people of the oppressed classes continue to be labourers. The rest of them are only small land holders. As the agricultural operations are seasonal, the demand for labour soars periodically. The use of modern machinery is feasible only for the elite. They are also able to gather labourers from all castes with their influence or intimidation. Therefore, the small land owners of lower castes are unable to utilize the landless labourers of even the same caste and their farming operations are impeded. During rotational irrigation for tank-fed lands, they face partisan attitude of the upper class people. They experience many hardships in the absence of social status.

Following scientific advancement and rapid industrialisation, the occupational division of labour on the basis of caste is already on the wane. But most of the employees from lower classes continue to be workers in the industrial sector for want of qualifications. Only a handful of them hold technical or managerial positions. A few self-employed people from lower classes are having only small industrial units and none of them could become a leading industrialist, because they are lacking in capital and coordination from industrialists of upper classes. In business sector, the cartel is maintained by the businessmen of upper classes, exchanging trade secrets only between them. So, those from lower classes are unable to manage any large business. A few persons who own petty shops or tea stalls have their customer base limited to the people of their caste, as they have no social status.

In politics, reservation provided for scheduled castes enables a few belonging to those castes to be elected as members of Parliament and State Assemblies and thence become Ministers. But even then they do not enjoy social status because their castes haunt people. Many of the 'Other Backward Classes (OBC)' are not represented in Parliament or State legislatures because the number of voters in their castes is very low and they can't get support from other castes. Thus the evil of caste has permeated the entire society in India. Only a casteless society could ensure social status for all the people of the country. Therefore, the elimination of the caste system will be the panacea for all the social ills of India. The time is now half past nine. So, I think we can disperse, OK?

Vijay: Just a minute, sir. As you are staying without family and have asked us to regard you as one among our family members, we will be delighted at your visit to each of our homes. All the students of + 2 desire for your visit.

H.M.: I shall honour your wish. I can visit one of your homes on every Sunday afternoon. As the 'parent-teacher association' is functioning, I would like to meet the head of each family. So, you must ensure that your family head, i.e. father, mother or brother as the case may be, is available and not disturbed by my visit on the particular day that will be decided on Friday every week, if I am not officially diverted. As I am not yet settled, I shall begin my visits next week. By then we shall decide the first house of visit.

All the students: (in one voice) Thank you very much, sir.

(The headmaster's domestic help Charli enters the hall)

Charli : Good night, sir.

H.M.: Good night; see you in the morning.

Charli : I have come here just now. Why are you driving me out, sir?

H.M.: You said 'good night'. So, I said 'goodbye' to you.

Charli : Is it wrong, sir?

H.M.: 'Good night' must be used to say 'goodbye' when you are leaving somebody late in the evening or when you are going to bed. You should have said 'good evening'.

(The students are laughing)

Charli : Oh, my goodness!

H.M.: Now, you are right. By the way, why did you come here?

Charli: You didn't return even after 9 O'clock. So, I was anxious for you.

H.M.: Were you anxious for me or anxious to have your dinner?

Charli : Are you making 'anaphora' by repeating the word 'anxious'?

H.M.: No. The same word gives varied meanings. The repetition here means your eagerness to eat.

Charli: Do you think I am a glutton?

H.M.: I don't worry even if you get that title.

Charli: If it is ture, why have you starved me for so long?

H.M.: Do you feel hungry? Don't be bothered about it. A quota has been reserved for you to devour.

Vijay : Who is this comedian, sir?

H.M.: Oh, I am sorry for my omission to introduce him. He is Charli, my domestic help, and Falstaff III.

Charli : I object to giving me this designation. I am your personal assistant out of school. Then who are other two Falstaff? That information is confounding me.

H.M.: The original Falstaff is a character portrayed by Shakespeare. Tony Lumpkin, a humorous character depicted by Goldsmith in 'She Stoops to Conquer' is dubbed as the kin of Shakespeare's Falstaff. He may be regarded as Falstaff II. Now, you may go and have the tiffin spared for you.

Charli: It is very late for all to leave. I shall take the food parcel with me to our temporary residence, namely the Panchayat Office. Ding-dong......... ding-dong...........ding-dong......

H.M.: Why do you make this sound?

Charli: It is the closing bell. All may go home.

(All the students, teachers and staff laugh and disperse)

2

TERRORISM AND ITS IMPACT ON PEOPLE

The headmaster in consultation with the students of +2 decides to begin his visits from the home of Vijay, the class pupil leader. Accordingly, he arrives at Vijay's house in the afternoon of one Sunday along with his domestic help Charli.

Vijay : Good evening, sir.

H.M.: Good evening, Vijay.

Vijay: (Turning to his brother Kumaresan) Meet our headmaster, dear.

Kumaresan: Hello, sir. Please be seated.

H.M.: Thank you. What about your family?

Kumaresan: Vijay is my only younger brother. We have no sisters. Our parents passed away many years before.

H.M.: Alas! Are you married?

Kumaresan's wife comes out of the kitchen, welcomes the headmaster and provides coffee for all.

Kumaresan: Yes, sir. She is my wife Santha and we have a girl child. I am serving as an Inspector in the Anti-Terrorism Squad in New Delhi. Now, I am on leave for 15 days. My wife is living here and she looks after Vijay and the child.

H.M.: Your service to the country is noble. Do you think that terrorism is on the rise in recent years? Could you elaborate on this grave threat?

Kumaresan : Terrorism is not a problem of only recent period.

In the early eighties of the 20th century, Sikh militants in Punjab indulged in terrorist activities demanding a separate State of Khalistan. On many occasions, they waylaid transport buses, paraded the passengers and shot them en masse. Thousands of innocent people were killed in their atrocities. With deadly weapons, the terrorists made the holy Golden Temple complex in Amritsar their haven. They were quelled and their leader Bhindranwala was killed in the army's 'Operation Blue Star' on 5th June 1984 which led to the assassination of Prime Minister Indira Gandhi. The consequent anti-Sikh riots in Delhi and elsewhere took a toll of more than 2000 lives.

The bombing of Air India-Delhi bound Boeing 747 by Khalistan terrorists in June-1985 killed all 329 passengers on board.

The serial bombings in Mumbai in 1993 killed hundreds of people. The main accused 'Mumbai underworld don' Dawood Ibrahim is believed to be enjoying shelter in Pakistan.

In 1995, the Harkat-ul-Ansar front organization-al-Faran kidnapped and executed U.S. citizen Donald Hutchings, German Drek Hasert and Britons Paul Wells and Keith Manigan. In 1997, FBI Investigators came to India, and on their interrogation of many persons, the arrested terrorist Mohammad Musaib of Pakistan divulged the tragic end of the tourists.

An Indian Airlines flight IC 814 was hijacked to Kandhahar in Afghanistan in December 1999. It was an operation masterminded by the Taliban with the active involvement of several ISI (Inter-Services Intelligence of Pakistan) linked figures. The five hijackers resorted to intimidation by slaying a newly wedded youth while his spouse was beside and threw his body out of the aircraft. During negotiations, they cowed down the Indian authorities to such an extent that three incarcerated crooks, namely Mohammad Masood Azhar Alvi- the Jaish-e-Mohammad chief, his lieutenant Syed Omar Sheikh and al-Umar chief Mushtaq Ahmad Zaragar were released and pathetically, a Central Cabinet Minister escorted them to Kandhahar and swapped them for the lives of the passengers on board the flight. It was akin to barter of goods. In the wake of this incident, India gave to Pakistan in 2000, a list of twenty most wanted terrorists and demanded to hand over them. But Pakistan did not respond to this plea.

Terrorists launched an attack on the Indian Parliament on 13th December 2001 killing seven security guards. The attack triggered the offensive deployment of troops on the India-Pakistan border and the suspension or reduction of diplomatic links and transport with Pakistan.

Terrorists caused a bomb blast in a bus in Ghatkopar on 28th July 2003. They carried out bomb blasts at the Gateway of India and Zaveri bazaar in Mumbai on 25th August 2003. The explosions claimed 54 lives and injured 244 people. A special Prevention of Terrorism Act (POTA) court convicted three persons including a woman and sentenced all of them to death in August 2009.

Terrorists attacked the Indian Institute of Science, a frontline scientific institution in Bangalore in 2005, in which attack Prof. M.C.Puri was slain. The train blasts in Mumbai in 2006 were severe and caused the loss of many lives. The serial blasts in Jaipur, Rajasthan on 13th May 2008 took a toll of 64 lives and injured 150 persons. On 25th July 2008, bomb blasts in Bangalore killed two persons. Seventeen serial blasts rocked different parts of Ahmedabad, Gujarat on 26th July 2008 killing 46 people and injuring over 200. Abu Bashar of Students Islamic Movement of India (SIMI), alleged mastermind behind this attack was arrested in the state of Uttar Pradesh after 20 days. The serial bomb blasts in Delhi on 13th September 2008 claimed 21 lives. On 30th October 2008, 75 persons were killed and over 300 injured in 12 high intensity blasts in the State of Assam. Again the serial bomb blasts on 1st January 2009 in Assam claimed 5 lives and left 62 injured. The New Year Day became a black day. The authorities suspected that United Liberation Front of Asom (ULFA) extremists were behind the attacks.

H.M.: The terrorist attacks in Mumbai, the financial hub of India on 26th November 2008 are said to be worse than the previous attacks. Why have they drawn the attention of the whole world?

Kumaresan: On that day, terrorists launched multiple attacks in eleven different places including the fivestar Taj Mahal Hotel, the Oberoi and Trident Hotels, Nariman House, Cafe Leopold and Chhatrapati Shivaji Terminus in Mumbai, taking a toll of 172 innocent lives including 21 foreigners and injuring 292 people as confirmed by the Health Department. The gun battle between the terrorists and security forces that consisted of 350 commandos of army, navy, National Security Guards (NSG) and 400 police personnel lasted for 60 hours. The gunmen attempted to identify Americans and Britons for hostage-taking. 8 Israelis were trapped inside Nariman House and many Israelis were held in Trident Hotel. The 21 slain foreign nationals included a Briton, an American, an Italian, three Germans, two Canadians, an Australian, a Chinese, a Thai, a Japanese, six Israelis and three from unidentified countries. Out of the 22 injured foreigners, there were five Britons, three Germans, an Italian, a Spanish, a Norwegian, a Finn, two Americans, a Canadian, a Jordanian, two Omanis, two Chinese, a Philippino, and an Australian. Ten employees of the Taj Mahal Palace and Tower lost their lives. Distressingly, the wife and two children of Karambir Kang, General Manager of the Taj Mahal Palace and some family members of employees were also killed. A few security men and a prominent Police Inspector were also killed in the attacks. The damage to the hotel building was so great that it required more than Rs. 500 crore for renovation during the subsequent months. During the attacks, the hotel guests were displaced in fear and panic, and when the turmoil was brought to an end, there were around 2,500 requests from the guests about their belongings and access to their rooms. The Taj management did everything possible to protect the guests during the attacks through phone, SMS, etc., and in the aftermath by providing medical, financial and other assistance. During the battle, 9 terrorists were killed and one captured alive. The attacks created several breath-taking and heart-burning narratives. One among them was the loss of six members of a Muslim family in the massacre at the Chhatrapati Shivaji Terminus Railway Station. Firoze, a five-year-old child, kept asking for his mother for five days. As he finally sensed that something was wrong, he could not be assuaged. Then relatives took the child to the cemetery and said to him, "Your mother and father are here." The child was crying and it took many days to placate him. The terrorist attacks in Mumbai therefore, plunged not only India but also all the peace-loving nations of the world in the doldrums.

H.M.: Who were those terrorists? Has their identity been established?

Kumaresan: Afghanistan's Ambassador to the U.S. T. Jawad told the 'Wall Street Journal' that intelligence gathered after the Mumbai carnage had linked Pakistan's ISI to the unprecedented strike. He pointed out the calls from a satellite phone left behind by the attackers to "people who were known ISI members or had very strong ties with the ISI". Mr. Jawad also said that there was evidence linking Yusuf Muzammil, identified by India as the attackers' chief organizer, to the ISI. British media quoted security sources as saying that targeting Western citizens suggested a "typical Al-Qaeda-style activity," reminding Al-Qaeda's attacks in the past on restaurants and clubs frequented by tourists. British intelligence agencies suspected Al-Qaeda in view of the coordinated operation possibly as a retaliation for American air attacks on its hideouts in the tribal areas on Pakistan-Afghanistan border, and CIA's anti-terror operations in Pakistan. The agencies also felt that India was chosen as a target because Al-Qaeda had sufficient resources to carryout an attack here. The lone surviving terrorist Mohammad Ajmal Amir Kasab was found to have hailed from Faridkot in Pakistan's Punjab province. He revealed that the 9slain terrorists also hailed from the same province. The 9-mm pistol recovered from slain Ismail Khan was manufactured at Diamond Nedi Frontier Arms Company in Peshawar (Pakistan). Toiletries, match boxes, medical kit, washing powder and food items found with them had markings of places in Pakistan. What else is required to establish their nationality? But Pakistan perversely denied any involvement of its nationals in the Mumbai attacks. 'The Observer' confirmed in London on 7th December 2008 that Ajmal had hailed from the village 'Faridkot' in the Okara district of Pakistan by the crucial evidence of the village's electoral list containing the names of his parents, namely Mohammad Amir Iman and Noor Elahi, and revelations by local persons. The report belied Pakistan's denial of its citizens' involvement in the heinous crime.

H.M.: Could there be any network behind the attackers who happened to be young youths?

Kumaresan: It is sure, of course. Rahil Abdul Rehman Sheikh was alleged to have played a key role in the 2006 serial bombings in Mumbai as well as abortive terror attacks in Gujarat and New Delhi. He enticed dozens of young men in Maharashtra into neoconservative organizations like the Students Islamic Movement of India (SIMI) and preacher Zakir Naik's Islamic Research Foundation. Later, those recruits travelled to Iran on pilgrimage visas, crossed into Pakistan and got into the Lashkar. He escaped police and was included in the list of India's most wanted terrorists. He is also believed to have been linked to Lashkar's networks in Kashmir which helped to facilitate the Fidayeen attacks in Mumbai also. According to India's Intelligence Services, Sheikh is holed up in Pakistan under the shelter of Lashkar military commanders known only by their pseudonyms 'Muzammil Yusuf' and 'Abu Hurrera' the very men suspected to have commanded the Fidayeen attackes in Mumbai. Investigators determined in late May

2009 that Ali Abdul Aziz al-Hooti, a top Oman-based jihad financier and businessman was in Mambai, days before the terror attacks. The police in both Oman and India determined that al-Hooti had direct links with several key suspects in the attacks.

H.M.: What is the action taken in this regard and how far it has progressed?

Kumaresan: After Indian investigators elicited vital information from the arrested terrorist Ajmal, India served demarche on Pakistan in early December 2008 demanding immediate action to handover the fugitives. It focussed on the Lashkar-e-Taiba and its founder-leader Hafiz Saeed, seen as perpetrators of the Mumbai attacks. Later, India exuded possession of proof of the involvement of Pakistan's Inter-Services Intelligence in the attacks. India had already demanded the return of Mumbai underworld don Dawood Ibrahim linked to 1993 serial bombings in Mumbai, and Jaish-e-Mohammad leader Maulana Masood Azhar of Pakistan in connection with the hijacking of Indian Airlines plane IC 814 to Kandhahar. But on 3rd December 2008, Pakistan President Asif Ali Zardari rejected any handover of the accused saying that if he had proof they would be put in the dock and sentenced in his country. In fact, the Pakistan Civilian Government's apparent willingness and sincerity to cooperate with India remain defunct since the democratic element is swayed by a convergence of the interests of the military, the jihadists and the right-wing political parties. As the democratic roots in Pakistan are neither strong nor consistent, the Government is diffident about its authority to execute its desires, although the links between the Lashkar-e-Taiba and the ISI are well documented. The Government therefore, tends to flinch from taking stringent action on or handing over the terrorists to India, which makes Pakistan a haven for them. The Editor-in-chief of 'The Hindu' Mr. N. Ram suggested that India should build international pressure on Pakistan to hand over those who masterminded the Mumbai terror attacks by going to the United Nations Security Council under resolution 1373, adopted by this world body in September 2001, since it is a counter-terrorism measure that is binding on member-countries of the UN to initiate steps to curb terrorist activities. He downplayed any reluctance to move in this direction due to speculation of a possibility to link the Kashmir issue with this plea. He cautioned that such attitude would amount to only a 'defensive state of mind' and not a determination to win the battle on a crucial issue.

Following international pressure, especially from the U.S., U.K., and other European Union nations, Pakistan began to probe the terrorist attacks in Mumbai. Pakistan acknowledged that some part of the conspiracy had taken place in that country. Rehman Malik, Adviser to the Prime Minister of Pakistan told journalists that a case of terrorism had been registered against eight Pakistani suspects and six of them had been taken into custody and some of them belonged to the banned militant group Lashkar-e-Taiba. On Pakistan's demand, India handed over dossier on evidence pertaining to Mumbai terror attacks to that country. As Pakistan asked for more information twice, they were also furnished by the Indian Government. Though there is persistent pressure on Pakistan from the U.S. and European Union countries to take speedy action, the criminals could be brought to justice only if that country shows alacrity on this issue which has rattled the entire world. On the part of India, steps were initiated for trial of the lone arrested terrorist Ajmal. Initially, Ms. Anjali Waghmare was appointed defence lawyer for him by a special court. Later, her appointment was revoked owing to her non-disclosure of facts about her representation of a victim of terror attacks in Mumbai in a compensation case. She was replaced by Abbas Kazmi as defence lawyer. When Ajmal, the accused, was produced before the special court for the first time on 15th April 2009, he retracted his confessional statement with the description on terrorist training sessions and the motive of the crime as 'freedom of Kashmir'. Ajmal told the judge that his confessional statement was taken under duress. He also stated that he was a minor, hiding his age. But medical tests of Ajmal done as ordered by the court revealed that he was not a juvenile. Ajmal made a U-turn and confessed to his crime before the Special Sessions Court at the Arthur Road jail in Mumbai on 20th July 2009. His statement about his training, joining the Mujahideen group in Pakistan, his journey from Karachi to Mumbai along with other terrorists and the execution of the carnage, lasted for about four hours. An Indian link emerged for the first time in the case. Ajmal mentioned the name of Abu Jundal as one who had taught them Hindi. In crucial testimony at the trial of Ajmal, an official of the US federal agency (FBI) told the special court on 12th August 2009 that its probe had established that the perpetrators had come from Karachi. Besides, the FBI filed a case in Los Angeles as six Americans lost their lives in the Mumbai terror attacks.

Hafiz Saeed, the chief of Jamaat-ud-Dawa (JuD) known as a front organization of the Lashkar-e-Taiba, was placed under house arrest in Pakistan in December 2008 during a government crackdown on the JuD following the Mumbai attacks and shortly after the UN Security Council 1267 committee designated him and the group as 'terrorist'. The LeT was blamed for the attacks in Mumbai on 26th November 2008 among other strikes. The Lahore High Court ordered the release of Hafiz Saeed along with Col. (retd) Nazeer Ahmed, another JuD leader on 2nd June 2009 saying that the Pakistani Government did not have sufficient grounds to detain the petitioners. India was startled by the court order. The US special envoy on Pakistan and Afghanistan Mr. Richard Holbrooke said, "Their release has disturbed us all." Pakistani Government said that it was considering an appeal against the release. In connection with the terrorist attacks in Mumbai, Pakistan arrested and kept in custody five men, namely Hammad Amin Sadiq, Zaki-ur-Rehman Lakhvi, Mazhar Iqbal, Abdul Wajid and Shahid Jamil Riaz. The Federal Investigations Agency submitted to the Pakistani anti-Terror court a charge sheet against these five men for their suspected involvement in the attacks, and 12 others who were declared proclaimed offenders in the case. 'The New York Times' said at the end of September 2009, "Pakistan's investigation concludes beyond any reasonable doubt that it was Lashkar militants who carried out the Mumbai attacks, preying on their victims in a train station, two five-star hotels, a cafe and a Jewish Centre over three days starting last November 26." The paper added that some people of the ISI had known about the plot but closed their eyes. 49-year-old David Headley Coleman was arrested by the FBI in the US in October 2009 for plotting a terror attack in India at the behest of Lashkar-e-Taiba. Headley was arrested at Chicago's O' Hare International Airport as he prepared to board a flight to Philadelphia on his way to Pakistan. The FBI also arrested Tahawwur Hussain Rana, aged 48, a Canadian citizen of Pakistani origin. The Central anti-Terrorism Cell of the Italian police, relying on information provided by the FBI and the dossier given by India, arrested two Pakistani nationals - 60-year-old Yaqub Janijua in the northern Italian town of Brescia on 21st November 2009 on charges of aiding and abetting the Mumbai terror attacks. They had reportedly made illegal money transfers through the agency they were managing. As for Ajmal, he had made a voluntary confession in the court on 20th July, 2009, admitting to everything, including the exchange of fire with the police at the Chhatrapati Shivaji Terminus. But he contradicted himself on 18th December 2009 stating that he had lied and his confession was not true, and he had admitted out of fear for the police. He said that his confession recorded before the magistrate was forcibly taken, following police torture. He also said that the "shorter person" as mentioned by eyewitnesses often, was not he but one "Abu Ali, who had died", and the police had fitted him in the case. He alleged that the police had tutored witnesses to identify him as one of the attackers at the train station. After a 271-day trial, the special court on 6th May 2010 sentenced Ajmal to death. The Bombay High Court on 21st February 2011, upheld the death sentence. Whatever may be the judgment, the perpetrators could be brought to justice only if Pakistan extends sincere support to India's efforts.

Notwithstanding the Government's vigilant actions after Mumbai attacks, terrorist activities have been found but at low level. Bihar-born Nepali national Mohammad Omar Madani, an alleged Lashkar-e-Taiba operative was arrested on 4th June 2009. He ran a logistical hub in Nepal to facilitate the transit of Jihadists to their targeted destinations in India. Madani provided LeT operatives with passports, cash and communication facilities that allowed them to travel from Pakistan to India through Kathmandu- and then escape by the same route.

Over 100 naxalites ambushed an elite police team that was conducting a routine exercise near the Laheri police outpost in Maharashtra on 8th October 2009. Seventeen policemen were killed in the attack. Maoists massacred 77 police personnel in Chhattisgarh State on 6th April 2010.

Two bicycle-bomb blasts in Nalbari, headquarters town of Nalbari district of Assam State on 22nd November 2009 killed 7 people and left 55 including minor children injured. The bomb explosion at the German Bakery in Pune killed 17 persons including 3 foreigners and injured about 40 people on 13th February 2010. The forces of Central and State Governments need to build greater coordination and step up concerted efforts to quell the terrorist threat to the country.

H.M.: Terrorists from Pakistan struck India. But that country also has not been spared from terrorism. what do you say about the happenings there?

Kumaresan: It is true, sir. The Pakistan People's Party chief and former Prime Minister Benazir Bhutto returned to her homeland on 18th October 2007 after many years of stay abroad. While attending the reception rally arranged by her supporters in Karachi, there was a failed bid on her life. Nearly 150 rallyists died and more than 450 were injured. Unmindful of constant threat to her life, Benazir participated in the electioneering campaign for over two months. After addressing an election rally in Rawalpindi on 27th December 2007, she was killed in a shooting-cum-suicide attack on her jeep. There was public reproach against inadequate security for her. But President Pervez Musharraf ascribed her death to her recklessness. However, he was alleged to have been part of a 'Broad conspiracy' to eliminate Benazir before elections, and an anti-terrorism court issued an arrest warrant for him in February 2011.

Twin suicide attacks were carried out in Lahore on 11th March 2008 in which 24 persons were killed and 170 injured. Following a massive blast outside the Marriott Hotel in Islamabad on 20th September 2008, around 60 persons including the Czech envoy Ivo Zdarek were killed and 266 injured. Unidentified terrorists ambushed the convoy of the visiting Sri Lankan cricket team in Lahore on 3rd March 2009. The attack launched by at least a dozen men who wielded guns and grenades took a toll of seven lives including six policemen and injured six cricketers. The entire world under shock, condemned the attack and stressed to root out the terrorist bases and infrastructure from Pakistan. Militants launched an attack on a Police Training School near Lahore on 30th March 2009, killing 8 police trainees and injuring 95 persons including some civilian bystanders. Pakistan security forces established control over the school after a grim eight-hour gun battle with armed militants. The Taliban claimed responsibility for the attack. In Pakistan's North-West Frontier Province, a suicide bomber rammed an explosives-laden vehicle into a police checkpoint in the Tangi area on 15th April 2009. Ten police personnel and six civilians were killed in the attack. The checkpoint of security forces in Doaba, a town in north-western Pakistan was subjected to a suicide attack on 18th April 2009. The attacker detonated a car bomb causing the death of 20 security forces personnel.

The hard-core and extremist Taliban of Afghanistan not only made the North-West Frontier Province (NWFP) including the fertile Swat valley of Pakistan their safe haven but also established their stronghold over the area. The Pakistan Government being unable to vanquish the Taliban, held talks with the outfit and reached a pact in February 2009 to bring about ceasefire in the trouble-torn province, evoking concern in India and many other countries. Even while the ceasefire was in force, the Taliban militants planted an improvised explosive device in a market selling music and DVDs in Takhtbhai town in north-west Pakistan on 4th March 2009 and blew up 16 shops overnight. In recent years, Islamic militants have bombed scores of entertainment shops in the NWFP of Pakistan, dogmatizing that music and films are contrary to the creed of Islam. The Taliban created unrest in the region, began to expand their base and influence to other parts, and posed a great challenge to the sovereign authority of Pakistan. In this context, President Asif Ali Zardari paid a visit to the US. On this occasion, the US officials, the Secretary of State Hillary Clinton and finally the US President Mr. Barack Obama impressed upon Zardari that the Taliban and Al-Qaeda were the great threats to the security and integrity of Pakistan and made him realize that it was absolutely imperative to eliminate these wicked forces from the Pakistani soil. The US leaders also coaxed him to believe that India would not be a threat to Pakistan's security. In the wake of these developments, Pakistan reduced its forces deployed along the border with India, and amassed the forces in the NWFP. The people vacated many villages and towns in the province in May 2009 and migrated to far-off areas apprehending battles. According to the data released by the United Nations High Commissioner for Refugees (UNHCR) on 22nd May 2009, over 17 lakh people had fled Swat, Buner and Dir. Over two lakh people registered in refugee camps, while the rest were staying with relatives and friends across the country or in schools and other communal buildings. The exodus was so massive that it forced the President to seek international aid to rehabilitate them. As expected, there was an intensive crackdown on the Taliban from mid-May 2009, and the army claimed to have killed hundreds of Taliban militants and destroyed their bunkers. Amid raging battle in Mingora, about 20,000 people were believed to be trapped in the city at that time. By the end of May 2009, Pakistan army claimed that it had wrested control of several places from the Taliban. In the first week of June, the army claimed to have killed over 1200 militants and lost 90 soldiers. Nevertheless, the Taliban attacks continued.

A powerful blast caused by an explosives-packed van at the police offices next to the provincial headquarters of ISI in Lahore killed 23 people and injured nearly 300 on 27th May 2009. The Government said that the attack was a retaliation to its offensive against the Taliban. A day after the Lahore blast, twin blasts followed by a gun battle in a crowded bazaar in Peshawar–the NWFP capital, killed 5 people and injured over 70. This too was viewed as the Taliban's retaliation. some students of North Waziristan's Razmak Cadet College left their school in a convoy of vehicles on 1st June 2009. Militants began to stop the vehicles and abduct the students. On noticing the trouble, many of the students were said to have escaped abduction as their vehicles turned back and slipped away from the scene. The military rescued all the 71 students and 9 staff who were abducted, after a firefight with their militant captors the next day. The suicide bombing of a five-star hotel in Peshawar in June 2009 by the Taliban using an explosives-packed vehicle killed 16 people and left more than 50 injured. Two of the dead were foreigners working for the UN relief agencies. The incident threatened the continuance of the ongoing humanitarian assistance to over 2 lakh displaced people. When worshippers poured out of a mosque in the NWFP on 5th June 2009, a suicide bomber struck and killed 40 people. Pakistan declared success in the three-month anti-Taliban operations in Swat on 9th July and said the nearly two million displaced people could start returning to their homes. The Tehreek-e-Taliban chief Beithullah Mehsud was reported killed in a US missile strike on 5th August 2009 and succeeded by Hakimullah Mehsud who was also reported dead in a shoot-out with a rival. But the Taliban denied the death of both.

Though Pakistan claimed to have vanquished the Taliban, the outfit's attacks continued. A suicide bomber blew himself up at a police training ground in Mingora in the NWFP on 30th August. 14 policemen were killed and about 20 persons were injured in the attack. A suicide car bomb blast killed 33 people and trapped many victims under smashed shops in Ustarzai–a small town in the NWFP on 18th September. There was a suicide car bomb blast in the Army cantonment area in Peshawar and another in a police station in Bannu in the NWFP on 26th September. At least 16 people were killed and more than 100 wounded in the two blasts. A suicide bomber gained easy entry into the highly guarded office of the United Nations' World Food Programme in Islamabad on 5th October and detonated himself, killing 5 people and wounding 3. 49 people were killed and over 100 injured when a suicide car bomb ripped through a busy market in Peshawar on 9th October. At least six insurgents armed with automatic weapons and grenades stormed Pakistan's Army headquarters in Rawalpindi on 10th October and took about 15 hostages. Six soldiers and four militants died in the exchange of fire. The driver of an explosives–packed car detonated in a crowded market place in Shangla adjacent to the Swat valley in the NWFP on 12th October. He had targeted an army vehicle carrying soldiers. The suicide attack killed 41 people including six security personnel and left 45 people wounded. The attackers managed to take 42 hostages and demanded the release of over 100 militants belonging to several groups in exchange for the hostages. A synchronised triple-attack by armed militants rocked Lahore on 15th October. Besides, two separate bomb attacks in the NWFP aggravated tensions in Pakistan. In all 39 people including civilians, security personnel and militants were killed and many people injured. A suicide bomber detonated his explosives-packed car in front of a police station at Peshawar on 16th October. At least 13 people were killed in the attack including a woman, a child and three policemen. Eleven people were wounded. Two suicide bombers detonated themselves in different parts of the Islamabad Islamic University campus on 20th October killing 5 students and wounding 29. In three separate incidents of Taliban bomb attacks in Pakistan on 23rd October, 23 people were killed and 15 injured. A massive bomb blast in Pashawar killed more than 90 people on 28th October. More than 200 people were reported injured in the blast. A fire from the explosion further ravaged the area. This attack was carried out while the US Secretary of State Mrs. Hillary Clinton was present in Islamabad. The incident cast a shadow on her three-day visit to Pakistan. A powerful explosion that was believed to have been caused by a suicide bomber took place in the parking lot of a hotel in Rawalpindi on 2nd November. At least 34 people were killed and nearly 50 wounded in the attack. Late in the evening, a suicide bomber detonated himself at a police checkpoint outside Lahore when his car was stopped. Seven policemen were injured and two of them seriously in the attack. A suicide car bomb in the NWFP town of Charsadda killed at least 30 people and left more than 40 wounded on 10th November. There was a suicide car bomb blast on the outskirts of Peshawar on 14th November. At least 11 people were killed and 26 others left wounded. Pakistani Taliban claimed responsibility for this suicide bomb attack. A suicide attack in Peshawar on 19th November killed at least 19 people and left 45 others injured. A suicide-cum-gun and grenades attack at a mosque in Rawalpindi at prayer time on 4th December killed at least 40 people and wounded scores including senior serving and retired army officers and their children. Pakistani Taliban claimed responsibility for the carnage. A suicide bombing-cum-rocket attack on the ISI headquarters in Multan in Pakistan's southern Punjab killed eight people and wounded more than thirty on 8th December. A powerful suicide car bomb detonated at a crowded market place in the Punjab town of Dera Ghazi Khan on 15th December killed 20 people and wounded more than 60. These reported data show that there were hundreds of people killed and injured in militant attacks in Pakistan during 2007 and 2008. In 2009, the situation worsened. During the period of 10 months from March to December 2009, there were 32 terrorist attacks in Pakistan in which 625 people were killed and more than 1400 injured. The last quarter of the year 2009 is notable for intensified terrorist attacks in Pakistan. The year 2010 also witnessed many attacks without an end. A teenaged suicide bomber clad in school uniform detonated himself at a military base in the north-western part of Pakistan on 10th February 2011. Over 30 soldiers were killed and more than 40 injured in this attack. I have revealed the datewise events to you with reference to the entries in my diary. I am unable to predict as to how long I will have to make such entries in the future.

H.M.: Does President Zardari make sincere attempt to quell terrorism in Pakistan and elsewhere?

Kumaresan: Mr. Zardari, in his article to 'The New York Times' published in December 2008, claimed himself to be an aggrieved person since his wife Benazir was a victim of terrorism. According to him, there were about 600 terrorism-related incidents in Pakistan during 2008 claiming a toll of 2,000 lives including 1,400 civilians and 600 security personnel. Mr. Zardari's information must be more precise than mine which is based on the media reports which usually cover only major attacks. The Pakistan President claimed to have countered terrorists by aggressive wars in areas bordering Afghanistan in which 600 militants were killed. He stressed that 'Pakistan was committed to the pursuit, arrest, trial and punishment of anyone involved in the Mumbai attacks'. He assured 'action against the non-State actors found within his territory, treating them as criminals, terrorists and murderers'. He also pleaded, "The world must act to strengthen Pakistan's economy and democracy, help us build civil society and provide us with the law-enforcement and counter-terrorism capacities that will enable us to fight the terrorists effectively". The President was honest and ingenuous in the admission of 'the legacy of dictatorship, the fatigue of fanaticism and the destruction of democratic infrastructure in Pakistan'. A group of civil servants met the President on 7th July 2009 to discuss national issues of Pakistan. Then he reportedly said that militants and extremists had been deliberately created and nurtured as a policy for short-term tactical objectives". This was the first candid admission of reality by Pakistan at the highest level. Only these militants produced by Pakistan carried out terrorist activities in that country and India as well. Even if Pakistan Government has tenacity of mind to annihilate terrorism, it needs to remain stable and strong and not fragile or brittle. Any jolt of the Government will be a threat to the democracy of that country. For instance, the 'National Reconciliation Ordinance' promulgated by the Pakistan People's Party Government was annulled by the Supreme Court in mid-December 2009. A spokesman of the anti-corruption National Accountability Bureau reportealy said, "The machine has started to move and the pre-NRO position is being restored. Those who had convictions, arrest warrants, or whose accounts were lying frozen before the NRO, they are all being restored to that position." Consequently, some Ministers faced possible arrest, summons from the accountability courts and restrictions on travel abroad. Such developments must be avoided and democracy should be enabled to take deep roots in Pakistan to tackle terrorism.

H.M.: I have understood that developed and developing countries were also subjected to terrorism. Could you please comment on that aspect?

Kumaresan: A bomb was planted aboard a London-New York Pan Am flight 103 which crashed over Lockerbie in Scotland on 21st December 1988, killing all the 259 people on board, besides 11 on the ground. The accused was reportedly sheltered in Libya. For many years, the Libyan Government refused to deport the accused. Later, it capitulated to the demand and handed over Abdel Baset Alial-Megrahi for trial in a special Scottish court sitting in the Netherlands. He was found guilty, sentenced to 27 years in prison, and jailed in 2001. As Mr. Megrahi suffered terminal prostate cancer, he was released on compassionate grounds in August 2009, though America deplored the release.

In the 1990s, a militant outfit called 'Felon Gong' indulged in terrorist activities in southern Philippines. The terrorists targeted mainly tourists including foreigners and killed many of them. In one of a number of instances of massacre, the militants handcuffed and blindfolded nearly 10 persons and beheaded them at the same time and that gruesome scene was telecast in some channels with a warning to the weak-hearted persons and children to aviod viewing the scene.

In 1998, the US embassies in Kenya and Tanzania became the targets of bombings. Osama-bin-Laden's lieutenant Abdul Rahman al-Safani of Yemen was believed to have been involved in these attacks.

The United States met with a holocaust that took a toll of around

3,000 lives when terrorists carried out aerial attacks on the twin towers of New York and the Pentagon near Washington DC on 11th September 2001. The alleged mastermind Khalid Sheikh Mohammad and his four associates were incarcerated in Guantanamo Bay, Cuba. During their trial before a US military tribunal, they indicated their wish to confess to terror charges.

The bombings in Bali, Indonesia in October 2002 killed 202 people. Bali was bombed in 2005 also. Three perpetrators of the crime were executed on 9th November 2008.

On 5th August 2003, a suicide bomber detonated a car bomb outside the lobby of the JW Marriott Hotel in the Indonesin capital Jakarta killing 12 people and injuring 150. Several explosions rocked the same hotel and the adjacent Ritz-Carlton Hotel on 17th July 2009 killing 9 persons and injuring 40 others. The Australian Embassy in Jakarta was attacked in 2004.

In October 2004, bombings at three sites on the east coast of the Sinai Peninsula killed 34 people. The Egyptian Government said that the mastermind was Palestinian and their targets appeared to be Israeli tourists.

On 9th November 2005, the Al-Qaeda conducted a series of coordinated bombings on three hotels in Amman, the capital of Jordan. The blasts at the Grand Hyatt Hotel, the Radisson SAS Hotel and the Days Inn killed 60 people and injured 115. One of the hotels was hosting a wedding with hundreds of guests.

On 29th June 2007, two cars laden with explosives were found in the West End area of London but the bombs failed to detonate. Had they gone off, the toll would have been heavy. The next day, a UK based Iraqi doctor Bilal Abdulla, accompanied by an Indian doctor Kafeel Ahmed, drove a burning jeep packed with explosives into the Glasgow airport's main terminal building in a bid to blow up the complex. Kafeel succumbed to burns. Dr. Abdulla and Dr. Mohammed Asha working together for the National Health Service (NHS) were charged with plotting a series of terror attacks across the UK by using bombs concealed in vehicles. While Asha was cleared, Abdulla was convicted of conspiracy to murder and bomb the Glasgow airport and public places in London, and sentenced to life imprisonment.

Canada proscribed the Lashkar-e-Taiba in 2003. 'National Post' reported in December 2008 that the LeT had been linked to recent terrorist plots in many Western Countries including Canada and the outfit's followers had been accused of contriving attacks in Toronto, the US, Britain and Australia. The report also stated that at least five suspects associated with the "Toronto 18"-described by police as a home-grown extremist group accused of plotting attack on Parliament Hill in Ottawa and to detonate truck bombs near the CN Tower in Toronto in 2006, allegedly travelled to Pakistan to train at Lashkar camps.

There was a car bombing outside a police barracks in Northern Spain on 29th July 2009. Interior Minister Alfredo Perez Rubalcaba said, "Forty-one children could have been killed." More than 60 people were wounded in the attack. Spain accused the Basque separatist group ETA of trying to kill women and children.

There was a bomb blast targeting the Indian Embassy in Kabul on 7th July 2008 that killed 60 people. The Embassy was targeted for the second time on 8th October 2009. A suicide car bomb blast took place near the Embassy in which 15 civilians and two Afghan policemen were killed and 76 wounded. Most of the wounded were civilians. A suicide bomber killed five top commanders of Iran's elite force 'Islamic Revolution Guards Corps (IRGC) on 18th October 2009. A powerful bomb derailed a speeding express train half way between Moscow and St Petersburg on 27th November 2009 killing at least 26 people and wounding nearly 100. Suicide bombings at two Metro stations in Moscow killed 39 people and injured more than 70 on 29th March 2010. Another twin suicide bombings on 31st March in North Caucasus of Russia killed 11 people including 9 policemen. A suicide bomb attack at Domodedovo airport near Moscow on 24th January 2011 killed 35 people including 8 foreigners and wounded 180 people. A bomb blast ripped through a hotel in the lawless Somali capital Mogadishu on 3rd December 2009, killing three Ministers and eight others.

Two leading security consultancy firms- 'Aon' and 'Janusian', created a 'Terrorism Threat Map' in which India, Pakistan, Afghanistan, Iraq, Yemen and Somalia had been classified under the most extreme category of 'severe threats'. The US and Canada were both classified under the middle category of 'elevated threats'. The map released on 2nd June 2009 listed Iraq, Afghanistan, Pakistan and India as the countries most afflicted by terrorist incidents in 2008. 'Aon' in its assessment of worldwide terrorism, said that South Asia was becoming the global hub of terrorist activities. An 'Aon' representative said that the global economic climate, with its concentration of wealth, could give rise to a more traditional, class-based form of terrorist activity.

H.M.: What is the cause of terrorism?

Kumaresan: Iranian President Mahmoud Ahmadinejad, while expressing "deep sorrow and pain" over the loss of lives and injury to Indians in the Mumbai attacks, mentioned that an "unfair international order" was the root cause of terrorism. He also attributed terrorism to the "occupationist and disuniting policies that tried to undermine regional security and stability". Though his comment is obviously a hit at some particular countries, his views cannot be totally repudiated. Besides, I feel that certain sections of people want others to follow their ways of life and fulfil all their wishes. Some harsh radicals are fierce in imposing their ideals on other people. While one cannot always act as he himself wishes, how can he expect others to emulate him? So, it is not possible for anybody to rope in all others to associate with him. People's feelings, mentality, interests, wishes, aspirations, aims, cultures, beliefs, faiths, etc. are very diverse naturally. So, it is always wise to find unity in diversity. But many people fail to realize this because they pant for sway over others. Selfishness, ego, intolerance and craze for power and money are inherent in them. So, they develop conflict of interests which leads to row over petty issues, animosity towards adversaries, wrangle with them over dissenting views, clash between them and finally internecine brawls. Such kind of persons identify like-minded individuals and are befriended by them. Most of them happen to be dropouts, the unemployed and loafers who become a sadistic group. Such groups in several places collude with each other in drawing and executing nefarious plans. In order to achieve their selfish goals, they entice youths and adolescents into violent means, taking the law in their own hands, to find remedy to any problem. The misguided youths are provided with money, training, modern arms and ammunition for terrorist activities. The established networks create all necessary infrastructure to aid, organize and facilitate high magnitude of terrorism in different parts of the world.

H.M.: Do the terrorists have any aims and objectives?

Kumaresan: Yes, they have their own objectives though they are neither sober nor noble.The objectives of terrorists vary in different places and contexts. Generally, they want to:

1. Create a sense of insecurity, defeat and despondency over life among the people of the targeted society or country.

2. Create people's profound hatred for political leaders and gradually for democratic set-up.

3. Destroy public properties.

4. Hamper peace, happiness and prosperity of people and stability of the nation as a whole.

5. Discredit, demoralize and cripple the Tourism Industry.

6. Threaten international sports and games.

7. Prevent investors' confidence and flow of foreign funds and thereby hinder the growth of industries, business and economy to ruin India's aim of becoming a superpower by 2020.

H.M.: Time is said to be the cure for all ills. Can we expect terrorism to come to an end in the near future?

Kumaresan: I don't think so, sir. According to 'The Washington Post' dated 2nd December 2008, a bipartisan task force created by the US Congress predicted that a weapon of mass destruction, either nuclear or biological would be used in a terrorist attack on a major city somewhere in the world by the end of 2013 unless the world community took an urgent and decisive action. That prophecy was ascribed to threats from rogue States, nuclear smuggling networks and the spread of weapons know-how. The panel's report further added, "In our judgment, America's margin of safety is shrinking, not growing". I therefore, think that vigorous and extensive actions based on meticulous strategies to wipe out terrorism will pay dividends.

H.M.: What suggestions do you propound to counter terrorism?

Kumaresan: Terrorists usually attack places where people gather so that casualties would be high. Among such places they consider hotels, especially star hotels as important targets because the guests belong to an elite class consisting of delegates, higher officials, business tycoons, foreign tourists, representatives, etc. So, at the time of checking into any hotel, everyone must be subjected to frisking, scanning of luggage and other hi-tech surveillance methods. Besides being kind and polite, the hospitality industry must step up security measures leaving no room for access to hotels without proper identity. Anyone visiting a staying guest must also be compelled to produce his identity card and undergo checks before allowing them in. Apart from hotels-railway stations, markets, office complexes and other public places with throngs must be closely monitored by specially trained armed police or security personnel.

The sources of finances to terrorists and distribution routes must be traced out and paralysed. We must make optimum use of the modern equipment of Information Technology to track down the source and destination of communications between terrorists. There must be close coordination of various intelligence and security agencies within the country. Beyond this, a strong and vibrant network of international intelligence agencies should be established and sustained. Expeditious exchange of information and instant actions must be ensured by framing governing laws. Further, the bunkers, training camps and supply routes of terrorists must be monitored by satellites and destroyed.

The Central Intelligence Agency (CIA) of the US deserves to be hailed for its delivery of two warnings in September 2008 of an impending terror attack on Mumbai through the Research and Analysis Wing (RAW). The agency specially warned that the Lashkar-e-Taiba was planning an attack on targets where large numbers of foreigners were present including the 'Taj Mahal Hotel'. The warnings corroborated the testimony of the lone apprehended terrorist Ajmal. However, the warnings turned futile due to laxity on the part of Indian authorities. Had they acted swiftly, the boon of such international links could have been brought to fruition. After the terrorist attacks in Mumbai, Mr. Barack Obama was asked whether India had the right to "take out" high-value targets inside Pakistan with or without the permission of Islamabad, falling in line with his own contention in regard to the US under his Presidency. He responded saying, "I think that sovereign nations obviously have a right to protect themselves". Endorsing his stand, a former US Secretary of State Ms. Madeleine Albright exactly reverberated Mr. Obama's comment. India should not hesitate to act in this direction if necessary.

On the other hand, religious leaders must exercise their venerable position and power to curb jihadi practices and instil non-violence, humane traits, compassion and universal benevolence in the minds of adolescents and youths. Every govternment could evolve counselling agencies to revert the misguided youths and put them back on the mainstream by providing suitable employment.

H.M.: Okay. By the way, there is another kind of terrorism, called 'State Terrorism'. Could you comment on that?

Kumaresan: A country's unprovoked attacks on an another

country is termed 'State Terrorism'. Though the attack is usually abrupt it is always deliberate because the attacker mulls it over for a long time. For instance, a taped Oval Office conversation that took place on 14th December 1972 and revealed on 2nd December 2008 throws more light on President Richard Nixon's slur. He had unveiled his intention to rain North Vietnam with bombs, to the National Security Adviser Henry Kissinger and adviser Alexander Haig. He had given orders to go ahead for one of the most controversial wars. Just after four days, the US unleashed a massive series of air strikes on Hanoi (now Ho Chi Minh city). Nixon's operatives embarked in mud-slinging on his critics and public figures, decrying even their personal matters and struggled to contain growing public unrest over the war in vietnam. With distrust in his aides, Nixon was sceptical of their loyalty. He had closed-eyes on, and deaf-ears to anti-war and civil rights protests. He had an obsession of foes all around and felt besieged. Ultimately, he made an unceremonious and premature exit following the busting of the Water-gate scandal. Even after pounding Vietnam for 12 years, the US could not vanquish its enemy and the State terrorism in the name of 'Vietnam War' could earn only the title 'bully' for the superpower.

H.M.: What is the role of the US in Afghanistan?

Kumaresan: The US and NATO forces deployed in Afghanistan in October 2001 to counter the Taliban and capture Al-Qaeda leader Osama-bin-Laden and his activists in the wake of aerial attacks in the US on 11th September 2001, continue to linger there for so many years. During their attacks on their targets, civilian deaths have become very common. In 2007, a US military convoy ploughed into several vehicles killing seven people including a family. The incident triggered riots involving thousands of irate Kabul residents. To quell the rioters, the security forces fired at the protesters on the streets killing at least 15 people. In the same year, a convoy of US marines hit by a bomb attack, subsequently opened fire in a bazaar killing 16 people. The guilty marines were dismissed and their officers charged, but they were later absolved. In July 2008, a bridal party was heading towards the groom's village in an area called 'Kamala' in the eastern province of Nangarhar on eve of the celebrations. Then a plane came pouncing low and dropped the first bomb which hit a large group of children who had run on ahead of the main procession, and killed most of them instantly. Within minutes, the plane returned to drop the second bomb right in the centre of the group, taking the lives of many women.

The bride and two girls who survived this attack, scrambled down the hillside to escape, but they too fell victims to a third bomb. Hajj Khan, an aged man who had led the bride's party said, "we were walking, I was holding my grandson's hand, then there was a loud noise and everything went white. When I opened my eyes, everybody was screaming. I was lying, metres from where I had been, I was still holding my grandson's hand, but the rest of him had gone. I looked around and saw pieces of bodies every where. I couldn't make out which part was which". Relatives from the groom's village being unable to identify the remains, buried the 47 victims in 28 graves. The air strike on the wedding party sparked riots that turned violent and the army had to be called in to bring the situation under control. The US military initially denied any civilian deaths in the Kamala bombing, but issued vague statements later.

In November 2008, 27 people were killed when a wedding party was bombed near Kandhahar. It was the 3rd wedding party to be hit in 2008 alone. Stories like this were quite common in Afghanistan. More than 600 civilians died in NATO and US strikes in 2008. According to the Afghan Independent Human Rights Commission, about 750 civilians were killed by foreign forces in 2008. A data indicated that the number of Afghan civilians killed in US-NATO military actions between 1st January and 8th April 2009 alone was around 200. The worst of the air strikes was carried out on two villages in Farah province that killed more than 100 innocent civilians including women and children on 4th May 2009. Humanitarian aid agencies reckoned higher figures since many victims branded as 'insurgents' were actually non-combatants. Most of the victims were killed in air strikes and the rest were shot dead by jumpy soldiers who opened fire in crowded public places after an attack on one of their convoys. Afghan civilians went down like nine pins. Informants for the foreign forces often provided misinformation both inadvertently and malignantly. Every day, terrified drivers in Kabul veered off the way as foreign troops hurtled through the streets in their armoured conoys training their rifles on the drivers and pedestrians. Afghans perceived that their lives were cheap in the eyes of the foreigners. Although they didn't suspect intentional killing of civilians, they lamented absence of care to spare them. But there were reports in September 2010 that some US soldiers allegedly killed 3 Afghan men for sport. A 'Human Rights Watch' report said that US investigations had been "unilateral, ponderous and lacking in transparency, undercutting rather than improving relations with people or the Afghan Government". The attacks by foreign forces were counter-productive. A Taliban commander in Oruzgan province had said that the attacks were sending recruits his way daily. He added, "There are now Taliban in every village, many of them have rejoined the movement after the savage attacks carried out by the Americans". Notwithstanding the presence of NATO forces, the Taliban continued its offensive many a time. For instance, an explosive-laden car was exploded by a suicide bomber outside the NATO military headquarters in Kabul on 15th August 2009. Seven Afghans were killed and 91 others injured in the attack. Suicide gunmen of Pakistani Taliban clad in police uniform stormed a UN guest house in Kabul on 28th October 2009, killing nine persons including six UN staff. In the American attacks on the suspected hideouts of the Taliban in the NWFP of Pakistan also, many civilians have been killed on several occasions. A suspected missile strike by the US killed at least five people in a tribal region on 14th June 2009. Drone aircrafts which were deployed by the US forces in the tribal region of Waziristan struck on 23rd June 2009 while hundreds of people gathered for a funeral, and killed upto 65 people. Pakistan Government protested against such incidents. There was concern that under the US President Barack Obama's surge, the civilian casualties would rise markedly. I don't find any fault with the efforts of American-NATO forces to destory the Taliban or Al-Qaeda, but their careless and indiscriminate attacks causing frequent deaths of civilians in Afghanistan and Pakistan deserve condemnation.

H.M.: Do you think that the American invasion of Iraq amounts to 'State terrorism'?

Kumaresan: Yes, indeed. The former US President George W Bush, in consultation with the former British Prime Minister Tony Blair, decided to attack Iraq alleging possession of 'Weapons of Mass Destruction (WMD)'. The US forces, joined by the British forces, pounded Iraq for about three months in 2003 in the name of 'Operation Desert Storm' and demolished Saddam Hussein's regime. Saddam went underground to avoid arrest while most of his aides were apprehended. The heavy bombardment created a holocaust-like situation in Iraq. As the main focus was on its capital Baghdad and other cities, there was huge loss of lives and buildings. Even after Iraq fell into the hands of the US, fights continued between its forces and the armed groups, especially Saddam's supporters posing stiff resistance. Hundreds of vehicles, many public properties, several market places, bazaars and even mosques were subjected to bomb blasts in which several thousands of innocent people including women and children were killed over a period of 5 years. Injuries, disabilities, deaths, screams and funerals happened almost every day. Shortage of food, milk powder and essential commodities on the one hand and scarcity of medicines and equipment to treat the wounded and sick on the other, caused by war and embargo, led Iraq to a humanitarian crisis. The belated 'Food for Oil Pact' arranged by the UN could not sustain the people. The Iraqi children were so traumatized by war, scenes of bloodshed and endangered life that they needed psychological counselling and treatment. Clashes broke out between 'Shia' and 'Sunni' Muslims. Saddam Hussein, who went underground was captured from a bunker after a few months and sued for ordering the death of nearly 200 Shia Muslims. It was a charge levelled against him and many of his close aides in a specially constituted court within Iraq. There was widespread criticism that the interim Iraqi Government allegedly set up by Mr. George W Bush and consisting of Saddam's opponents had appointed a farcical court and the trial was biased against the accused. During the trial, one of Saddam's lawers was killed and some others were intimidated into withdrawing from the case. The trial was said to be hasty, giving not enough time or scope for the defence lawers to analyse the case in detail. It was a travesty of justice. The judge pronounced doom against Saddam and other accused. But the US authorities who scoured entire Iraq for 'Weapons of Mass Destruction' could not detect any. Mr. Tariq Aziz, Foreign Minister and Deputy Prime Minister during Mr. Saddam's rule, was jailed for 15 years in March 2009 for the execution of 42 Iraqi merchants. The Iraqi High Tribunal later in the last week of October 2010, sentenced Mr. Aziz to death along with four others for committing crimes against humanity by elimination of religious parties. However, Iraqi President Jalal Talabani expressed compassion for Mr. Aziz, adding that he would never sign the order to execute him. Even after Saddam Hussein and most of his close aides were sent to the gallows, violence and unrest continued in Iraq. More than 2,000 members of the foreign forces also lost their lives.

During their actions in Iraq, some of the US troops committed many war crimes. As one of the most chilling crimes, five American soldiers gang-raped a 14-year-old girl and killed her along with her parents and six-year-old sister in March 2006. Three soldiers were given life sentence by a military court. The fourth who acted as lookout, was jailed for 27 months. The leader of the gang rape Steven Dale

Green, convicted of rape and murders, faced death penalty. He was declared guilty on 17 charges by a federal jury in a Kentucky civilian court on 7th May 2009. Iraqis strongly demanded execution of Green and fulfil America's humanitarian responsibility. Master Sergeant John E. Hatley, a senior US soldier was accused of shooting four blindfolded prisoners in March 2007 in south- west Baghdad. According to witnesses, the bodies were dumped into a canal and never retrieved. The soldier was jailed for life in April 2009.

Abraham Lincoln said, "No man is good enough to govern another man without that other's consent." The presence of US-led forces in Iraq was decried worldwide. The US people held huge protest rallies against President George W Bush and clamoured for withdrawal of their forces, and the British people followed suit against Prime Minister Tony Blair. After change of guard in Britain, as decided by Prime Minister Gordon Brown, the British troops commenced pull-out from Iraq at the beginning of April 2009. Since 2003, 179 British troops were reported killed. But there was no let-up in violence. In Southern Iraq, the market at Al-Bathaa, a Shia Muslim town, was crowded with people. On 10th June 2009, a car bomb ripped through the market, killing 32 people and wounding 70 others. The hospital officials struggled to cope with the injured. Four US soldiers were killed in combat on 29th June 2009 in Baghdad. The next day witnessed killing of at least 24 people in a car bomb explosion in a crowded outdoor market in the northern city of Kirkuk. Over the last week of June 2009, there was a surge in violence in Iraq leading to 250 deaths. This had generated apprehensions whether there would be a resurgence of near civil war conditions because the Iraqi Government dominated by 'Shias' could alienate the 'Sunni' community. Iraq and the US signed a troop pull-out pact under which the US soldiers are to be withdrawn by the end of 2011. However, Mr. Bush's successor President Barack Obama had expressed his desire for troop pull-out by the end of 2009. America had signed the Status of Forces Agreement (SOFA) with Iraq under which the US troops had to pull out of urban areas. Accordingly, American soldiers were withdrawn from all Iraqi cities and towns on 30th June 2009 and continued to operate outside city limits. Still, incidents of violence were reported. There were two suicide bomb attacks in the northern town of Tal Afar in Iraq on 9th July 2009. Besides, two bombs exploded in a market in Sadr city. A roadside bomb exploded in the Karrada business district of Baghdad. 42 people were killed in these attacks. Trucks laden with explosives blew up outside the key Ministries of Finance and Foreign Affairs in Baghdad on 19th August 2009. 86 people were killed and nearly 300 injured in the explosions. Dozens of cars parked outside were also set ablaze. This was the worst violence since the US troops vacated Iraq's cities. A suicide bomber walked into the Sunni mosque in Tal Afar on 16th October 2009 and started firing on worshippers with an AK-47 rifle. When he ran out of ammunition, he detonated his explosive belt, killing 11 people and wounding 42 others. Two suicide car bombs, which targeted the Justice Ministry and the Baghdad provincial administration, exploded in Baghdad on 25th October 2009 killing 136 people and injuring nearly 600. At least 25 staff members of the Baghdad Provincial Council were killed in the bombing. Sunni militants, seeking to overthrow the Shia-dominated Government, were suspected to be the perpetrators. A string of car bombings in Baghdad on 8th December 2009 killed 112 persons and left 207 injured. Terrorist attacks in Iraq happened often in 2010 also. Suicide bomb blasts on an Iraqi recruitment centre and army headquarters in Baghdad in August 2010 killed 61 persons and wounded 125 others. The most heart-rending tragedy was witnessed on 31st October 2010.

On that fateful day, an alleged Al-Qaeda group in uniform, took over a Catholic Cathedral in Baghdad-killed the priest and held more than 100 worshippers hostages inside. The militants contacted the Iraqi authorities over mobile phone and demanded the release of Al-Qaeda prisoners in Egypt. Since the negotiations were fruitless, security personnel stormed the church. The grenades and explosions of suicide bombs killed 52 people and wounded many others. Following this carnage, insurgents- suspected as Al-Qaeda-linked Sunni militants, carried out coordinated rapid-fire bombings and mortar strikes in 13 separate neighbourhoods of Baghdad on 2nd November 2010. 76 people were killed and more than 200 wounded in the attacks. Christians were again targeted in the 2nd week of November 2010 with 13 bomb and two mortar attacks on their homes and shops in which six people were killed and 33 injured.

Terrorist attacks in Iraq continued in 2011 also. A suicide bomber detonated his explosives-packed vest in Tikrit on 18th January targeting police recruits. At least 50 people were killed in the attack. After mere two days, a triple suicide bombing along two highways leading to the holy city of Karbala on 20th January, targeting Shia pilgrims, killed 56 people and injured 180 others. Two car bombs on 24th January, struck Shia pilgrims in the same Karbala, killing 18 people and wounding 55 others. A car bomb ripped through a funeral tent in a Shia area of

Baghdad on 27th January, killing 40 people and wounding 78 others. A suicide bombing outside the city of Samarra on 12th February, killed at least 27 Shia pilgrims travelling in a bus.

Terrorist attacks are likely to continue as long as the US troops stay in Iraq and the Shia-Sunni animosity persists. So, withdrawal of US forces from Iraq was expected to take place earlier than the time stipulated in the accord. The combat troops were withdrawn in August 2010. Mr Obama stated that all the US troops would leave Iraq by the end of 2011. Nevertheless, the travails of state terrorism will haunt the people of Iraq. Mr. George W Bush, just before laying down office as President, admitted that he was "unprepared for war" when he joined Oval Office and said that his "biggest regret" during his eight-year tenure was the "intelligence failure on Iraq." He said that many people and a lot of leaders of nations around the world were all looking at the same intelligence. I feel that any expression of remorse after wreaking havoc on Iraq is akin to praying the Sun after losing the eyes.

H.M.: Is there any means to prevent State Terrorism?

Kumaresan: The people of every country always desire peace and friendship with all other people in the world. But unfortunately, a few individuals without universal brotherhood and possessing Big Brother attitude and tendency to hold sway over others, occasionally become national leaders. Such leaders, being intolerant, are easily perturbed by any conflicting views or actions of their counterparts in other countries. It is only these bullies who indulge in State Terrorism. This problem could be solved if the leaders of powerful countries are resolute in avoiding interference in the affairs of other countries. Any row between countries must be resolved only through the United Nations and never by any sort of direct action. In order to play an effective and successful role, the UN must have teeth. Its laws and regulations should be strengthened with necessary modifications or amendments to make them binding on all countries. To fulfil this purpose, all nations must usher in vigorous UN reforms expeditiously.

H.M.: Thank you for your narration. Let us take leave of you.

Kumaresan: It is very late for dinner. So, please have your dinner here, sir.

Vijay: We shall be glad if you dine with us, sir.

Charli: Yes, with pleasure.

H.M.: Keep quiet. Are you hungry?

Charli: I am always hungry. I have been keeping quiet all along your conversation. Had I intervened, I could have given a novel suggestion to end the threat of terrorism.

H.M: Who did prevent you from giving suggestion?

Charli: I was mute because you had gagged me.

H.M: It's okay. What is your suggestion?

Charli: I shall tell about it after having dinner.

Vijay: Why do you defer airing your views?

Charli: Because I may be left bereft of my dinner by being driven out by my boss.

Kumaresan: He will not leave you to starve. So, you may utter your novel suggestion vociferously.

Charli: My suggestion is just that every household in the world must possess lethal weapons so that none will dare to attack others and peace will prevail in every nation.

H.M.: Do you propose to proliferate weapons all over the world?

Charli: No. My suggestion is a paradox. If it is followed, nobody could be a bully like........

Vijay: Like whom?

H.M: He makes a satire on me. He deserves the punishment expected by himself. So, you may send him out.

Charli: No, Sir. It is a folly to call you a bully since you are holy.

H.M.: Don't feign in vain but now turn one of swine to dine.

Charli: That's fine and relieves all pain. You may call me 'Thotty' but pay me forty. (You may call me a scavenger, provided you give me money).

All are laughing. After having their dinner, the headmater and charli return home.

3
GLOBAL WARMING AND CLIMATE CHANGE

The headmaster and Charli arrive at Rahul's home.

Rahul: Good evening and welcome, sir.

H.M.: Good evening Rahul.

Rahul: (Turning to his father Madhavan) Meet our headmaster, Dad.

Madhavan: Hello, sir. Please take a seat.

H.M.: Thank you. May I know about you?

Madhavan: I am an assistant manager in the Ministry of Environment and Pollution Control. Now, I am on leave for a week. My wife is staying here to help my aged father in maintaining our lands. Rahul is our only son.

Rahul's mother greets the headmaster and provides a drink.

H.M.: The global climate change, the greatest challenge of the 21st century, is attributed to the polluted environment. What are the present trends in this regard?

Madhavan: A 30-year map of the Earth's climate changes has indicated that the planet's atmosphere warmed on an average of about 0.4 degree Celsius. Some top scientists opined at the end of November 2008 that the Earth's climate appeared to be changing more quickly and deeply than a UN report for policy makers predicted. Dr. P.V. Joseph, the former Director of Indian Meteorological Department said, "A new finding is that the sea surface temperature of the equatorial Central Indian Ocean [south of Sri Lanka] has had a phenomenal increase of about 1.5 degree Celsius during the last 50 years. This might weaken the monsoon heat engine [the vertical Monsoon Hadley Cell that drives the monsoon circulation over the Indian subcontinent]".

He added that latent heat released through the condensation of moisture would heat up the atmosphere over the part of the ocean tampering with the seasonal pressure gradient that pulled the moisture-laden winds towards the subcontinent. The number of depressions [that form over the Bay of Bengal] during the monsoon season had come down in the recent decades. Monsoon rainfall over South Kerala, the gateway of the Indian monsoon, too was on the decrease. The strength of the low-level monsoon winds over peninsular India had fallen by nearly 20 per cent over the last 50 years. The data for the last 100 years showed that while rainfall in certain meteorological divisions such as Kerala was on the decreasing trend, in centain other regions such as Maharashtra it was on the increase. The pace of the ocean growing acidic is faster than ever. Scientists have ascribed this phenomenon to the increase of carbon dioxide in the atmosphere. Their finding is that the ocean acidity is proportionate to the level of carbon dioxide in the atmosphere.

In 2008, there was spiralling air pollution from transporting a record 622 million passengers and the highest loss of Amazon and other tropical forests. Scientific reports revealed that Arctic ice was melting faster than ever and 'methane', one of the most damaging climate change gases, was found bubbling up from the tundra and the Arctic Ocean. There were record temperatures and near-record hurricane seasons. It became clear in 2008 that climate change was disproportionately impacting on the poor. Farmers around the world reported a pattern of increasingly unpredictable seasons and social problems linked directly to water and higher temperatures. North-east Brazil, persistently drought-prone, recorded a temperature rise of 1°C in 30 years. Now, more than 1.5 million people face water scarcity and forced to migrate to southern parts of the country to seek employment in the biofuel fields. The people of Nepal, Bangladesh, Niger, Malawi, Uganda and elsewhere are experiencing hotter temperatures and very less predictable rains. Rapid industrialisation in developing countries and growing pollution contribute to global warming.

The United Nations said in November 2008 that emissions from industrialised countries were static in 2006 after six years of growth. But some countries including large emerging economies like India and China did not report on their emissions since 2007. Among the 40 industrialised countries that reported to the United Nations, emissions had increased by 2.5 per cent from 2000 to 2006 viewed as "continued growth" by the climate panel. The UN officials expressed concern that the global economic slowdown would add a new layer of uncertainty about salvaging the appalling situation, because many of the programmes to curb the emissions that cause global warming, required financing and credit.

H.M.: Can we hope, the situation could improve soon?

Madhavan: Unless intensive and concerted efforts are made, the situation is likely to be exacerbated by increasing pollution. Dr. Chris Field, a senior scientist has told that a surge in the use of coal in countries such as China and India impelled soaring greenhouse gas emissions threatening temperature rises. A large-scale melting of the Arctic tundra, releasing billions of tonnes of carbon into the atmosphere, will accelerate warming even further. Lots of forested areas that had been acting as carbon sinks could be converted into carbon sources. Tropical forests, instead of absorbing carbon dioxide from the atmosphere, would release it. All these factors will lead to the tropical forests drying out and becoming vulnerable to devastating wildfires. There is a prediction that the Earth's temperature is likely to rise between 1.1°C and 6.4°C by 2100, depending on future global carbon emissions.

A report by the Intergovernmental Panel on Climate Change (IPCC) said in 2007 that sea levels would rise by 15-59 cm this century, an average of 38.5 cm. But some others disputed this, saying that the panel was underestimating the risk, as an IPCC report in 2001 had predicted 48.5 cm. In September 2008, a team led by Tad Pfeffer at the university of Colorado, published its calculations. It concluded as true, a scenario that thermal expansion due to warming waters would lead to a total sea level rise of roughly 100-200 cm by 2100.

According to new NASA satellite data that shows the latest signs of global warming, more than two trillion tonnes of land ice in Greenland, Antarctica and Alaska have melted since 2003. Between Greenland, Antarctica and Alaska, melting land ice has raised global sea levels about one-fifth of an inch since 2003. Sea levels also rise from water expanding as it warms. There are more melting concerns from global warming, especially with sea ice. The satellite images clearly showed the shift in the location of the Himalayan glaciers since 1937, confirming the fact that 450 glaciers across the Himalayas are melting fast. The glaciers have been reduced in their area from 2,000 sq. km. to 1,600 sq. km. showing a reduction of 20 per cent. Research shows that the Gangotri glacier has retreated 2 km further inwards in the past 180 years at an alarming speed of 17-20 metres/year. Glaciers such as Kafni in Himachal are shrinking at an alarming rate of 20 metres a year. Melting of these glaciers has led to drastic climate changes such as rise in temperature and decrease in snowfall.

H.M.: What are the threats posed by climate change and how do they impact upon human life?

Madhavan: A 12-day United Nations conference on global warming was convened from 1st to 12th December 2008 in Poznan, Poland, in which delegates from 190 nations participarated. The purpose of the meeting was to hold preparatory talks aiming to clinch a global treaty on climate change at the Copenhagen summit in December 2009. Plenty of grim warnings were sounded at the very start of the talks. The forum was cautioned that war, hunger, poverty and sickness would stalk humanity if the world failed to tackle climate change. Polish Environment Minister Maciej Nowicki, who was elected to chair the meeting said, "Humankind in its activity just reached the limits of the closed system of our planet. Further expansion in the same style will generate global threats of really great intensity-huge droughts and floods, cyclones with increasingly more destructive power, pandemics of tropical disease, dramatic decline of biodiversity and increasing ocean levels."

The United Nations Food and Agriculture Organization (FAO) said in a new report entitled "Climate Change and Food Security in Pacific Island Countries", that climate change-related disasters had already seriously constrained the development of the Pacific island nations-and ocean warming, frequent tropical cyclones, flash floods and droughts were likely to bring a devastating impact on food production systems in these countries. Increasing coastal inundation, salination and erosion as a consequence of sea level rise and human activities may contaminate and reduce the size of productive agricultural lands, thus threatening household and local food security as revealed in the report. Alexander Muller, Assistant Director General in the FAO said, "It is critical to build resilience of the food systems to avoid enormous future economic losses in agriculture, fisheries and forestry."

The pace of climate change and the resultant rising sea levels pose a great threat to the inhabitants of many low-lying islands across the world. The expert notion is that monsoon deluge and fall in food output may force nearly 25 crore people into diaspora by 2050.

Migration of people in large numbers from coastal areas, and small island nations becoming desolate will be on the rise. The Maldives, in the close vicinity of India, has initiated creation of a sovereign fund to resettle its population of 3 lakh people abroad, being apprehensive of one-metre rise in sea level and near-total immersion. The island nation has pleaded for treating climate change as a human rights issue at global level. Bangladesh is also under heavy risk as millions of people who are living close to the sea, may resort to migration. The pivotal cause of the problem, namely the soaring level of global atmospheric carbon dioxide that was recorded as 379 parts per million (ppm) in 2005 by the Intergovernmental Panel on Climate Change which was far from 350 ppm considered as safe by climatologists, must be addressed effectively. Building coal-based power plants everywhere aggravates emissions. The poor people fall easy victims to climate change in terms of starvation or displacement. All the world countries should therefore, act swiftly in letter and spirit to cut emissions, contain pollution, conserve water resources, spread green cover and sustain agriculture. The United Nations Framework Convention on Climate Change was expected to usher in wholesome strategy with alacrity at its meeting in Copenhagen.

Health experts say that climate changes increase vector density and it leads to more vector-borne diseases like Malaria, dengue and chikunguna. The Indian Council of Medical Research (ICMR) decided to form a separate cell to study climate change and its impact on public health. The link between climate change and health will be analysed in detail through this proposed cell by forming a network of national level laboratories, researchers, entomologists and State Governments. So, climate changes are likely to pose challenges to human health also. Apart from human beings, marine lives are also facing great risk. An international panel of marine scientists said that the increased acidity of sea water, caused by dissolution of greenhouse gas carbon dioxide by absorption, threatened the survival of coral reefs, shellfish and the marine food web generally. Carbon dioxide is the major component of greenhouse gas emissions which have risen steadily since the beginning of the Industrial Revolution in the 18th century. Acidity of ocean surface waters has increased by 30 per cent since the 17th century. As the gas dissolves in the oceans, it produces carbonic acid. The growing ocean acidity is an environmental threat and severe damages are imminent as warned by the panel on 30th January 2009. It called for urgent actions to reduce emissions of carbon dioxide sharply. The acidification could be controlled only by limiting future atmospheric levels of the gas.

The UK Meteorological Office's Hadley Centre presented a study at a conference on global warming in Copenhagen on 11th March 2009. Vicky Pope of the Hadley centre said that the impact of climate change on the Amazon rainforest was much worse than they thought. Tim Lenton, a climate expert at the University of East Anglia, England, called the study a "bombshell" saying, "When I was young, I thought chopping down the trees would destroy the forest but now it seems that climate change will deliver the killer blow." The research by British climate change specialists shows that even severe cuts in deforestation and carbon emissions will fail to save the rainforest. Upto 85 percent of the forest could be lost if greenhouse gas emissions are not brought under control, the experts said. Though experts had previously prophesied that global warming could cause significant destruction of the Amazon, the new research is the first to quantify the long-term effect. It found that a 2°C rise above pre-industrial levels-the target for ambitious international plans to curb emissions, would still see 20-40 per cent of the Amazon die off within 100 years. A 3°C rise would see 75 per cent of the forest destroyed by drought over the following century, while a 4°C rise would subject 85 per cent of Amazon to perish. As an alarming situation is apparent, it cries for immediate attention. Otherwise, the loss of Amazon is likely to change the tropics–the drivers of the world's weather systems for ever, leading to more extreme weather.

An international agency 'Oxfam' projected that the number of people affected by climate disasters would rise by 133 million to 375 million a year on average by 2015. The agency used the best-available data of 6,500 climate-related disasters since 1980 to reckon the figures shown in its report, "The Right to Survive." The pace of increase in the number of affected people could overwhelm the humanitarian aid system. The projected rise is mainly due to a combination of entrenched poverty and people migrating to densely populated slums which are susceptible to the increasing number of climatic events. The problems could be compounded by the political failure to address these risks and a humanitarian system that is wanting. The world needs to re-engineer the way it responds to, prepares for and prevents disasters. Just to deal with the higher numbers, the world will need to increase its humanitarian aid spending from 2006 levels of $ 14.2 billion to at least $ 25 billion a year. Even this higher amount-the equivalent of only $ 50 per affected person–will still be inadequate to meet their basic needs. While giving aid to the affected people, political or other preferences play influential roles causing unfair practices. The international humanitarian system needs to act swiftly and impartially after disasters, investing money and effort commensurate with need, Oxfam said.

H.M.: What are the proceedings under way to tackle this world problem?

Madhavan: Agreed in 1997, the Kyoto protocol aimed to cut emissions of greenhouse gases across the developed nations by about 5 per cent on 1990 levels. It introduced mechanisms such as carbon trading to help countrties meet their targets. It also put in place monitoring and verification systems, carbon markets, technology transfer and funds for adaptation. But the protocol does not cover the United States which never ratified it, or some developing nations like China. As it ends in 2012, the deadline for the legally binding cuts to be made is 2008-12. The countries capable to make cuts were asked to do so sparing many countries including all those in the developing world. Emissions by the 40 industrialised nations that agreed binding cuts in pollution, are down 5 per cent on 1990 levels. But the decline was attributed not to climate policies but to the collapse of the Soviet Union and the subsequent economic decadence in Eastern Europe in the 1990s. The United Nations climate secretariat said that emissions in Eastern Europe were rising again and the industrialised nations had seen a rise of 7.4 per cent in greenhouse gas emissions within the 2000-2006 time frame.

In 2007, EU nations agreed a broad plan to cut carbon dioxide levels by 20 percent in 2020 compared to 1990, make 20 percent cut in energy use through efficiency measures and to meet 20 percent of energy from water, wind, solar and other renewable sources by 2020. EU Environment Ministers held a meeting in Brussels on 4th December 2008 as a prelude to the EU summit on this subject. They felt the scheme of 'pollution trading rights' as an obstacle in clinching a major accord on climate change at the summit. Germany and Poland were leading the opposition to the scheme that enabled purchase of pollution rights. Poland and other Eastern European nations also wanted special dispensation in the carbon dioxide emissions rules due to their dependence on coal for power.

At the UN meeting on climate change convened in Bali in 2007, the negotiators evinced keen avidity for the Bali road map. The same meeting in December 2008 for 12 days in Poznan (Poland) was a prelude to negotiations for a new UN Climate Treaty as I told already. But this meeting showed a downgraded spirit with the participants taking a light view of the proceedings and desiring to defer pragmatic decisions on a post-2012 road map to fight climate change globally, to the following year. They were tardy in heading towards concrete decisions. They only discussed the inputs to go into the negotiating text for an agreeament in Copenhagen. Many developed nations kept their commitments to cut their greenhouse gas emissions on the back burner, on the pretext of the global economic downturn.

The executive secretary of the United Nations Framework Convention on Climate Change Yvo de Boer in an interview, rejected forcusing on the short-term and ignoring the long-term issue because these decisions would be with us for 30 years. This notion conforms to that of the European Union and the US President Mr. Barack Obama who has vowed to cling to the commitments to cap emissions of carbon dioxide. Mary Robinson – former President of Ireland, Margot Wallstrom – Vice–President of the European Commission and Gro Harlem Brundtland–former Prime Minister of Norway, in a jointly authored article, suggested government action and investment in new green technologies and renewable energy to stimulate the economy and create new jobs, i.e. smart growth. They pointed out that the poorest people and countries–those least responsible would be the hard-hit by the ongoing climate change. They added that the climate change impacts would hamper achievement of many of the United Nations Millennium Development Goals (MDG) including those on poverty alleviation, control of child mortality, and combating HIV/ AIDS, malaria and other diseases. They stressed on innovative ways for capacity building and technology transfer, and the need to ensure availability of fair and proportionate funds for adaptation measurs in developing countries. They exhorted industrialised countries to take swift and strong steps to increase assistance to the least developed countries for adaptation. The trio envisaged the Copenhagen Treaty-2009 in prospect to take shape with more stringent focus on the human and social implications of climate change and based on human progress and justice. Realizing the utmost need to increase assistance to the Third World, the European Union on 30th October 2009 reached a ‘conditional deal’ on funding the efforts by developing countries to tackle global warming. The EU agreed to a ‘fair’ share of an estimated

100 billion euros a year needed by 2020 to fight climate change, though the amount was not specified.

H.M.: Could you please outline the possible remedies for climate change and the means to reverse the present trend?

Madhavan: To combat and minimize the emission of carbon dioxide, extensive and wholesome measures should be taken globally. Power generation using coal must be phased out and replaced by alternative sources of energy. China was averse to a short-term timetable for reduction of emissions contending that development goals needed priority and that developed countries like the United States had not performed enough. But Western countries viewed that China's acceptance of emission cuts was imperative to meet global reduction targets, especially because of its biggest emission of greenhouse gases. For the first time, a government body hinted at a possible time frame for reducing emissions. The "2050 China Energy and Carbon Dioxide Emissions" report released by a government panel on 18th August 2009 envisaged a scenario where the emissions could fall beyond 2030, and predicted slowdown of its emissions growth by 2020, citing its significant investment in renewable energy. This report augured well for future success in containing emissions.

Wind power can greatly contribute to the prevention of climate change. The 'Global Wind Energy Outlook 2008', published by the Global Wind Energy Council and Greenpeace International, looks at the global potential of wind power upto 2050 and found that it could avoid as much as 1.5 billion tonnes of carbon dioxide emissions every year. The report also explains how wind energy can produce 12 percent of the world's energy needs within 12 years and provide upto 30 percent of the world's electricity by the middle of the century. Wind energy has already become a mainstream power generation source in many regions around the world and it is being deployed in over 70 countries. China has the world's fastest growing wind power market and is expected to become the biggest manufacturer of wind energy equipment very soon. The existing power sector as in 2008-09 is responsible for around 40 percent of global carbon dioxide emissions and there are only three options to reduce this by 2020, namely energy efficiency, fuel switching and renewables, predominantly wind power. Governments worldwide should therefore, step up actions to augment generation of wind power.

Solar power is another source of energy which could be exploited.

This kind of energy can be used for various purposes, especially domestic needs. A 36-year-old Swiss school teacher Louis palmer, starting from Lucerne in Switzerland in 2007, travelled around the world in the first solar-powered compact car developed by scientists at Swiss Universities. His adventurous journey of 52,000 km that lasted for 17 months covering 38 countries, culminated on 4th December 2008 at Poznam, the venue of the United Nations Climate talks. It was the maiden global journey by a solar-powered car gliding sans noise with a speed of upto 90 kmph and capability to cover 300 km on a fully charged battery. Having given rides to about 1000 persons-officials and commoners including New York city Mayor Michael Bloomberg and the UN Secretary General Ban Ki-moon. Mr. Palmer titled the car a 'solar taxi'. He was optimistic at the viability of the technology. Seeing it as a 'panacea' to counter global warming, the enchanted adventurer prophesied, "Here at the conference, we are talking about reducing emissions by 10 or 20 percent. I want to show that we can reduce emissions by 100 percent–and that's what we need for the future." Solar–powered vehicles like this must be extensively popularised, manufactured in plenty and their sales boosted.

Accordingly, the Chinese automaker BYD Co. Ltd. has developed a purely electric car. Named as 'e6', it has a range of 400 km on a single charge and claimed to be unique. The car, which could comfortably seat five passengers, drew much attention from both the media and the industry at its debut at the 'North American International Auto Show' in Detroit in January 2009. The Chairman of the company Wang Huafu said, "The core enabling technology is the BYD Fe Battery, applied in its all three electric vehicles. The Fe battery is extremely safe, environmentally friendly and affordable. It has a lifetime of over 10 years". BYD brought another newly-developed plug-in hybrid car to the Auto show. Many auto companies including the big three in the US, Japanese Toyota and Korean Hyundai are competing to develop the plug-in hybrid technology. Such innovative efforts could provide positive contributions to environment protection.

Pollution control is imperative in the present context. To complement the mitigation of emissions, some geo–engineering options might be taken up which could together cool the climate, according to British researchers. 'Geo-engineering' provides large-scale schemes such as erecting sun-shades or mirrors in space, sowing the stratosphere with white particles or whitewashing building roofs to reflect sunlight or scattering iron filings in the ocean to promote carbon-gobbling algae. Massive futuristic schemes to spur land and the sea into sucking up greenhouse gases may help fight global warming.

India produces around 250 million tonnes of solid waste every day. To ensure clean air and curb environmental pollution, projects for effective solid waste management are essential in urban and suburban areas. Rural areas should also be gradually brought into this fold. Separate dustbins for decomposable and non-decomposable solid wastes in different colours must be adequately provided at all establishments, public places and streets. They must be cleared daily and disinfected for neat maintenance, by the civic sanitary staff, as done in the Western countries. Above all, the people should be trained to use only the dustbins for solid waste disposal through awareness programmes and even by means of law that may be binding on everybody. In the State of Tamil Nadu, there is an age-old practice of burning old and worn out things during 'Bhogi' on the eve of 'Pongal' festival celebrated in January every year. As this act causes environmental pollution, the people must be coaxed to dispense with this practice. For efficient management of solid waste, a common compost plant and sanitary landfill facility has been established at Venkatamangalam village in Kancheepuram district of Tamil Nadu. This facility has been installed to cover three adjoining municipalities, namely Alandur, Pallavaram and Tambaram, which visually extend Chennai city. Such solid waste management cluster is worthy of emulation by all States across the country. It will greatly contribute to environment protection.

The importance of toilets must be focussed in all the villages for a healthy and hygienic living. The ecosan toilet technology is ideal for sustainable environment and prevention of contamination of air, water and soil.It facilitates reuse of human waste for farm production. This technology is making toilets aesthetically appealing and enables using the compost and urine as fertilizer for raising the kitchen garden. Orientation meetings for masons on constructing toilets and how the toilets could be made more beautiful and cost effective, were held in some places in Tamil Nadu. There was a plan to provide Rs. 10,000 to each participating mason to construct ecosan toilet in his own house. 'Friend-in-Need', a Non-Governmental Organization based in France, proposed to organize ecosan toilet construction competition for masons and beauty contest for ecosan toilets, announcing cash prizes. Such positive and productive steps, if taken up extensively, will boost ecosan toilet construction and contribute greatly to environment protection.

It has been found that corpulence of human beings also has a bearing on climate change. Phil Edwards from the London School of Hygiene and Tropical Medicine has said, "Population fatness has an environmental impact." According to a study, high rates of obesity in richer countries cause upto one billion extra tonnes of greenhouse gas emissions every year, compared with countries having leaner populations. Scientists have expressed concern because obesity is on the rise in many rich nations. Intensive and widespread awareness campaigns are necessary to contain fatness among human beings. Besides people, animals also cause environmental pollution. The US Supreme Court ruled in 2007 that greenhouse gases emitted by belching and flatulence amounts to air pollution. Following this, the 'Environment Protection Agency (EPA)' put forward among others, a notion to charge fees for air-polluting animals. If the Government proposal becomes a law, it would require farms or ranches with more than 25 dairy cows, 50 beef cattle or 200 hogs to pay an annual fee of about $ 175 for each dairy cow, $ 87.50 per head of beef cattle and $ 20 for each hog. But there was bitter opposition against this move from livestock owners. An EPA spokesman said that the fee was proposed for farms with livestock operations that emit more than 90 tonnes of carbon emissions in a year and fall under federal Clean Air Act provisions. A spokesman for 'People for the Ethical Treatment of Animals' said in Washington, "It makes perfect sense if you are looking for ways to cut down on meat consumption and recoup environmental losses." I feel that tax imposed on farms may yield revenue receipt for the Government but can't solve the problem. Gas emissions by animals is natural which cannot be avoided. To deal with this issue, Stonyfield Farm, the yoghurt manufacturer initiated at the Vermont farms in the US, a programme of experiment to determine whether a change in diet would help cows belch less methane, a potent heat-trapping gas that has been linked to climate change. Since January 2009, cows at 15 farms across Vermont had reportedly had their feed adjusted to include more plants like alfalfa and flax seed that mimic the spring grasses that the animals are used to eating since long ago, rather than corn or soy which do not act so. As per the calculation made in a particular herd in May 2009, methane output had dropped by 18 per cent. Meanwhile, the change in feed did not affect the milk yield which remained static. Scientists must take up research to invent suitable remedy, either some chemical or a contrivance that could neutralize the impact of gases emitted by farm animals.

If we can have any chance of keeping global temperature increases below a 2°C tipping point, greenhouse gas emissions will have to fall by over 50 per cent by 2050. On current trends, they will rise by 50 per cent by 2030. Such an outcome would lead to unprecedented reversals in human development in our lifetime followed by ecological catastrophe for future generations. To avert such disasters, effective strategies to contain global warming need to be evolved and carried out. The World Economic Forum, while meeting in Davos on 29th January 2009, opined that the Earth might be spared from an unsustainable increase in global temperature by investing more than $ 10 trillion in clean technology between then and 2030. The WEF study stressed that countries needed to vastly increase spending on safeguarding the environment. It said that at least $ 515 billion should be spent annually on measures to limit carbon emissions. It added that in the light of the global financial crisis, it was crucial that every dollar was made to 'multi-task' to create a sustainable low-carbon economy. One day, economics can recover from a financial crisis. But there is no antidote or rewind button for global warming. So, this burning problem needs to be given top priority in spite of the global economic slowdown.

H.M.: Your exposition of the issue evidently throws light on the need for a multi-pronged approach to tackle global warming. But this problem has not yet drawn the attention of the common people whose support and cooperation are vital to the success of any endeavour. So, I feel that creation of public awareness of the issue may be required. What is your idea on this aspect?

Madhavan: Yes, sir. You are absolutely right. The people's awareness of this problem and their active involvement in tackling it are very important. Awareness compaigns therefore, form part of the remedies. The world displayed its sensitivity to the challenge of climate change by positively responding to the exhortation of the 'World Wildlife Fund' to turn off lights for a full hour on 28th March 2009. Several illuminated landmarks across the globe went dark that night to highlight the threat of climate change. Nearly 4,000 cities and towns in 88 countries dimmed non-essential lights from 8.30 p.m. to 9.30 p.m. That 'Earth Hour' was termed 'a huge success' by environmental activists. Kim Carstensen, leader of WWF's Global Climate Initiative, in a statement said, "Last night's message from the masses was loud and clear: Delay no more, real action now!" In Bonn, Where negotiators form 175 countries gathered on 29th March 2009 for talks on control of emission of gases that are responsible for global warming, German boy and girl scouts presented the top UN climate official Yvo de Boer, with a blue 'ballot box' symbolically representing the world's vote the night before to save our planet. Diverse campaigns including 'Earth Hour' must be juxtaposed with vigorous efforts by the Governments worldwide to achieve fruitful results. The Cabinet of Maldives held the world's first under water meeting 6 metres below the surface of the sea on 17th October 2009 to highlight the danger posed to low-lying nations by the rising seas as a result of global warming. A declaration approved at the end of a 25 minute meeting, presided by President Mohammad Nasheed, called for global action to combat climate change. The Nepali Cabinet held a historic meeting on 4th December 2009 at the Everest Base Camp in Kalapatthar at an altitude of 17,192 feet, to send a message to the world that the Himalayas in Nepal are meeting because of climate change triggered by carbon emissions in big countries. These unique and novel events could create awareness of global warming among the leaders and people around the world. Kashmiri boats known as 'Shikaras' took planned positions and formed the number 350 in the Dal Lake in Srinagar on 24th October 2009 to highlight the safe upper limit for carbon dioxide in the atmosphere suggested by scientists. Such spectacle could motivate people to ponder over their role in containing climate change.

Mr. Al Gore's film 'An Inconvenient Truth' presents convincing statistics, facts and graphic delineation of the approaching doom in the wake of global warming that has resulted in climate change. Film director Ms. Franny Armstrong, in her 90-minute documentary on climate change 'The Age of Stupid', attacks broader attitudes of consumerism, exploitation and the tendency of the human race to ignore impending unpleasant realities. The documentary was screened at the Poznan meeting-2008. Ms. Franny planned for its worldwide screening not only in theatres, but also through online DVD purchases. People at large evince keen interest in their own affairs, but show apathy towards common causes. Most people deserve a cynical view because of their selfishness. They don't keep a balance between personal and common interest. For instance, a teacher usually displays fervour in making his own kids brilliant. But the level of his enthusiasm in respect of his class pupils is often less. A building contractor is meticulous while constructing his own house. But in case of public buildings such as school, office complex, hospital, etc. built under contract, he performs the same works with less standards. An official in competent position, while purchasing materials for office use, does not ponder over the cost and pays what is demanded. But when he purchases materials for his domestic use, he bargains with the seller and behaves like a miser. People's usage or maintenance of public properties like Government buildings, lounges, office vehicles, etc. is not as good as that of their own assets. These are only pointers to the disparity shown between personal and public matters. Such society therefore, won't respond to public problems with the same alacrity shown on personal problems.To bring about a change in the mindset of the people who are insensitive to the impending pitfall, films and the media could play a positive role. So, Mr. Al Gore's film and Ms. Franny's documentary are worth emulating by professionals in the cine field. They could illuminate the many threats to our environment and enable the majority of the world people who are still ignorant of the approaching miseries, wake up to them. The theme for World Environment Day 2009 is 'Your planet needs you – Unite to Combat Climate Change.' It means every individual has to protect the environment from being polluted and keep it green. Films can be the apt tools for educating people to realize their responsibility to safegurad our environment from pollution for the sake of the present and future generations.

In the State of Tamil Nadu, eco clubs have been formed in schools. By the end of 2008, 4,200 eco clubs were functioning in government higher secondary, high and aided schools, so as to create awareness among children, of environmental issues. The clubs would help children follow environment-friendly practices, besides teaching them how to maintain their school premises clean, planting of saplings in schools, recycling of degradable waste from schools into manure, raising of herbal gardens and desilting of rainwater harvesting structures. The State Government proposed to extend formation of eco clubs to cover all the Government schools. The School Education Department proposed to appoint postgraduates with science background as co-ordinators to monitor the functioning of these clubs. The co-ordinators would be appointed in every district as revealed by the School Education Minister. It was also planned to appoint a State co-ordinator in the rank of District Education Officer. The department was also planning to enhance the assistance provided to the clubs under the National Green Corps. These are very useful efforts to create awareness of climate change and all the State Governments in India and elsewhere may follow suit.

H.M.: I think many world leaders evince keen interest in solving this problem, isn't it?

Madhavan: It's sure. French President Nicolas Sarkozy said in a speech in the second week of September 2009 that France would introduce a carbon tax to slash its greenhouse gas emissions. He expected to raise 3 billion euros, which would be returned to households and businesses through a reduction in other taxes. The result would be a shift of the tax burden from other revenue sources to energy derived from fossil fuels to discourage their use. Exempting electricity which is mostly generated via nuclear power in France and does not emit greenhouse gases, gasoline, diesel fuel, coal and natural gas were proposed to be subjected to the tax. A similar tax exists in some European nations including Denmark, Sweden, Finland and Slovenia. France would be the largest economy to impose such a tax. Although the imposition of this tax was reportedly opposed by 67 per cent of the French population and Mr. Sarkozy's conservative colleagues, he sought to convince them of the need for such a tax and likened it to other major reforms elsewhere. But the designated court rejected this reform as unfair and ruled carbon tax invalid.

The US House of Representatives passed a legislation by a 219-212 margin to limit pollution that is blamed for global warming. The American Clean Energy and Security Act aims to reduce greenhouse gas emissions by 17 per cent on 2005 levels by 2020, and 83 per cent by 2050, create 'green' jobs and wean the US economy from oil imports. This was considered a historic enactment in the right direction to tackle the global problem of climate change. The President of the United States Mr. Barack Obama convened the Major Economies Forum summit in L' Aquila in Italy in July 2009. The group, accounting for 75 per cent of global emissions and comprising the G8, the G5 and other major economies, agreed on several contentious issues for the first time. In the declaration issued at the end of their meeting, all nations recognised the imperative of not letting the global average temperature to rise beyond 2 degrees Celsius over the pre-industrial levels. The leaders agreed that both aggregate and national emissions should start falling as soon as possible with a different time frame for the developing countries, bearing in mind that social and economic development and poverty eradication are the first and overriding priorities. The industiral nations meeting in the G8 summit had committed themselves to reducing their emissions by 80 per cent by 2050 and called on the rest of the world to move towards the goal of reducing overall global emissions by 50 per cent by 2050. The G5, representing China, India, Brazil, Mexico and South Africa, in their declaration called upon the industrial countries to reduce their emissions by 40 percent in the medium term by 2020. The agreement enabled making emission reductions "measurable, reportable and verifiable."

A high-level climate summit was convened at the United Nations by the Secretary General Ban Ki-moon in September 2009. Addressing the summit, the US President Mr. Obama affirmed his country's determination to act on climate change and said, "We will meet our responsibility to future generations." Chinese President Mr. Hu Jintao pledged support for action to combat climate change and announced four kinds of measures that China would adopt. India and Japan also made positive and significant contributions at the summit. China, for the first time, announced a target to reduce its carbon dioxide emissions to 40-45 per cent of 2005 levels by 2020. On 26th November 2009, the State Council, China's Cabinet declared, "This is a voluntary action taken by the Chinese Government based on our own national conditions and is a major contribution to the global effort in tackling climate change". On 3rd December 2009, India announced 20-25 per cent carbon emission cuts on 2005 levels by 2020. These are all optimistic response of the leaders and countries. But reversing this optimistic trend, the world's key industrialised nations said that they had abandoned hope of a legally binding treaty at the Copenhagen summit in December 2009 and had begun to plan only for a meeting of world leaders. Senior negotiators and politicians conceded on 5th November 2009 that a global treaty to fight climate change would be deferred by at least six months and possibly a year or more.

During the 12-day UN summit on climate change that began in Copenhagen on 7th December 2009, negotiators from 192 countries involved themselves into seeking compromises on carbon emissions and funds for poor countries to tackle the global problems, with an aim to finalise a deal. The European Union on 11th December pledged $ 10.6 billion to help poor nations battle global warming. Britain alone pledged $2 billion - more than any other EU member State. Indian Environment Minister Jairam Ramesh made it clear that India would not compromise on its three key principles - no legally binding emission cuts, no peaking year and no international review of domestic-funded mitigation actions. The official draft treaty circulated on 11th December created clear divisions among the participants. China, India and other developing nations demanded that rich countries must discuss much deeper cuts in their greenhouse gas emissions. They wanted to extend the 1997 'Kyoto Protocol', which imposed penalties on rich nations if they did not comply with its strict emissions limits but made no such binding demands on developing nations. They also boycotted the talks on 14th December. Negotiators worked through 15th night but could not succeed in finding consensus on the most fundamental questions, namely how much greenhouse gas emissions be cut, by which date and who would pay for the cost of mitigation and adaptation to the effects of climate change. Though a two-track negotiating process was back on stream on 17th, fundamental disagreements over these issues persisted and the climate talks were in disarray at one stage. There was concern among developing countries that rich nations were pushing for a new single agreement, ignoring the 'Kyoto Protocol'.

Besides a stormy overnight session held by the negotiators, there were personal negotiations between President Obama and the political leaders of China, India, Brazil and South Africa. Finally, they reached an agreement that fell short of a 'legally binding treaty' and was viewed as a reference document. It was not adopted by consensus, due to strong objections by some countries. The accord promised a mobilisation of $ 100 billion in annual funding for developing countries to meet the challenges of climate change from 2020 and also pledged about $ 30 billion by 2012. It set a target limiting temperature increases to a maximum of two degrees celsius, but failed to specify the greenhouse gas emission cuts to be adopted by nations. It did not create any scope to ensure drastic reductions of emissions by developed countries. No deadline was fixed for global emissions to peak, which left many scientists, activists and vulnerable countries disappointed. The accord had less than full formal recognition. The European Union later lamented that the 'Copenhagen Accord' had missed out ambitious emission reduction targets. Agricultural scientist Mr. M.S. Swaminathan, who was at the summit, said that the response of the climate change conference to the magnitude of the threat was faulty. As Mr. Obama said, the 'Copenhagen Accord' may be perceived as a beginning of constructive actions in the future. A legally binding and wholesome treaty needs to be achieved at the earliest.

H.M.: Thank you Mr. Madhavan. Charli........ Charli........ What happened to you? Are you asleep?

Charli: Why do you raise this question? You could have understood it from my snoring.

H.M.: I couldn't hear you snoring.

Charli: Then you'll have to wear a hearing aid.

H.M.: It is an absurd idea. Besides, how could you sense your own snoring?

Charli: I knew that because I had just a doze and not a sound sleep.

H.M.: Stop your senseless talk.

Charli: You have asked me not to participate in your discussions which I have not flouted. Why should I be silent now?

H.M.: Allowing you to comment on important topics would be a folly.

Charli: No. Such attitude keeps me free but makes you the loser.

Madhavan: How does he become the loser?

Charli: He has troubled you for two hours on the issue of climate change. Had he allowed me, I could have suggested a recipe for overcoming global warming. Now, he is deprived of that chance.

Rahul: You may shed your inhibition now and propound your recipe.

Charli: I can't do so now because it was an oracle I heard in sleep and most of the points have slipped out of my memory since my boss interrupted my sleep.

H.M.: Do you think that your dream-soaked imagination might have produced another 'Kubla Khan' if I had not interrupted you?

Charli: Why not? Should I not be an heir to S.T. Coleridge?

H.M.: Oh, yes. You may become even a swallow or a skylark. By the by, what are the remnants of your dream in terms of measures to tackle global warming?

Charli: I remember only two points, sir. First, the entire atmosphere must be kept air-conditioned. Secondly, our food items for breakfast, lunch and dinner must be cool.

H.M.: You are now on the road to a lunatic asylum. Finally, you have come to your targeted point. Rahul....... could you provide 'cool' dinner for Charli?

Rahul: Oh, yes sir. We have ice cubes for him.

They all go to dinner in a joyful mood.

After dinner, the headmaster and Charli return home.

4

HUNGER AND FOOD SECURITY

The headmaster and Charli arrive at Sudha's home.

Sudha: Good evening and welcome, sir.

H.M.: Good evening Sudha.

Sudha: (Turning to her father Rajaram) Meet our headmaster, Dad.

Rajaram: Hello, sir. Please be seated. As Sudha apprised us of your visit, we have been eagerly waiting for you.

H.M.: Thank you. how many children do you have?

Rajaram: We have a son and a daughter. Our son is elder than sudha and working as a civil engineer in a private construction company in Kochi. I am an Agriculture officer in the State Government service.

H.M.: I am pleased at your profession which aids to produce food-the foremost need for existence of mankind. We painfully learn that the global food security has been under threat since a few years, and now on the road to a crisis. Could you please expound on the present state of the issue?

Rajaram: Oh yes, sir. The year 2008 started facing rice shortages in the Philippines, Nepal and Bangladesh which are among the rice–producing countries. Hoarding of food grains by traders in at least 12 sub-Saharan African countries caused soaring maize and rice prices that led to political instability. Governments had to intervene to contain prices and ensure supplies. Analysts ascribed the problem to poor harvests in major grain-growing countries like Australia, that resulted from climate change and extreme weather. But planting of maize, wheat and other crops on millions of acres in the United States and elsewhere in 2007 to provide biofuels for cars rather than food for people was also blamed. According to the United Nations Food and Agriculture

Organization's preliminary data, more than 960 million people–one in every six people in the world go to bed hungry and 40 million suffered malnourishment in 2008, the highest figure in decades, due to higher food prices. Rapidly growing world population much exacerbates the food crisis. According to a report prepared by the US-based International Food Policy Research Institute (IFPRI) in collaboration with Welthungerhilfe and Concern Worldwide, California, Madhya Pradesh in India has the most severe level of hunger in the country, followed by Jharkhand and Bihar. Punjab, the granary of India, ranks below countries like Honduras and Vietnam in terms of hunger levels. The India State Hunger Index (ISHI) measures hunger on three leading indicators, namely prevalence of child malnutrition, rates of child mortality and the proportion of people who are calorie deficient, and combines them into one index. This approach is similar to the 2008 Global Hunger Index that was released for World Food Day on 16th October 2008. The ISHI wehich was released in New Delhi on 14th October 2008 by Mr. G.K. Chadha, member of Prime Minister's Economic Advisory Council, on the eve of World Food Day expressed the same view. The report found that 12 States fell in the 'alarming' category, and one State, namely Madhya Pradesh fell in the 'extremely alarming' category. Four States–Punjab, Kerala, Haryana and Assam-were in the 'serious' category. India is home to the world' largest food insecure population, with more than 200 million people who are hungry. The country's poor performance is driven by its high levels of child under-nutrition and poor calorie count. Its rates of child malnutrition are higher than those of most countries in sub-Saharn Africa, the report said. India, which ranked 66th among 88 countries in the 2008 Global Hunger Index of the FAO, does not have a single State in the 'low hunger' or 'moderate hunger' categories. Figuring amongst the 88 countries itself is shameful for the country after years of strong economic growth. High growth of Gross Domestic Product (GDP) is not sufficient and inclusive growth is essential. The country has a poor record on distribution of wealth. The report also identified that strong economic growth does not necessarily translate into lower hunger levels. Even States with higher rates of economic growth in recent years, such as Gujarat, Chhattisgarh and Maharashtra, have high level of hunger, while States with relatively slower economic growth, such as Punjab, achieved a lower hunger level.

Several countries across the world are struck by food shortage and spiralling food prices. The Rome summit on food security held in December 2008 deliberated the situation at length and resolved to take remedial measures. As for India's situation, 77 percent of the population spends less than Rs. 20 per head a day as estimated by the Arjun Sengupta Commission on organised workers. It is a testament to under-feeding that grips the majority of the population. India therefore, has the highest malnourished population in the world. The utter failure of the Government to control the prices of farm inputs and farmers' agitations resulted in higher Minimum Support Price (MSP). It has led to the rise in food subsidy estimated to reach Rs. 50,000 crore for the year 2008-09. Still, it is just 1.32 per cent of GDP. Elimination of starvation should be the top priority for every nation. To achieve this, one of the multi-pronged effort is an effective administartion of the Public Distribution System (PDS) through fair price shops. The Government must always have enough buffer stock of food grains as per norms. From 2005 to 2007, India's food stocks dwindled to a level below the buffer norm due to abated procurement, forcing the Government to import six million tonnes of wheat in 2006-07 and one million tonne in 2007-08 from foreign corporates at prices higher than procurement rates to meet the shortages in the PDS. As imports were dear, public protests erupted which impelled the Government to gear up for higher procurement that achieved about 30 million tonnes of wheat and rice in 2008-09. Because of lack of storage space, about 5 million tonnes of food grains were exposed to risk of loss at open space. The Food Corporation of India (FCI) was in a bid to offload its wheat stocks by floating tenders. It amounted to sale of surplus stocks in the market. The ideal action to dispose of these grain stocks would be to allocate them to the States. Earlier, the household quota was slashed from 35 kg per family to 20 kg. Whenever quotas are curtailed, the market prices soar by 20-30 per cent. The quota of 35 kg may therefore be restored. Further, the Government had eliminated a section of beneficiaries from the PDS citing wheat shortage as the reason. Now, they must be brought back into the ambit of the PDS. They will not only ensure surfeit of offtake and avoid glut of wheat but also stabilize market prices.

A two-day international conference on 'Food Security' was held in Madrid (Spain) in January 2009. On this occasion, the head of the United Nations Food and Agriculture Organization Mr. Jacques Diouf said that the food crisis pushed another 40 million people into hunger in 2008. That brought the global number of undernourished people to 97.3 crore out of a total population of around 650 crore. He focused on the challenge ahead to ensure food not only for 97.3 crore hungry people but also for 900 crore population in 2050 which compels to double the global food production by the middle of the 21st century. Many countries and international organizations pledged $ 22 billion during and after the 2008 Rome summit in development aid to alleviate hunger. The hardship in getting farm loans caused by the global economic crisis was undermining efforts to tackle food insecurity. The frontline global crusaders against hunger are baffled since the financial meltdown has overshadowed the food crisis, pushing millions towards starvation.

According to the UN food agency, which issued a report on World Food Day on 14th October 2009, thirty countries require emergency aid to tackle hunger, including twenty in Africa. Parents in some of Africa's poorest countries strive to provide a meal once a day to their children at the cost of education, clothes and basic medical care. Mr. Otive Igbuzor, the head of international campaigns for 'Action Aid International' said, "It's actually a world emergency that calls for action from both developing and developed countries. We know, a child dies every six seconds of malnutrition." The FAO's estimate revealed that the number of people suffering from hunger and malnutrition in the world was reckoned at close to 100 crore in 2009. Asia and the Pacific region had the largest number of hungry people followed by sub-Saharan Africa. It was far more than the figure that stood at 82.5 crore a decade before. The number will increase if Governments do not spend more on agriculture. The UN Secretary Genenal Ban Ki-moon observed a 24-hour fast on 14th November 2009 in solidarity with the hungry people worldwide. There is a high growth of population in developing countries at an average rate of 8 crore every year. But investment in agriculture has decreased over the past 30 years. The rising challenges of climate change, global economic crisis, a limited resource base and a high-volatile food prices have combined together and raised the level of global food insecurity. The organization's twice-yearly 'Food Outlook' report released on 4th June 2009 said that international prices of most agricultural commodities had fallen in 2009 from their 2008 levels, indicating the gradual return of many markets to balance. The bumper crop had also facilitated replenishment of global reserves to pre-crisis levels. At the same time, food prices remained high in many developing countries, and acces to food for the poor also continued to be threatened by loss of employment, income and other effects of the global economic crisis, the report said. The forecast for 2009-10 predicated a reduction in production of wheat and coarse grains and a marginal increase in rice output.

H.M.: Could you predict the possible scenario?

Rajaram: Well, sir. Though precise prediction is not possible since making headway or suffering deterioration will largely depend on how the world countries might act to salvage the situation, there is a vision of some bottlenecks and probabilities. An alarming population explosion is likely to worsen the food insecurity. The 'United Nations Population Fund' said in a report released in November 2008 that India would become the most populous country by 2050 overtaking China. Its population of 118.6 crore in 2008 is projected to be 165.8 crore in 2050 as against 140.8 crore projected for china. The 'State of World Population Report, 2008' released in New Delhi by Planning Commission member Mr. Syeda Hameed, said that the world population would increase from 674.9 crore to 919.1 crore by 2050. According to the FAO, the world population of 600 crore in 2000, may rise to over 900 crore in 2050. The Indian Government and the FAO have expressed almost the same view vis-a-vis the world population in 2050. The FAO felt that the 1996 World Food Summit's target of halving the number of hungry people by 2015, and the first Millennium Development Goal of halving the prevalence of hunger and poverty might not be accomplished.

The global warming has an adverse impact on food security. A study in the US journal 'Science' found that by the end of the century, the coolest temperatures in the tropics during the crop growing season would exceed the hottest temperatures recorded between 1900 and 2006. In moderate regions like Europe, previous record temperatures could become the norm by 2100. Scientists David Battisti at the University of Washington and Rosamond Naylor at Stanford University in California, have warned that the rising temperatures would take their toll on farmers' crops resulting in severe food shortages that could starve half of the world's population. The production of staple food such as rice and maize could fall by 20 to 40 per cent due to higher temperatures. The tropics and subtropics must also experience drought, exacerbating the situation. Those who would suffer the most would be the poor, densely inhabited in the equatorial regions where a rapid growth in population has already pushed up the demand for food. The researchers, before making these prophecies, have analysed relevant impact of rising temperatures in the past. The record heat wave across Western Europe in 2003 killed around 52,000 people and also cut the yields of wheat and fodder by a third. In 1972, a temperature rise between 2 and 4 degree celsius above the norm caused by a prolonged hot summer in the south-west Russia and south-east Ukraine cut down wheat and coarse grain yields for the whole of the erstwhile Soviet Union by 13 per cent. These precedents precisely corroborate the predictions on food crisis for the 21st century. A report released by the UN Environment Programme (UNEP) has warned that if major changes are not made in food production and processing system, food prices may increase by 30-35 per cent within the next 10 years, forcing those living in extreme poverty to spend 90 per cent of their income on their bread.

H.M.: What is the strategy to eliminate hunger and ensure food security for the people of the whole world?

Rajaram: To face this challenge, effective schemes must be operated to contain human population, especially in the developing and the undeveloped countries. Besides, all nations must strive to augment food production. To achieve this goal, farmers need to be trained and involved in adoption of modern farming technologies and the research inventions should be transmitted to the fields then and there through professionals. Scientists emphasize to attain the state of food security transcending the level of self-sufficiency in food production and ensure quality food for all the people. To fulfil this ambition, large-scale organic farming is imperative. Expert notion is that organic farming practices are conducive to enrichment of soil health, and sustainable yield and income, besides being eco-friendly. Such farming yields quality produce sans any residual poison, which could fetch higher price. These facts have been confirmed by researchers across the world. But the majority of farmers do not adopt this method due to insufficient availability of specific farm inputs and lack of credit and marketing facilities which cry for attention. Production of wheat, rice, pulses, vegetables, fruits and tea through organic farming accounts for only 2.5 per cent. To create more awareness on organic farming which enables sustainable agriculture, training programmes for farmers are conducted in selected areas under a project jointly implemented by 'Aide-et-Action', Chennai and 'Bharati Women's Development Centre' with funding from European Commission. Booklets on organic farming are distributed to farmers. As it is a wise recipe, the training may be imparted extensively to the farmers of all areas under crops.

The 'National Agricultural Development Programme' (NADP) is being implemented in various parts of India. It has tried to address the twin issues of water and power by conservation in an integrated manner. The concept of the programme is 'less water and more productivity'. A major highlight of the NADP is its emphasis on precision farming practices that comprise micro-irrigation management techniques such as drip irrigation, sprinkler irrigation and drip fertigation (mixing fertilizer in water and feeding the land with it through drip irrigation) which are more productive and useful. For joint efforts and wide coverage, precision farming societies have been formed in several pockets of many States. Under precision farming programme, sugarcane, banana, maize, tapioca, groundnut, spices, vegetables, turmeric, cotton, herbs and flowers have been included. The method is good for vegetables and all crops in raised-bed formation. The quantum of water required to irrigate an acre under the flooding system can be used to irrigate at least three acres under micro-irrigation systems such as the drip irrigation. Well-to-do farmers raising sugarcane, coconut and betel vine have found drip irrigation successful. It is enough if the field is irrigated once in three days. The micro-irrigation management techniques facilitate high moisture retension. Therefore, the intervals between irrigations are wider vis-a-vis the flooding system, leading to a huge saving on power and water. While adopting this method, power cuts do not affect the farmers because long duration of power supply is not required. Since the system prescribes chisel ploughing, aeration of soil takes place to the desired level, facilitating better roof penetration. Hence it is possible to get higher yield. So, precision farming would help farmers produce world-class agricultural products by implementing the latest technologies to maximise the yield and get higher profits. They could get upto 60 per cent more upon the usual yield. About 90 per cent of the produce would have marketable quality. There is a possibility of the produce having a higher shelf life. Farmers must be extensively coaxed to undertake precision farming and they must be trained to adopt the new techniques. The cost of laying the drip irrigation system works out to Rs. 85,000 a hectare. Government subsidy amounts to Rs. 40,000 per hectare and the balance could be met through bank loan. There is also an additional grant of Rs. 25,000 for installing the water-soluble fertilizer distribution method.

The Agriculture Department has been popularising the 'System of Rice Intensification' (SRI) technique in the recent past to gain higher productivity at lesser cultivation costs. Popular varieties such as 'Improved White Ponni', BPT-5204 known as 'Andhra Ponni' and Ambasamudram varieties, namely ASD-18, ASD-19 and ASD-20 are cultivated using the SRI technique, and a record yield of 12,700 kg per hectare has been registered. To implement this method, clusters were formed, each cluster comprising 10 hectares in some areas. Such advanced techniques are worthy of vigorous extension over all the areas under paddy cultivation. To fetch high yield, fertilizers and manures are essential along with fertile soil and irrigation. Chemical fertilizers have not only become dear but also fallen in crunch. Notwithstanding a high cost, such chemical salts do not ensure good yield but their constant application gradually wreaks havoc on soil fertility over years and land reclamation becomes difficult and delayed. Natural farming is the only alternative that could boost the crop yields. Farmyard manure and green foliages are the safest for the soil. Above all, the produces from natural farming cause no harm to the consumers. Even if the soil is alkaline, its fertility can be improved by multi-seed sowing with various minor legumes and grains in the land. After a month, the germinated seeds must be mulched back into the soil. The soil fertility could thus be sustained. Every farmer needs to be motivated and guided to reap high yields. So, there is a need for greater coordination between farmers and Agriculture Department officials. Over half of the food produced is lost, wasted or discarded. Food wastage due to lack of proper processing and storage is a major problem faced by India. Realizing the importance of food processing, a separate ministry was formed at the Centre and a Cabinet rank Minister was appointed. According to Mr. Ashok Sinha, Secretary, Union Ministry of Food Processing Industry, various measures have been taken after the ministry came into existence, to develop food processing in the country. The country is in the forefront of production of fruits, vegetables, milk, food grains, fish, etc. But due to lack of processing, wastage is enormous. Food worth Rs. 33,000 crore is wasted. Mr. Sinha added that the ministry was in the process of establishing mega food parks across the country. Besides extensive efforts to boost farm yields, perfect and loss–proof systems must be devised and implemented in the realms of storage, transport, distribution, sale and consumption of food grains.

H.M.: Suicide by farmers in some areas have been reported. Is there any decline in the grievous events?

Rajaram: According to available data, there were 2,16,500 farmer suicides in India from 1997 to 2010. In the five years till 2001, the annual average of farmer suicides was 15,747. For the six years from 2002, it had gone up to 17,366. The distressing increase has been recorded in the vulnerable States of Maharashtra, Andhra Pradesh, Karnataka, Madhya Pradesh and Chhattisgarh. Among them, Maharashtra is the worst-hit which mourns more than 4,000 deaths every year since 2004. Its 2007 figure was 4,238 even after the Prime Minister's consoling visit to the distressed Vidharbha region in mid-2006 and a Rs. 5,000 crore 'farm relief package'. The impact from several studies, official reports and commissions of inquiry between 2005 and 2007 failed to contain the problem. The farmer suicides at national level was 16,632 in 2007, 16,196 in 2008 and 17,368 in 2009. In the Union budget presented in Parliament on 6th July 2009, the Finance Minister of India proposed to set up a task force to study farmers' debt to moneylenders in some regions of Maharashtra. Though the proposal is wise, its fruitful results depend on suitable constitution of the task force and its effective functioning. If it is zealous for the welfare of farmers, their suicides can be prevented. All the States which recorded farmer suicides must be covered by the task force. Mr. Nitish Kumar, Chief Minister of Bihar State, on 11th October 2009, ordered a probe into reports alleging that people died of starvation in the districts of Sitamarhi and Gaya. He also directed to fix responsibility for the starvation deaths on the officials who supply food grains to 'Below the Povety Line' families. This dismal trend must be reversed at once and gradually eliminated through sustained efforts on a war-footing. Provision of funds to the affected areas can't be the sole remedy to the problem of farmer suicides. Most of the officials in the Government administrative machinery have no zeal for selfless service or concern for the suffering poor. They use their official positions only for their own prosperity and basking in comfort and ostentation. For instance, there are government servants who demand money from destitutes for inclusion in the Old Age Pension Scheme. Children, widows and physically disabled persons are also forced for bribe, whenever they seek a certificate, at various levels. Obtaining even a death certificate entails payment of kickback. In such a situation, how is it possible for the financial allotment to reach the targeted people in the grip of penury, in full? Suppose a Chief Engineer orders release of water from the dam under his control. The released water gushes out of the sluices and traverses a large number of weedy channels that impede its flow. It is unable to permeate the fields freely. The tail end delta is deprived of water and the farmers are frustrated. The Prime Minister may be likened to the Chief Engineer and the poor farmers to the targeted beneficiaries. It is needless to say who the weedy channels are. To prevent farmer suicides, the root-cause of every case must be probed, though a general opinion points to poverty and being subjected to usury. Other causes must be dealt with according to the case. The causes of crop failures that cripple farmers, plunge them into poverty and impel them to have recourse to usury, should be identified and addressed in an integrated manner. As it requires wholehearted service, Social Welfare Organizations could be involved in the evaluation of farmers' problems, finding out the fruitful remedies, suggesting measures to the Government and implementation or monitoring of announced programmes. Political interference and foul play by middlemen should be ruled out. The Government must ensure that its entire assistance in terms of cash or kind reaches the affected people without any erosion. However, an all-party committee consisting of persons known for their honesty and probity in pulic life may be constituted to coordinate the efforts and hold periodical reviews on the progress made in association with Social Welfare Organizations. Besides, psychological counselling to face challenges in life, is essential for farmers in vulnerable regions. If comprehensive infrastructure is created for profitable agriculture and farmers' income is guaranteed, farmers' suicides will become past history. Sage-Saint Ramalingam (5.10.1823 - 30.1.1874) passionately said in Tamil - "Vadiya Payirai Kandapothellaam Vadinayn" (Whenever it happened to see withering crops, I myself was withering). But today's modern generation has completely failed to cherish compassion for the hapless poor. Is it not a matter of shame for the society to let several thousands of fellow citizens commit suicide every year out of povety, debt, squalor and starvation? Is it not a disgrace to the nation that brags itself about its scope to attain superpower status in a decade?

H.M.: Time and again, this tragedy has disturbed my sleep whenever it came to my mind. At all costs, the tendency among farmers in some areas to commit suicide has to be eliminated. Otherwise, it may spread to the farmers of other regions, whose woes continue to be on the rise. Generally, farmers encounter many problems and the majority of them struggle to make both ends meet. So, they are driven to other occupations wherever possible. Will it not produce an adverse impact on food security?

Rajaram: Yes, of course. But this trend can be changed by proper planning, covering all aspects of agriculture. As for India, more than

75 per cent of the population depends on agriculture. The extent of uncultivable lands such as moors, rocks, forests, etc., is very limited. Even in hills, we find diverse plantations. The vast area of cultivable plains is the primary asset of India, that needs to be protected from any harm. But since around 1970, the area of cultivable lands has been shrinking day by day due to various factors. The 'Real Estate' business has grown enormously, converting farm lands into layouts and then apartments or individual houses. We can now see buildings of many sorts on vast areas, in all parts of the country, previously under crops. Cultivable lands continue to be acquired by the Central and State Governments for laying of roads and railway lines, and establishment of industries, small industrial estates, special economic zones, IT Parks, airports etc. Instead of utilizing barren lands for such purposes, fertile lands are often acquired according to the whims and fancies of those in power. The so called urbanization is constantly swallowing the lands under crops recklessly. The foremost task is to protect the farmlands from abuse and use them only for cultivation. Governments of all the countries need to enact stringent laws and frame policies to ban misuse of farmlands and enforce them in a strict and unbiased manner. Those who flout the norms should be severely penalized.

While safeguarding the farmland asset, extensive measures for boosting the yields and profits must be undertaken jointly by the Government and farmers. A series of actions would be required to achieve the desired results. Initially, soil testing must be carried out at least survey-numberwise. Plotwise test may be done for special crops or reasons. For proper analysis and quick coverage of vast areas, a soil testing laboratory needs to be set up in each district. The soil samples must be collected by the field staff of Agriculture Department and taken to the district lab. Testing of soil samples should be done by well-trained personnel and checked by an expert to keep up standards. It has to be done with care and not considered as a routine formality. Any error in soil testing would mislead the professional and the concerned farmer akin to errors in medical laboratories which at times lead to incorrect prescriptions. On the basis of lab findings, professionals could advise the concerned farmer on soil treatment for any abnormality such as alkaline soil, etc. and on enrichment of soil's nutrition that will be ideal for the particular crop to be raised. Periodical soil testing with the advice of professionals can be very useful. The district level labs may be upgraded into multi-purpose labs to deal with pests and diseases in crops. Soil test and technical advice for restoration of soil health must be available to farmers free of cost. Land reclamation is also important to enhance the extent of farmlands wherever possible. These measures would ensure availability of stupendous area of farmlands.

The Agriculture Department experts may advise farmers on suitable means of irrigation in terms of open well or bore-well, required depth, etc. that may very from place to place. Source of irrigation and method of irrigation prescribed under modern farming must be ensured. Delta regions are mostly dependent on river water, the supply of which is very uncertain in the wake of monsoon failure now worsened by climate change, and poor storage in dams. In India and elsewhere, government spending on 'drought relief' and 'flood relief' is very huge. This expenditure paves way for 'seasonal earnings' of politicians, engineers, contractors and some relief distribution staff. As usual, the surviving victims remain homeless in case of deluge, take shelter in public buildings or under trees and dwell in open yards even with infants and pregnant women for a long period. After flood or drought, the affected people are disabled to resume their works, especially agricultural operations and suffer underfeeding or starvation. When they return to normality after several months, they face the next calamity. This state of affairs is prevailing in many States of India and other south/south-east Asian countries. The best panacea for these twin problems is linking of rivers. Though dear, it is surely possible, provided that politicians push their political and personal interests aside and uphold the national interest.

Once the rivers are linked and weirs built across them, the surplus water could be harnessed to produce power and provide enough irrigation. A guaranteed water supply would be a morale booster to the farmers who are apprehensive of water shortage. Linking of rivers is an ambitious project that could put an end to 'flood relief' and 'drought relief', thereby saving a huge sum to the Exchequer, and avoid crop failures. Besides ensuring water supply, adequate power has to be distributed to farmers. Power supply by turn-system is suitable but supply during night hours must be avoided since it involves many risks including snakebites. Announcing free power for farmers is an attempt for political gains. It gives room for abuse of power and installation of motor with higher horsepower than the one for which sanction is obtained. The Electricity Board/Department authorities are winking at this malpractice for reasons known to anyone. Announcement of free power with unannounced power cut and frequent interruptions in supply is futile. Further, farmers are dragged for many months and even years to give new power connection to their pumpsets. Besides wastage of time and energy, the expenditure their attempt entails, is known to all. The Government should curb unhealthy and detestable practices, and ensure early power connection to pumpsets. The ideal approach is to levy concessional tariff which any prosperous farmer can afford to pay, and provide power in a very useful manner.

There are many farms and research stations functioning under government control. They can produce quality seeds of various food grains, cereals and pulses, and distribute them to farmers in time through agriculture depots. Thrusting unsold and stale seeds on farmers is unwise. Farm machineries and implements may be arranged with bank credit. Agricultural inputs such as fertilizers, pesticides, etc., must be made available to farmers at subsidized cost without scarcity in accordance with the technical specifications relevant to the particular crop and cultivated acreage. Each farmer must be provided with a 'Farmer Card' similar to 'Family card' which must be designed to contain details like year, season, crop, extent, date of – sowing, transplantation, issue of fertilizers and pesticides, date of usage, date of visit by officials with their remarks and sign, date of harvest, yield and disposal of the produce. The card will enable the officials to verify the proprieties regarding the kind, quantity and usage of inputs. The complaints of supplying impertinent fertilizers as the kind-component of crop loans can thus be averted. Moveover, such cards will help to establish close coordination between farmers and professionals, which is vital for successful agriculture. This system may initially be troublesome to farmers as well as the departmental establishment. However, farmers will get accustomed to deal with the cards in the course of time if properly guided, and the establishment will essentially be disciplined and streamlined. To adopt this method, the Agriculture Department will have to be refined and expanded with more professionals and staff who should work with dedication. They may hold meetings of farmers in villages in the evening and provide technical guidance to them. The problems in the fields may be ascertained and solved quickly by visiting the lands. A sincere service of, and not mere inspection by higher officers can be valuable. We can find many officers in various departments who do not devote much time to their official duties. They concentrate more on their private affairs. They just visit their subordinate offices, pick holes in the work, issue orders or instructions and leave quickly. Their purpose is to record camps and project themselves as working hard. Some officers would visit many offices on the same date but sign the records showing different dates. Their idea behind this act is quite obvious. Such visits, by no means amount to a service, but lead only to a waste of travelling allowance allotment and petrol. The Agriculture Department, having a noble goal to ahieve food security, can't afford to accommodate such individuals. The higher officers of this department should not confine themselves to signing of files and inspections. They must chart out a fixed programme of visit to villages for at least 20 days in a month and adhere to it strictly. If there is any unavoidable deviation, the visit may be deferred to a date not covered in the programme. During the visit, the officer must stay in the village for a few hours-interact with farmers and field officials–identify the problems while assessing various aspects of cultivation–and exemplify a fine guide. The head of the department should make the officers accountable for food output in their respective areas and hold periodical reviews of the progress. With these arrangements, farmers can get necessary guidance and help at every stage of the crop, covering application of fertilizers and plant protection. After harvest, the produce must be safely preserved, avoiding wastage. Threshing floors need to be formed as part of post-harvest management. Farmers have to look into this aspect and follow proper practices until the grains are sold either to government Direct Procurement Centres (DPC) or to other agencies.

That poverty is the cause of hunger and malnutrition, cannot be rejected. But what causes poverty? In agriculture-oriented countries like India, poverty has to be mostly attributed to crop failures. Besides, if our country records high level of industrial production and free circulation of money but fails in food production, what could be the situation? We can't eat manufactured goods or currency that are useful for comforts in life. We can live without these things like ancient people but never without farm produce. All the countries across the world have developed a disposition to focus on other sectors of development, neglecting agriculture. If this trend cuntinues, the entire mankind will have to starve by the end of this century. If agriculture flourishes in all cultivable areas, it can eliminate poverty as well as hunger and malnutrition.

Therefore, increasing investments in agriculture is a must. Mr. Hafez Ghanem, Assistant Director General of the FAO said, "Investment in sustainable agriculture is the key to ensuring the food security of present and future generations". A 'Green Revolution', similar to the one which produced foison of cheap food 50 years ago in India needs to be repeated without delay. A former President of India Mr. K.R. Narayanan, in his 'Republic Day' speech on 25th January 2002, quoting from a poet said, "The cry of a child on the roadside mars the harmony of the Universe". This has to be borne in mind while making our endeavour to eliminate hunger from the world with an eternal food security.

H.M.: Thank you Mr. Rajaram. Where is Charli?

Sudha: He had gone out an hour before. He is now approaching our house, sir.

Charli: Have you finished your conversation, sir? Shall we go home?

H.M.: Where have you been to?

Charli: I have been roaming this mini-town to beguile the evening.

H.M.: It's okay........ but have you beguiled any students into some misdeed?

Charli: No, sir. Why are you suspicious of my behaviour?

H.M.: Because I always remember the past.

Rajaram: What is wrong with him? Has he made any mistake?

H.M.: In my previous station, he led five students into a forest on the pretext of showing a pair of tiger cubs and hoodwinked them into collection of firewood.

Sudha: Did all of you see the tiger cubs? (towards Charli)

Charli : No........ they had gone underground. However, I showed the students a litter of kittens behind a hut, on our way back.

H.M.: How absurd it was! Fortunately, no forest is available here.

Charli: You never commend me for my sagacity.

H.M.: It was not sagacity but deception. It was a hap that you were not flogged.

Charli: I would contend that collection of firewood at no cost is a wise act. But the boys, instead of bashing me, spoiled my lunch by adding abundant salt covertly, leaving me bereft of my lunch.

Sudha: Is it not better than physical assault?

Charli: No. To be smitten is better than losing my lunch.

H.M.: You are really wise. Why did you move out during our conversation?

Chali: I wanted to escape ennui.

H.M.: You are disinterested in agriculture but relish its produce.

Charli: You may take it as you like. Anyway, thanks for reminding me what we should do next.

Rajaram: (laughingly) Our dinner is ready. Let us all have it.

After dinner, the headmaster and Charli take leave of them and return home.

5

ENERGY SECURITY

The headmaster and Charli arrive at Emili's home.

Emili: Good evening, sir.

H.M.: Good evening, Emili.

Emili: (Turning to her brother Robert) Meet our headmaster, dear.

Robert: Hello, welcome sir. Please take a seat.

H.M.: Thank you.

Robert: (Turning to his wife Maria) Meet the headmaster.

Maria: Hello, sir. We are fortunate to have you here.

H.M.: I am also glad to meet you.

Robert: She is my wife Maria. She is a clerk in the Postal Department. I am an Assistant Engineer in the State Electricity Board.

H.M.: It's nice. Could you enlighten me on matters pertaining to your profession please?

Robert: Oh, yes. I am pleased to convey the matters as far as I know about.

H.M.: Many intellectuals and experts in your field often stress the need to increase power generation in the context of our soaring needs. What are the steps so far taken in this regard and is there scope to ensure energy security?

Robert: As you know, there are conventional modes of energy such as hydroelectricity, thermal energy, etc. apart from nuclear power. Besides, non-conventional energy sources are also available.

Among various types of energy, the main focus is now on nuclear energy since its production is clean and so, not hazardous to environment. India has 17 operating nuclear reactors now with a total installed capacity of 4,120 MW. Most of them are running at half the capacity due to fuel shortage. The nuclear power programme was hitherto constrained by limited fuel supplies. In this context, after marathon process amid controversies in both the countries, the India-United States Civil Nuclear Cooperation Agreement was signed in 2008. Under this nu lear deal, India envisages guaranteed supply of nuclear fuel from the U S. On the other hand, India was negotiating with Russia to clinch agreements that could bridge the demand-supply gap in uranium and enable the setting up of more state-of-the-art nuclear power plants in India. After final touches were put on by Prime Minister Dr. Manmohan Singh and Russian President Mr. Dmitry Medvedev, a mega $ 700 million agreement to supply nearly 2,000 tonnes of unanium, was signed by the two countries in December 2008. This will cover not only the reactors run on Russian Technology but also the US-origin Tarapur nuclear plant, and raise the capacity utilization of the other existing plants to 90 per cent from an unhealthy 40 to 60 per cent due to shortage of the raw meterial. The agreement will be for 5 years which is extendable. Analysts hoped that the deal would immediately boost electricity generation by at least 1,000 MW. The two sides agreed to set up four more power plants at Koodankulam in Tamil Nadu where Russia is already assisting in installing two plants. Russia also desired to install 10 nuclear reactors along the east coast of India. The French company 'Areva' has come forward to set up two 1,000 MW plants at Jaitapur in Maharashtra's Ratnagiri district, for which an agreement has been reached involving a supply of 300 tonnes of uranium. India envisaged to sign another contract for supply of uranium with Kazakhstan. It also intends to set up technical collaboration in a wide range of nuclear-related activities including uranium mining and processing. India has also devised strategies to enhance domestic uranium supplies. Import of uranium for nuclear power generation will obviate the need for import of coal. According to Atomic Energy Commission Chairman Anil Kakodkar, two-three nuclear power units will be connected to the national grid soon and they would add about 1,500 MW. The country's first fast breeder reactor was under construction and on schedule to get commissioned in 2010-11. Dr. Kakodkar envisaged building of nuclear power plants comprising 6-8 units of 1,000 MW each over the years upto 2020. It was aimed to generate 20,000 MW of nuclear power by 2020. Half of this would come from indigenously developed Pressurised Heavy Water Reactors (PHWR). He said, " We aim to produce 10,000 MW through PHWRs, about 5,000 MW through imported reactors and about 2,500 MW through Fast Breeder Reactors. India was in discussion with several foreign nuclear vendors. An inportant guarantee it was seeking from any vendor was, life-time uninterrupted supply of fuel and the right to re-process the spent fuel as the country had developed recycling capabilities. This was important because for delivering a sustained growth of 8 per cent through 2031, India would need to grow its electricity supply by 5-7 times". He has also said that there would be a ten-fold rise in India's power requirement in the next four decades. With the signing of agreements with foreign countries and expectation of regular supplies of uranium, India envisages the biggest power capacity addition during the XI five-year plan period. There is confidence to achieve the target of 78,000 MW of capacity addition since the country is making rapid strides in building super critical power plants. Yet, the country is buying the technology and many of these units are being awarded to Chinese companies which is not an optimistic trend. Bharat Heavy Electricals Limited (BHEL) should be encouraged to build India's own strenght in this vital field of power engineering. India's first 'Super Critical Test Facility' commissioned at the Tiruchi unit of BHEL is of great importance from the strategic and economic point of view.

H.M.: What is the advantage of solar power and is there any effort to exploit the sun's energy for our requirement substantially?

Robert: Among the non-conventional energy sources, solar power is the most important. According to experts, though cogeneration and biomass types of renewable energy were firm sources, their variable cost had been hiked in recent years. But in respect of solar, wind and geothermal energy, the variable cost was virtually nil. Further, solar termal plants of only 200-250 MW are cost advantageous and not smaller plants of 1 MW or 5 MW. To popularise this technology, the country's expertise must get a boost. The United States plans to establish plants of an aggregate capacity of 4000-5000 MW. The developing nations also must follow suit to meet the growing energy needs. In the 1970s, the international township 'Auroville' near Puducherry, embarked on an ambitious paln to make the entire township dependent on renewable energy. Initially, the residents desired to reduce power consumption through energy efficiency devices. As their plan worked out, they decided to generate power using renewable energy systems such as solar photovoltaic, wind pumps and biomass-based generators. All these efforts resulted in the establishment of the Auroville Centre of Scientific Research and five commercial units engaged in the promotion of renewable energy. By using a combination of systems, the township could reduce consumption and meet around 20 per cent of the total energy requirements. Further, they could enjoy light facilities at times of power disruption in the wake of cyclone, power-shut-down, etc. Auroville has developed the required equipment such as wind pumps, solar pumps, solar warter heaters and solar homes. The solar pumps could be an ideal means of getting water for irrigation and drinking, and are suitable for use in lieu of diesel pumpsets. A decision was taken to give one lakh solar lamps free of cost to economically weaker sections of society who were using kerosene lamps in Tamil Nadu, under a memorandum of understanding between the Non-Governmental Organization 'Exnora International' and Solkar Solar Industry Limited, signed on 7th July 2009. Each lamp could light up an area of 200 sq.ft. It could be used for six hours. It had provision for charging instruments such as mobile phones. Once this target is achieved, about 45 lakh litres of kerosene can be saved annually. The NGO also planned to approach philanthropists or social service organizations to join it in this endeavour. Bharat Heavy Electricals Limited (BHEL), a Government of India Undertaking, said on 2nd June 2009 that it had completed two 100 KWp (Kilo Watt peak) solar power plants in the Lakshadweep islands. With this, BHEL has commissioned eleven solar power plants in the islands.

The Government of India has finalised the draft for the 'National Solar Mission'. The Government outlay will be Rs. 85,000 crore to Rs. 105,000 crore over a period of 30 years. The project will be implemented in three phases. The first phase of solar development will spur domestic manufacturing in urban and rural areas. It will promote commercial-scale solar utility plants, compel installation of solar rooftop in buildings of government and public sector undertakings. The first phase of the Mission to be implemented between 2009 and 2012 will make it compulsory to install solar water heaters for all hospitals, nursing himes, hotels, guest houses and residential complexes with a minimum plot area of 500 sqm. It is estimated that an area of 40-50 million sq. metres is currently available for installation of solar collectors. The target for solar heating application is 7 million sq. metres by 2012. In about 2,000 to 3,000 buildings and establishments with 500 sq. metres of rooftop, roughly 3 million sq. metres can be used for solar application. Use of solar photovoltaic (*PV*) panels will also be encouraged to charge existing inverter systems both in the residential and commercial buildings that would help to save 30 per cent of grid power that is wasted in charging the current models of inverters. In the second phase, the Mission will focus on the commercial deployment of solar power plants. This will involve storage options, and the promotion of solar lighting and heating systems on a large-scale through micro-financing. In the final phase, the target is to achieve tariff parity with conventional grid power and an installed capacity of 20 GW (Giga Watts) by 2020. The installation of one million rooftop systems with an average capacity of 3 KW is also envisaged. A Solar Energy Authority of India is proposed to monitor various aspects of the Mission. Specialised personnel and technicians will be produced by education and training. The Mission will require about one lakh personnel. It aims to make India a global leader in solar energy and envisages an installed solar generation capacity of 20,000 MW by 2020, of one lakh MW by 2030 and of two lakh MW by 2050.

The first findings of a major research effort by the 'International Institute for Applied Systems Analysis' in Africa, together with experts at the 'European Climate Forum' and the 'Potsdam Institute for Climate Impact Research' revealed that the sun over North Africa is very strong and very reliable and rarely blocked by clouds even in winter. So, the dependable sunshine could be a constant resource to generate solar energy. The cost of moving electricity througth long distances has come down. So, Dr. Anthony Patt of the International Institute propounded a scheme involving government investment of 50 billion pounds over the next decade in a giant network of solar panels in the Sahara desert, during the conference on global warming in Copenhagen on 11th March 2009. Only a fraction of the Sahara would need to be covered to produce enough energy. The expert reckoned that such a plan combined with strings of wind farms along the North African coast could supply the whole of Europe with all the energy it needs. He hoped to present full details of the scheme to the Governments in 2009 itself. Such concrete proposals must be given priority by the concerned Governments. Thus, it is vivid that there is a keen interest to produce as much solar energy as possible for the benefit of the whole world.

Besides solar power, wind power also provides a sustainable solution to the problems of energy insufficiency and fluctuating fossil fuel prices. Its production can provide 3.5 lakh 'green collar' jobs through direct and indirect employment. The number is expected to increase beyond 20 lakh by 2020, paving the way for economic development. Apart from this, wind energy helps to keep the environment clean. Biomass power is another source of energy, produced from paddy straw, paddy hay, sugarcane tops, coconut rachies and stem, pulse stalks and tapioca stems. Biomass gasifier units are fuelled by wood like Julia Flora, casuarina, etc. Biomass power could be utilized for street lights, motor pumpsets, kitchen use, etc. Such lights function even during load-shedding. It facilitates savings in power bills. It is eco-friendly because of the reduction in the emission of carbon and soil erosion. Biomass power projects also boost industrialisation of rural areas. Commercial exploitation of biomass power is under way in Sweden, Brazil and the Philippines. In India, biomass units have been established in some town panchayats at a cost of around Rs. 4 lakh per unit and beneficially utilized. It may be extended to all the civic bodies. Hostels in government and private sectors must be encouraged to use biomass gasifiers for their kitchen needs. The Central Ministry of New and Renewable Energy and the Energy Development Agencies in States should take expeditious steps in this regard.

H.M.: Which sector among 'Agriculture' and 'Industry' consumes more power?

Robert: The pattern of consumption by various sectors has not been static at all times. As per the data of the Tamil Nadu State Electricity Board, the percentage of power consumption by different categories over the years has been in this pattern:

Category	1970-71	1980-81	1990-91	2000-01	2005-06	2006-07	2007-08
Domestic	5	9.55	16.21	20.82	24.78	23.99	24.35
Agri	25.12	28.45	24.47	27.47	21.99	21.15	20.47
Industry	50.10	48.97	42.09	35.43	36.58	38.35	39.54

It is clear that agricultural consumption has not increased and instead slightly decreased since 2005-06 though the supply is free of cost. The variations in industrial consumption are not significant though its share of revenue is 51 per cent. But the domestic category which accounts for 18 per cent of revenue, has steadily and drastically raised its power consumption. The causative factors for this trend are notable. First, while there are 18.4 lakh farm connections, 4.64 lakh industrial low-tension connections and 6,700 high-tension connections in the State, the number of domestic consumers which was 72.4 lakh in April 1998 has soared to 1.3 crore in April 2008. Secondly, the domestic consumers in the slab over 600 units bimonthly have recorded 44.6

per cent increase in their consumption during 2006 via-a-vis 2005. About 1.17 lakh domestic consumers consumed over 750 units a month as in 2008. All these have happened mainly due to a boost in the personal income of the middle-class people and consequent jump in the demand for electrical appliances. The sale of air-conditioners has trebled in 2008. To reverse this alarming trend, the State Government proposed to levy higher tariff for those who consumed over 600 units bimonthly but flinched from ordering an upward revision of tariff following criticism from political parties and legislators in the opposition benches. Power saving strategies are very important. Further, the 600 unit-limit is not going to affect the poor or middle-class people. Well-to-do people can afford to spend a little more for their power consumption. The Government therefore, should remain steadfast in its reasonable decisions and boldly order for higher tariff in respect of consumptions of 600 units and above bimonthly.

H.M.: Could you please expound the means of saving energy?

Robert: As advised by energy experts, all consumers must prefer purchase of energy-efficient products unmindful of higher cost, bearing in mind the scope to reduce their power bills. Usage of electronic choke instead of wire-wound choke in a four feet tube light can save 28 units of power in a year. A switch from the traditional T8 40-Watt light to T5 28-Watt fluorescent lamp can save 65 units. The use of 'compact fluorescent lamp (CFL)' for bath rooms instead of ordinary bulbs can save 137 units. Use of electronic regulator in lieu of conventional regulator for fan will save 50 units. Use of Light Emitting Diode (LED) lamp as night lamp would ensure saving of 47 units. In case of computer monitors, use of the Liquid Crystal Display (LCD) monitor will save 86 units. Most of the people are not aware of these wonderful benefits. Civic authorities are using the old incandescent lights and sodium vapour lamps which consume more power. These could be replaced by 'Compact Fluorescent Lamps' which provide more light and longevity. Such a move has been followed in many rural areas in Tamil Nadu and consequently, the power bills of the panchayats have come down by more than 50 per cent. All the officials of the Local Administration Department should therefore be instructed by government to emulate this practice.

Energy saving is at the centre of attention in the Western countries. The European Union decided to ban the sale of incandescent light bulbs and replace them with fluorescent bulbs as part of an energy saving plan, intending to save 7.7 to 12.4 billion euros by less energy consumption. In spite of higher cost, the energy – saving bulbs last 10 times longer. China was taking the lead in energy security. Improving energy efficiency has become a priority for the Chinese Government. The local government in Beijing began a 'green lighting' project in 2004. Since then, around 3 million energy-efficient lamps have been installed in public service buildings, schools and hospitals. The Chinese Government provided subsidies, on energy–efficient light bulbs, of 30 per cent on wholesale and 50 per cent on retail purchases since April 2008. In spite of huge investment in renewable energy, coal consumption in China grew by 7 percent in 2008, even as prices rose, and accounted for 43 percent of global coal consumption. So, the Government envisages energy conversion programme as an important way of controlling consumption in cities. The programme is part of the Chinese Government's plan to distribute 100 million energy-friendly light bulbs in cities across China. The programme is partly funded by China's massive $ 586 billion stimulus package, which earmarked $ 30 billion exclusively for green energy projects. China has set an ambitious target of producing one-fifth of all its energy needs from renewable energy by 2020. Lighting accounts for 19 per cent of the country's energy needs, according to the Joint US-China Cooperation on Clean Energy (JUCCCE), a non-profit organization that is working to promote clean energy and energy efficiency in China. The Government has taken much pains to woo residents in cities to swap incandescent bulbs for greener alternatives in the context of the comparatively higher prices of energy-efficient lamps. Distribution of ten million energy-saving lamps in replacement of incandescent lamps on the streets of Beijing started on 22nd June 2009. This initiative made the lamps available for sale at a much-reduced price of just 1 yuan (Rs. 7) - i.e. 10 per cent of the market price. The JUCCCE in association with the Shanghai Municipal Government, distributed 10 million energy-saving lamps free of cost to the city's residents. It was one of the largest ever energy conversion exercises of its kind. It could save $ 35 million a year in electricity bills as reported.

Buildings could be designed with vents that allow in, natural light during the day and fresh air always. The materials used for construction can also keep the building's inner temperature at low levels. The spectacular building that houses the Salim Ali Centre for Ornithology and Natural History (SACON) at Anaikatty in the Western Ghats near Coimbatore has been designed in such a way that natural light is utilized to the maximum. Measuring a built-up area of 36,000 square feet, the buildings on the SACON Campus are red-brick circular structures with courtyards, arched corridors, clay tile flooring and tiled roof. The main walls are almost 40cm thick. Most of them are not plastered (exposed brickwork) and some are made of coarse, random rubble. The filler slate roof has two layers of tiles with reinforced concrete grids. The design and materials used for construction ensure ample lighting and ventilation. The features reduce heat radiation in the building. The campus also has 30 solar lamps. The campus includes the main block, laboratory, canteen and students' hostel. Several kinds of office equipment such as computers are used. The laboratory needs 24-hour power supply. An air conditioner keeps the temperature at the required level for precision equipment inside. In spite of all these facilities, the need for using electrical lights and air conditioners is reduced substantially. The average power consumption of the campus has been at 6,500 units to 7,000 units a month, and has been steady since it came up in the late 1990s. According to a SACON employee, the Centre's buildings save nearly 60 per cent of electrical energy vis–a–vis conventional buildings. Mr. P.B. Sajan, Joint Director and Architect at the Kerala-based Centre of Technology for Rural Development says that advantages of such buildings include energy saving in the use of air conditioning and daytime lighting. The courty–ards, filled with trees and shrubs, keep the environment cool. The buildings were designed by Laurie Baker and constructed by the Centre of Technology for Rural Development. It has constructed several such buildings in Kerala State. Environment-friendly and energy conservation features characterise all these buildings. While a normal, non-air-conditioned conventional building consumes nearly 47 units of energy per square metre a year, the energy consumption at the SACON buildings works out to just 28 units. Such energy-efficient buildings may be popularised for construction in all areas while taking up new buildings.

Above all, government and service organizations need to inculcate energy-saving habit in every citizen of the country. If public awareness of energy economy is created, women and children will adopt it well, making the effort successful. The Electricity Department/Board may grant suitable incentive for consumers using power at low levels. A disciplined and judicious use of energy, avoiding wastage, will certainly lead us on the road to energy security.

H.M.: I have grasped useful information on energy sector from you. Thank you very much.

Charli... Are you lounging or dozing? Your act is useless.

Charli: I had a useful study while dozing.

H.M.: What could you study without any book in hand?

Charli: It was not a book-study but brown study.

H.M.: How is it useful to you?

Charli: Because I could hear an oracle through seraph while feeling to be in Athens.

H.M.: What did you hear?

Charli: I heard that I would be subjected to three-pronged attack by someone close to me.

H.M.: Who is that 'someone'?

Charli: He was not identified as oracles are always implicit.

H.M.: Are you able to guess as to who might attack you?

Charli: I could guess the guilty instantly and imagine about his three-pronged attack.

H.M.: Then why do you say as 'someone' in a clandestine manner?

Charli: If I am explicit in revealing his identity, I may be subjected to four-pronged attack.

H.M.: Don't be silly. Tell me who he is. And, how would he attack you from three angles?

Charli: If you insist, I shall shed my inhibition and divulge everything to you. (Suddenly, he switches the lights off) If I go somewhere with students, I am assailed. If I participate in any conversation, I am pulled up. If I remain a mute spectator or slumber, then too I am decried. Since it is the 'prerogative' of my assailant, I can't rant.

H.M.: Why do you resort to such euphemism as 'prerogative' and 'assailant' for a candid mention as 'imperious headmaster'?

Charli: Thank you, sir. I shall do so in the future.

H.M.: Even in your perception as attacks, the treble attacks do not happen at the same time. So, how can you term them as 'three-pronged attack'?

Charli: Whenever an attack targets me, it is reminiscent of the others. So, at that moment I feel three-pronged attack. In my case, it has never been a separate attack and none can dispute my contention.

H.M.: Are you restive because of the so-called attacks?

Charli: No, I am following in a stoic's footsteps.

H.M.: Who is that stoic?

Charli: Matthew Arnold. Nevertheless, I am an outcast during your conversations in the students' households.

H.M.: I asked you not to intervene in the discussions because your comments might botch up them. But I never asked you to go out. Have you not watched me uttering only a few words and listening to others' views?

Charli: My comments wouldn't botch up the interactions between you and the hosts but would grace them.

H.M.: How could your scanty views adorn a chat?

Charli: It can be likened to a pinch of salt that makes food palatable.

H.M.: If you add it in excess, the whole food will have to be discarded.

Charli: As you have reminded me about food, I feel hungry. Shall we go home?

H.M.: It is not I but you, who used the word 'food' first.

Charli: Hunger buries all human qualities including memory. Your repetition of that word makes me hungrier.

Emili.: Our dinner is ready. All of you may have it now.

Charli: Thank you.

Emili.: Not at all. Providing food is only a matter of routine.

Charli: My thanks is not for providing dinner but for sparing me from cooking tonight.

Robert: You are really clever. By the by, why did you switch the lights off?

Charli: You emphasized the importance of saving electricity. My boss is only a man of words but I am a man of action. We have already seen each other and hearing does not need any light.

All are laughing.

After dinner, the headmaster and Charli take leave of the hosts.

6

HUMAN RIGHTS VIOLATIONS DUE TO GENOCIDE

The headmaster and Charli arrive at Sanjay's home.

Sanjay : Good morning, sir.

H.M. : Good morning, Sanjay.

Sanjay : I expected your visit only in the evening. It's nice to see you in the morning, sir.

H.M. : Today, I am free in the morning. So, I have come now.

Sanjay : I am happy about it, sir. (Turning to his father Ashok). This is our headmaster, Dad.

Ashok : Hello, sir. Please be seated.

H.M. : Thank you. Are you in the Government service?

Ashok : I was a government pleader and retired two years ago. I am now a member of the State Human Rights Commission (SHRC).

H.M. : It's a pleasing matter. Could I get some information on your present task?

Ashok : Oh, yes. By all means.

(Mrs. Chandra Ashok welcomes the headmaster with a hot drink and gets introduced to him).

H.M. : How did human rights crop up in mankind and why are they much focused on?

Ashok : The tradition of human rights emerged from several political fights including the 'French Revolution' of 1789 and the freedom struggles in India and elsewhere. The Human Rights

Movement gained momentum in the aftermath of grave injuries inflicted on humanity by the World War II. It bloomed into the proclamation of the Universal Declaration of Human Rights by the united Nations General Assembly in 1948. Having been authored by many architects from diverse origins, the Declaration transcends race, gender, and fundamental freedoms with universal hue. As fundamental freedoms are cardinal in the minds and humour of Europeans, the freedoms adorned the Union's founding treaty of Rome and they were strengthened further by the 2000 Charter of Fundamental Rights. The European Union enjoins 'respect for human rights' for its membership and adopts it in the forefront of its global policy. Given many social, political and economic challenges burying human rights, the Union is consolidating actions to uphold the rights all around the world. Further, it has contrived projects and programmes to achieve this noble goal and spends 140 million euros annually in this realm under 'European Instrument for Democracy and Human Rights'. The spirit of the European Union needs to be kept up by all nations across the world. Nevertheless, we witness human rights violations worldwide. All countries focus on human rights mainly because of their violations due to genocide, racism and other crimes. It is similar to being on the lookout for shade while suffering a scorching hot day.

H.M. : Do you think that genocide is a perennial problem affecting many countries?

Ashok : 'Genocide' is not new to this world. History speaks of several ethnic massacres around the world. For instance, Adolf Hitler's Nazi regime carried out carnage of millions of innocent Jews in the late 1930s and the early 1940s, which is known as 'the Holocaust'. Bangladesh seceded from Pakistan after 1971 Liberation War, that witnessed mass killings. An international conference in Dhaka, held at the end of July 2009 and attended by historians, academics and international legal experts, called for a campaign for the United Nations' recognition of the mass killings as genocide. Of late, the ethnic strife and the consequent genocide of Tamils in Sri Lanka attracted the attention of the whole world because of its spanning nearly three decades and its heavy death toll.

H.M.: Could you please elaborate on the Sri Lankan imbroglio?

Ashok: There were constant grievances and complaints that ever since independence from the British rule, there was discrimination against the Tamils in Sri Lanka and they were neglected by the majority

Sinhalese and the Government dominated by them. The Government was allegedly biased against the Tamils in terms of their rights, political power, financial allotments, development schemes, welfare schemes, infrastructure creations, employment and so on. They were denied jobs in vital sectors including the armed forces. The Jaffna region in the North and the Batticaloa region in the East were kept apart, rejecting the plea of the Tamils for unification of these regions mostly inhabited by them. These factors eventually led to hatred towards the successive governments and a desire for emancipation in the minds of the Tamils. A few Tamil political parties and groups wanted to fulfil their aspirations by virtue of forming a separate 'Tamil Eelam' after secession from the unified Sri Lanka. However, their efforts were not active. But the 'Liberation Tigers of Tamil Eelam (LTTE)', an organization formed in the 1970s with an emancipatory political vision and idealism, launched the freedom struggle. As other means of fight didn't produce the desired results, the LTTE resorted to an armed struggle. The first full-scale war between the LTTE and the Sri Lankan army erupted in July 1983. There were continued fights. Both sides suffered heavy casualties. Thousands of civilians were also killed. Following India's efforts to end the ethnic strife in the island nation, the 'India-Sri Lanka Agreement' was signed in Colombo on 29th July 1987 by the Indian Prime Minister Rajiv Gandhi and the Sri Lankan President J.R. Jayewardene. As per the agreement, the Sri Lankan troops were ordered back to barracks and the Indian Peace Keeping Force (IPKF) with a strength of one lakh soldiers were deployed in the Tamil States of Sri Lanka. But ironically, the Indian troops couldn't restore peace. Instead, the IPKF and the LTTE were fighting against each other from 1987 to 1990 until the former was withdrawn. India was spending about Rs. 1 crore per day to maintain the IPKF in Sri Lanka. Many Indian leaders and people therefore, questioned the wisdom of the agreement. As the LTTE was accused of conspiracy in the assassination of Rajiv Gandhi on 21st May 1991, enraged India refrained from interfering in the ethnic conflict. The LTTE had allegedly killed many of their adversaries including Sri Lankan leaders, for example the Foreign Minister Lakshman Kadirgamar, and leaders of Tamil Political parties, namely A. Amirthalingam (1989), Neelan Thiruchelvam (1999), Padmanabha, etc. The organization was proscribed as a terrorist outfit, first by India and then by the United States, Canada, the European Union, etc. After withdrawal of the IPKF, fights recurred between the Sri Lankan soldiers and the LTTE which developed into another Eelam War in the 1990s. Apart from LTTE cadres and soldiers, thousands of Tamil civilians were also killed. During their battles with the LTTE, the Sri Lankan army ruthlessly killed a large number of innocent Tamils with an obvious intention to eliminate the race from the Sri Lankan soil. In some places, the Sinhalese soldiers had reportedly displayed sign boards reading "the Tamils' meat is available here." The army took over Jaffna from the LTTE in 1995. 'Hero's Day' was observed by the LTTE as an annual ritual on 27th November every year since 1989. In his 'Hero's Day' speeches, the LTTE Chief Velupillai Prabakaran averred that 'Eelam' was the only solution to the problems of the Tamils and vowed to achieve it at all cost. Norway involved itself in mediation and strove hard for many years to restore peace in Sri Lanka. Norwegian Minister Eric Solheim constantly negotiated with the LTTE and the Sri Lankan Government and its leadership separately. Braving the appalling atmosphere in the war-zone, he travelled many a time into the jungles to meet the LTTE leaders. In fact, he spent most of his days in Sri Lanka during the periods of negotiations. His involvement, dedication and goodwill were unparalleled. As a result of an active and persistent role by Norway, the Eelam War III came to a halt and the Sri Lankan Government reached a ceasefire agreement with the LTTE in 2002. Hats off to Norway and its negotiators for their zeal in world peace and unflinching efforsts to achieve it, amid the daunting task in a challenging situation in Sri Lanka. A Monitoring Mission was set up for proper implementation of the accord. However, frequent violations of ceasefire with recrimination by the LTTE and the Sri Lankan army made the ceasefire fragile. Time and again, there were skirmishes between the soldiers and the LTTE cadres. The Government unilaterally withdrew the ceasefire agreement, declaring it "invalid" on 2nd January 2008. Norway intervened immediately to save the hard-fought pact. But the Government was rigid and didn't relent. As the agreement ended, the Monitoring Mission wound up its operations. A free-for-all emerged for the antagonists. 'Occasional' fights turned 'frequent'. The situation therefore, began to deteriorate.

In April 2006, Army Chief Sarath Fonseka sustained grievous injuries in a suicide-bomb attack by a woman LTTE cadre but survived the attack. Following the closure of the sluice gates of Maavilaru in the East by the LTTE, hostilities intensified in July 2006. At this stage, the Rajapaksa Government determined to eliminate the LTTE militarily. The fighting escalated into the full-scale Eelam War IV in Argust 2006. Mr. Sarath Fonseka drew up a grand plan with the backing of the political leadership to oust the Tigers from the East first, and take the war into the LTTE heartland in Wanni in the North. The 57 Division of the Sri Lankan Army (SLA) was created in February 2007 with a firm strategy to advance in a methodical manner from the west of Vavuniya into the LTTE strongholds. The SLA which was already engaged in ousting the Tigers from the East, declared some LTTE bases "liberated" in July 2007. Batticaloa was also wrested from the Tigers by the military. The LTTE was ousted from the East in 2007. However, violence, killings and abductions rose alarmingly in the Eastern Province. The nature of the crisis could be grasped from the decision in the last week of November 2008 by the 'Association of Government Doctors' to withdraw its members from hospitals in the East if the Government did not agree to its demand for a Rs. 1 billion Life Insurance Scheme for doctors. The doctors revolted after one of their colleagues was shot dead in Batticaloa. Human Rights Watch (HRW), in its report released on 24th November 2008, called upon the Government to take immediate steps to address the deteriorating human rights situation in the Eastern Province. The LTTE had not been able to regain its lost bases in the East.

The 57 Division and 58 Division that was elevated from Task Force I covered a distance of 63 km and 82 km respectively in their march before closing in on Kilinochchi. The crawled their way through, amid fierce resistance from the Tigers. Having learnt lessons from past mistakes, the troops operated in small batches of four to eight and avoided battalion marches into possible Tiger traps, which paid dividends. The two Divisions wrested many areas from the Tigers. It was evident that the Tigers had suffered heavy casualties. The SLA was advancing through many LTTE-held areas. The LTTE and the Sri Lnakan Government always gave conflicting versions on deaths and injuries suffered by either side in the battle zones. In 2008, the SLA gained control of many areas held by the LTTE, and by the year-end, launched a massive attack to capture Kilinochchi–the stronghold of the Tigers, and faced stiff resistance. In such situation, Human Rights Watch (HRW) accused the LTTE of "widespread abuses" against Tamil civilians trapped in Wanni and warned that the lives of "hundreds of thousands" were at risk. HRW claimed to have found "extensive evidence" of forced recruitment of civilians including childeren, widespread use of abusive forced labour and unjustified restrictions on civilians' freedom of movement. All these amounted to severe blow on human rights. Kilinochchi, the administrative and political capital of the LTTE, proved to be the toughest target for the troops in their entire campaign. In the last phase, it took over one and a half months for the troops to gain entry into Kilinochchi as the Tigers did all they could to halt the march of the army including raising a 40-km-long ditch-cum-wall stretching from Kilaly to Kilinochchi. The entire infrastructure of Kilinochchi town was either dismantled and carried away or destroyed. The town's main water supply tank with a length of 40 feet, was blasted and power-supply cables were slashed. Even the revelations of the LTTE tallied with the fact that the civilians had fled long before the military reached there. In spite of stiff resistance from the Tigers, Kilinochchi was captured by the SLA on 2nd January 2009. It was a devastating blow to the Tigers politically and militarily. Since then, many villages, towns and LTTE bases including Elephant Pass and Muhamalai were brought under the army's control. The area under the LTTE control began to shrink. The Mullaithivu forest alone became the shelter for the Tigers. To help the civilians stranded in the battle zones, India sent a shipment of humanitarian aid in December 2008 to Colombo for distribution by the International Committee of the Red Cross. India further announced its second instalment of humanitarian assistance worth $ 3.64 lakh in January 2009. But the ICRC, the only link to the displaced people, said that it had not been able to secure 'safe passage' to the conflict zone since January 2009.

Tamil United Liberation Front (TULF) leader Mr. V. Anandasangaree said in December 2008 that war between the LTTE and the Sri Lankan forces had reached the final stages and the trapped citizens were desperate to escape the clutches of the outfit. He added that if Tamil Nadu in India was sincere in helping the Sri Lankan Tamils and had any sympathy for over 3 lakh people trapped in the areas under the control of the Tigers, it should pressurize the outfit into releasing them without using them as a shield. He conceded that there were a number of human rights violations in the island nation. The Sri Lankan Government reproached the LTTE on 27th January 2009 for holding 300 patients in Mullaithivu district at gun point which disabled the officials of the ICRC and the UN to take them for treatment. According to the ICRC statement, hundreds of people had been killed and wounded in the Wanni region following intensified battle, and violence was blocking evacuation of the wounded. People were being caught in crossfire, hospitals and ambulances had been hit by shelling, and several aid workers had been injured while evacuating the wounded. The violence was preventing the ICRC from operating in the region. The ICRC added that an estimated 2.5 lakh people were trapped in a 250 sq. km area subjected to heavy fighting. The UN office in Colombo stated that it would attempt again to evacuate hundreds of critically wounded civilians including at least 50 children by convoy. The Government announced 48-hour crasefire by the end of January 2009. Utilizing the ceasefire, the ICRC transported 226 patients to Vavuniya for treatment. The Sri Lankan Air Force attacked a Home for the Aged destitutes, killing four of them on 14th February 2009 in Wanni. The ICRC revealed that Putumattalam hospital in Wanni was hit by shelling which killed 16 patients and it was forced to shift 240 sick and wounded persons. It is vivid that the Government and the army had little or no concern about the safety of the people. Paul Castella, the head of the ICRC delegation in Colombo said, "We are shocked that patients are not afforded the protection they are entitled to." The ICRC was pointing out the human rights violations in the war-torn areas of Sri Lanka then and there. In the first week of February 2009, a member of the Janatha Vimukthi Perumuna (JVP)-a Sinhalese organization, accused the ICRC local head of presenting an exaggerated picture of the plight of those stranded in the war zone and demanded his deportation. Within hours of his comment, the ICRC main office in Colombo was attacked.

The continuous offensive and advancement of the Sri Lankan army from all sides, shrinked the area under the LTTE's control. The Government demarcated an area of 17 square-kilometre as 'No-Fire Zone (NFZ)' to enable the trapped civilians estimated around one lakh to move out. President Mahinda Rajapaksa ordered a two-day halt to the military offensive on 13th and 14th April 2009 on the occasion of Sinhala and Tamil New Year. The Government of India exerted pressure to extend the ceasefire, but in vain. Britain's plea to extend the ceasefire was also rejected. In the first week of May 2009, the Sri Lankan Government offered amnesty to the lower rungs of the LTTE on condition that they should give up their arms and surrender to the military. The Government added that the offer was not applicable to the top rung of the LTTE including its Chief V. Prabakaran and all others against whom criminal cases were pending. The military believed that an estimated 300 to 400 LTTE leaders and cadres had taken shelter in the remaining area of the 'No-Fire Zone' and held 15,000 to 20,000 civilians as human shield. The UN and other international agencies put the figure at 50,000. The LTTE maintained that the number of people stranded was over 1.5 lakh.

Even after announcing an end of combat operation with heavy

weapons on 27th April 2009 in response to constant pressure from the Indian Government to stop the war, the Sri Lankan forces continued their offensive against the LTTE. The sufferings of civilians during the final stages of the war in Sri Lanka were awful. During the period of three months from February to mid-May 2009, 15,000 people-including 2,000 Children had been killed. The pitched battle reached its peak on 18th May 2009. The next day, the Sri Lankan President informed the death of the LTTE Chief V. Prabakaran to the Indian External Affairs Minister. The army announced the end of Eelam War and claimed to have identified the bodies of many LTTE leaders including Charles Anthony-the elder son of V. Prabakaran, the Tiger Intelligence Wing chief, Pottu Amman–the Political Wing head, B.Nadesan- in charge of the Tigers' Peace Secretariat and S. Pulithevan. The militrary collected at least 250 bodies of the Tiger cadres and expected many more bodies could be lying in bunkers inside the war zone. Most of the leaders reoportedly died either of gun wounds or in suicide blasts by the Tiger cadres. A few appeared to have swallowed 'Cyanide capsules' to escape capture by the military, as per the conditions of the LTTE organization. The curtains came down on the nearly 3–year long Eelam War IV. The war took a heavy toll on the SLA also. Sri Lankan Defence Minister Gotabhaya Rajapaksa was quoted in the local media as having said on 21st May 2009 that since military operations began in August 2006, 6,261 security personnel died and 29,551 were injured, with 2,556 of them left disabled. These figures were confirmed by the Sri Lankan Military Spokesman Udaya Nanayakkara who also revealed that the Sri Lankan forces had killed over 22,000 Tigers. He also told that over 9,100 LTTE cadres had surrendered. The defeat and destruction of the LTTE and its proclaimed goal of 'Tamil Eelam', are widely attributed to the disunity and rivalry within the Tamil factions in Sri Lanka. The exit from the LTTE of Vinayagamoorthy Muralitharan alias Karuna following dissidence within the outfit and his induction into the ruling combine was also a heavy blow to the organization.

H.M.: How is the post-war situation and what are the conditions of the Internally Displaced Persons (IDPS) in Sri Lanka?

Ashok: According to a survey by the Colombo–based Medical Research Institute in March 2009, in six out of the then 13 Relief Camps, 25.5 per cent of children were suffering from acute malnutrition, of which 5.2 per cent were severely malnourished and needed immediate rehabilitation with therapeutic food and treatment.

14 foreign citizens were also found in the camps at the time of survey. The United Nations Secretary General Ban Ki-moon was on a visit to Sri Lanka for a first-hand assessment of the post-war situation. On 23rd May 2009, he visited one of the government-run Relief Camps for the displaced in the war-torn North. After spending 20 minutes walking through the camp, he said to the journalists, "I am very moved after what I have seen. I have seen so many wounded". Later, he had a meeting with President Mahinda Rajapaksa in Kandy which focused on the need to - give the UN agencies and international humanitarian organizations, immediate and unhindered access to all areas where there were displaced people, fast-track the screening and processing of refugees as quickly as possible, take immediate steps to initiate a political process of dialogue- accommodation-and reconciliation. After the meeting, Mr. Ban revealed that Mr. Rajapaksa had told him that his government had prepared a plan for settlement of the nearly 3 lakh war-displaced civilians within 6 months and also apprised him of the steps taken to initiate a political dialogue for a solution acceptable to all parties to the ethnic conflict. The Secretary General welcomed the Sri Lankan President's assurance in Parliament on 19th May 2009 that a national solution acceptable to all sections of people would be evolved, and the Government's announcement expressing its intention to dismantle the welfare camps at the earliest as outlined in the plan to resettle the Internally Displaced Persons (IDPs), and called for its early implementation. Expectant and nursing mothers were also among the IDPs in the welfare camps. There were appeals to consider their plight and release them for handover to their relatives or friends who were prepared to look after them. Hundreds of government officials including at least two Sri Lankan Administrative Service (SLAS) officers who were engaged in various services in the erstwhile LTTE-controlled territory and subsequently either forced or voluntarily moved deeper into the Tiger territory as the troops advanced, were also sheltered in the camps. As many as nearly 3 lakh Tamils were being held in camps behind barbed wire. Interviews with civilians detained in the camps were conducted by a reliable third party whose identity was reportedly known to the 'Guardian Newspaper' despite government restrictions on access to the camps. The inmates had described the dismal conditions inside the internment camps where, as told by them, food, water and medicines were desperately inadequate. A lady had told that only those with money were able to buy access to water. One of her children, who fell sick due to unhealthy environment, had been sleeping on a mat outside the tent, covered from head to toe with a blanket to

keep off flies. She had spoken in frustration revealing that her children were begging her for food and water and such condition was killing her. A 58–year–old woman had narrated her plight of wading through chest-deep water for three and a half hours to reach a camp near Vavuniya. She had termed it as a horrible endeavour to save five of her eight children and four of her seven grand children whom she had escorted. She had not known what could have happened to the rest who got separated from them during the shelling. She had cried, yearning for their reunion which was not certain. One health official had told that as his daughter had fallen ill in February 2009, he had arranged for her shifting out of the area by the sea with doctors but he had not seen them since. He had stated that doctors put patients on mattresses under the trees for want of proper hospitals inside the 'No-Fire Zone.' One day in April 2009, patients with limited mobility had struggled on the ground in the wake of heavy rain and flood, and 10 patients had died of drowning that night. The official had also told that a make-shift hospital that was set up in a school in Mathalan had been shelled thrice and there had been attacks with multi-barrelled rocket launchers, rocket-propelled grenades and white phosphorus and he had seen people with burnt-skin as they had been affected by chemical bombs. He had also claimed that he and his wife along with their two children aged one and three, had been running from artillery fire for nine months, had lived in many bunkers and had been displaced 13 times.

Mr. Sarath N. Silva, the Chief Justice of Sri Lanka's Supreme Court told a news conference in Colombo on 5th June 2009 on the eve of his retirement that it was time to build a nation with one people, irrespective of religion, colour and race. He was also quoted as saying that if there were no proper judicial and social mechanisms to grant the Tamils their due protection by law, there was the possibility of another uprising, though not an armed struggle. Justice Silva further said, "Law of the country does not show any interest in these IDPs. I openly say this. The authorities can penalise me for telling this. I visited relief villages where Wanni IDP families are sheltered. I cannot explain their suffering and grief in words. It is an utter lie if we continue to say that there is only one race and no majority or minority in the country". The Centre for Policy Alternative (CPA), an independent Colombo-based think-tank, which was critical of the Government's approach on Eelam War IV, filed a petition in the Supreme Court of Sri Lanka challenging the restrictions on the free movement of the 2.8 lakh war-displaced people sheltered in government-run camps spread across three districts in the Northern Sri Lanka. The IDPS had begun arriving in government-controlled areas in March 2009 and they were housed in camps encircled by barbed wire with no permission to leave the camps unless approved by military officials, the petition said. The CPA stated that restriction of free movement of IDPs was a violation of their fundamental rights. It mentioned that as in June 2009, the IDPs included 3,100 public servants 6,700 persons over the age of sixty, 780 pregnant women and disabled persons. The application also mentioned that the Vavuniya Magistrate had recorded the death of 30 senior citizens due to starvation and malnutrition, and even the UN and ICRC officials were not allowed into the camps without the permission of the military. The CPA reportedly said to have received an anonymous letter threatening the worst if the organization did not mend its ways. The letter written in Sinhalese was titled as "Notice to the traitors". It showed vanities of the Governments' triumph over the LTTE and the military's heroism in ending the thirty-year-war and defeating what it termed "wretched traitors" and likened the CPA to them. The letter also commanded the CPA, viewing it as a bane to Sri Lanka, to close down its institute for a week-display the national flag-bestow its honour to the warriors along with the Government on 3rd June 2009 - and donate one million rupees to the 'ApiVenuven Api' account as an honour to the warriros. Further, it intimidated the CPA into stopping all the anti-national programmes of its institute and cautioned that the sender mentioned as 'Sri Lankans affectionate to the motherland', was keeping close tabs on the organization. From this letter, anybody could grasp the partisan mentality prevailing in Sri Lanka with no concern for the consequences of Eelam War including the ineffable sufferings of lakhs of displaced Tamils.

Amid mounting pressure from within and outside to investigate 16 major cases of human rights violations in 2006, President Mahinda Rajapaksa appointed a Commission of Enquiry in 2007. The eight-member Commission headed by former Supreme Court Judge Nissanka Udalagama lasted one year and five months. The Judge said to 'Daily Mirror', "We completed investigation into seven cases and reports on five were finalised while the rest remain uninvestigated". While the probe remained unfinished, curtains came down on the investigations on 14th June 2009. It is a vivid testament to the Sri Lankan Government's indifference to human rights and the farcical investigation by the Commission. There were widespread allegation of human rights violations that led to the killing of several thousands of innocent Tamils during the Eelam War IV, and demands for investigation into the issue. The United Nations Human Rights Chief Mr. Navi Pillay had told the UN Human Rights Council that there was credible evidence of gross violation of international humanitarian laws. When the Council meeting was convened on 27th May 2009, a Swiss-European Union draft resolution calling for an investigation into possible war crimes in Sri Lanka was dropped after it was put to the vote. The Canadian representative commented that the defeat of a justified resolution was a challenge to the UN body's credibility itself. The Sri Lankan Government presented a counter-resolution condemning the Tigers and welcoming what it called the "liberation by the Sri Lankan Government of tens of thousands of its citizens kept by the LTTE against their will as hostages", and its resolution was adopted. The Tamil Nadu Chief Minister Mr. M. Karunanidhi, in a letter to the Indian Prime Minister Dr. Manmohan Singh, focused on the belief of millions of Tamils spread across the world that the Sri Lankan Government's resolution was largely against the interests of Sri Lankan Tamils, with a request to take appropriate decision in this regard, having in mind, the sentiments of the Sri Lankan Tamils and their future welfare. The Government of Sri Lanka has a tendency to view anybody raising their voice in support of the tormented Tamils in that country, as the supporters of the LTTE and the foes of the Government. For instance, Mr. Bob Rae, a Member of Parliament in Canada belonging to the opposition Liberal Party arrived at Colombo airport on 10th June 2009 with required visa to visit Sri Lanka. But he was briefly detained at the airport and later deported. The Controller-General of Immigration was quoted as saying that the decision to deport Mr. Rae was based on a government Intelligence report. According to the report, Mr. Rae had been accused of being a pro-LTTE character. He was viewed as an opposition Member of Parliament and hailing from Greater Toronto area inhabited by a large number of Tamil people. Such mindset of the Sri Lankan Government apparently indicates its aversion to Tamils.

H.M.: What role has India played to resolve the ethnic conflict in Sri Lanka?

Ashok: After the ethnic strife broke out in Sri Lanka, the LTTE began to reinforce itself militarily. In the 1980s, the then Chief Minister of Tamil Nadu Mr. M.G. Ramachandran displayed a true spirit and alacrity on finding a solution to the ethnic conflict in Sri Lanka. He was distressed at the failure of the tripartite talks held in Bangalore in the early 1980s. India mediated the peace talks held in Thimpu, Bhutan, in 1985. That was also fruitless. On an occasion when the Sri Lankan Tamils suffered for want of food and essentials due to stoppage of supplies from Colombo, Prime Minister Rajiv Gandhi ordered the Indian Air Force to air-drop them into the areas of the Tamils. The Sri Lankan Government was startled by this action. Afterwards he reached the 'India-Sri Lanka Accord' which I have narrated about, a little while ago. The IPKF-LTTE clashes and subsequent assassination of Rajiv Gandhi in 1991 created an unpleasant atmosphere which impelled India to distance itself from the ethnic conflict since early 1990s. In the wake of proscription of the LTTE, their cadres were denied entry into India. Patrolling by Coast Guard vessels was intensified along the Indian, especially Tamil Nadu coast and transport of essentials by the sea to the Tigers' areas was curbed. As for political leaders in Tamil Nadu, none after late M.G. Ramachandran evinced keen interst in the burning problem. The political parties which came to power in the State alternately could never reach a consensus on this issue, or rather, didn't concentrate their efforts on it. They were adopting recriminatory posture on this problem also as in all other local issues. A few resolutions were passed in the State Assembly, some letters were sent to the Prime Minister, token strikes were observed, and human chains were formed over a period of about 18 years, demanding action to end the ethnic strife. But never did all the parties join together to launch strong and wholesome efforts to diffuse the grave situation in the island nation. The measures, which the parties claimed to have taken, were only formal and not robust to resolve the conflict. For many decades, every ruling party in Tamil Nadu had an alliance with that in the Central Government and was working with New Delhi closely in pursuit of their own ends. But they failed to exercise their influence and impress upon the Central Government to force Sri Lanka to halt the war at any cost in view of heavy loss of lives. If Tamil Nadu had withdrawn its support to the coalition government at the centre at any point of time in the past, especially when the LTTE-SLA war was underway, the situation would have been different. Had the Central Government taken a decision to snap India's diplomatic ties with Sri Lanka, as soon as the war was resumed in August 2006, such action would have come to fruition. But India did not contemplate such move. Besides, it provided arms supply at the request of Sri Lankan authorities which enabled them to intensify the war. The political leaders in Tamil Nadu would usually express their serious concern over the plight of the Sri Lankan Tamils on the eve of elections to woo the voters. On many occasions, Sri Lankan Tamil MPs stressed the need for an active role by India to restore peace there. Even the LTTE leaders stated that the resolution of the ethnic conflict was not possible in the absence of India's 'vital role', and requested for its intervention. But India was indifferent to those appeals for a long time. It was only by the end of 2008 when the war had taken a heavy toll on Tamil civilians and created unrest in Tamil Nadu, the State leaders revived their attention to the sensitive issue. Even by that time, the general elections in India scheduled for May 2009 had been announced. Some parties made it an election issue for fishing in troubled waters. As done in the past, the Tamil Nadu Assembly passed a resolution urging the Government of India to take necessary action to stop the war in Sri Lanka. An all-party delegation of Parliament Members from Tamil Nadu and Puducherry called on Prime Minister Dr. Manmohan Singh on 1st December 2008 and sought the Central Government's serious intervention to restore ceasefire in Sri Lanka. In response to this plea, Indian Foreign Secretary and National Security Adviser paid a few periodical visits to Sri Lanka and held talks with the President and concerned officials. What transpired in their talks were not clearly divulged. The Indian Minister for External Affairs also visited Colombo and held talks with the President. In spite of all these belated efforts, there was no let-up in the war situation. The daily reports of civilian deaths continued and triggered human chains, rallies and agitations across Tamil Nadu at various levels, namely students, lawyers, workers etc. Some small parties who were not in power but the real sympathizers of the Sri Lankan Tamils were indeed pained by the human slaughter in that country. They too resorted to agitations all over the State. Several thousands of the Tamils living in the United States, Canada, European Union countries, etc., held rallies and agitations decrying the brutal killings of their brethren in Sri Lanka and clamoured for halting the military operations. But the Sri Lankan Government turned a blind eye and a deaf ear to the developments in Tamil Nadu and elsewhere since it was tenacious to destroy the LTTE unmindful of sheer civilian deaths. When the war had reached its final stages in the first week of May 2009, the Tamil Nadu Chief Minister Mr. M. Karunanidhi went on fast in Chennai that was given up after a few hours following an information that Sri Lanka had decided to desist from using heavy weapons. But this assurance was allegedly not kept up. Indian External Affairs Minister Mr. Pranab Mukerji also went to Colombo in the terminal stage of war. But all these steps failed to be a deterrant to the Sri Lankan war and its very harmful impact on the Tamils trapped in the war zone. If India had embarked on positive steps well in advance, especially in the early stages of Eelam war IV, to achieve a political solution instead of the military solution to the ethnic conflict, about 1.5 lakh lives could have been saved and all concerned might have enjoyed peace and happiness.

H.M.: In the wake of elimination of the LTTE, will the post-war situation facilitate a free, mixed-community of the Sinhalese and the Tamils?

Ashok: If it happens like that in good spirit and both the ethnic groups live in peaceful coexistence and brotherhood, it will certainly exhilarate everyone in the world. It is the wish of all the people across the globe. But some Sinhalese organizations continue to sow in their minds, the seeds of hatred for, and discrimination against the Tamils and strengthen the inveterate racist tendencies. A rapport between the two ethnic groups could therefore, be achieved only if the political leaders, monks and social activists work vigorously to dispel the evil thoughts and unify the minds of all the people. The destruction of the LTTE and displacement of a large number of the Tamils should not be exploited to grab the lands held by them for the benefit of the sinhalese. Mr. V. Gopalsamy, popularly known as 'Vaiko'–the leader of Marumalarchi Dravida Munnetra Kazhagam (MDMK)–a political party in Tamil Nadu, aired concern that there was a great danger of Sinhalese colonisation on a massive scale in the Tamil-dominated areas of Sri Lanka. He added that over 1.45 lakh Tamils had been killed in the war and the majoritarian Sinhalese had devised an intrigue to occupy the Tamil space and change the demographic profile of the country after annihilating the Tamil population in the Northern and Eastern parts of the island nation. If this prediction is vindicated, the animosity between the Tamils and the Sinhalese will grow fast and peace will never return to Sri Lanka.

H.M.: Has the exodus from Sri Lanka to Tamil Nadu been a relief to the refugees?

Ashok: The affected or terrified Sri Lankan Tamils began to flee their motherland and take shelter in Tamil Nadu as refugees, ever since the war between the SLA and LTTE broke out first in the 1980s. As there was a steady flow of refugees, camps were established for them in Tamil Nadu. Whenever SLA-LTTE clashes intensified, refugees were pouring in large numbers. The Government provided them with accommodation, relief in cash and kind and some concessions. However, many of them struggled to adapt themselves to the new situation, especially because of a change in the nature of their manual jobs. But in the course of time, they got accustomed to some unfamiliar works. Nevertheless, they find it difficult even to make both ends meet. Though they had a passionate interest in their homeland, they didn't dare to return there. The Tamil Nadu people at large liked them because of such innate qualities as frank talk, harmless nature, meek behaviour, sincerity in work, truth and dependability. The refugees were never alienated from the local people. It is unfortunate that such amiable people have been forced to suffer. The refugees had crossed over to Tamil Nadu in small or large groups over a long span of time. They had sailed by small boats after paying heavy charges for which they had to sell what they possessed. Every group of refugees had left even without enough clothes. Every adult person had in his hand, not any valuables but such family members as excited children, infants, pregnant woman or senior citizens. Very often, sick and wounded people had fled. The sailing experience at night happened to be a nightmare for most of the refugees. On many occasions, boatmen had forced the refugees to disembark on some uninhabited islets where they were stranded. They had to remain there without food and water for many days until they were noticed and rescued by either fishermen or the Coast Guard. Many a time, refugees were drowned following boat capsize. Sometimes, they missed their destination because of losing direction or fierce wind and roamed about. The most horrible event of this kind happened at the end of April 2009. As a fierce battle between the SLA and the Tigers was going on, a small group of 21 Tamil fishermen and women left behind everything in their native place Mullaithivu and set sail on a fibre boat in the Bay of Bengal with an intention to take shelter in a refugee camp near Rameswaram in Tamil Nadu. But the boat went adrift as they lost their direction and sailed for 10 days. When they reached the faraway coast of Uppada in Andhra Pradesh, they were rescued by local fishermen on 29th April 2009. As the war forced them to flee their homes in a hurried manner, they had nothing to eat and drink. Besides, they should have anticipated a less-than-12 hour sail to reach Rameswaram. The gruelling sea trip along with an unfavourable weather had exhausted their energy and made them fatigued. The rescued people suffered severe dehydration and the ordeal had pushed them into a state of shock. The Kakinada district administration officials took urgent steps for their admission in the Government General Hospital. Seventy-year-old Kamala Devi was lying in a critical condition in the Intensive Care Unit (ICU). A one-year-old boy was seen curled in his mother's lap. Patima, one of Mary Joseph

Benny's two daughters was barely able to speak due to shock. A survivor Ms. Benny, while narrating their tale of woe, lamented that ten persons on the boat had died due to starvation and she had lost her husband Maria Das, two sons and a daughter during the ordeal. Ms. Mary, who drank only the sea water on the ill-fated boat and died on way, did not miss suckling her 12-month-old baby Kubera. Her act enabled the child to remain alive and healthy. All the ten corpses including that of Mary had to be thrown into the sea as they would cause harm to those alive. At the moment of every death and disposal of the body into the sea, the victim's kith and kin with parched throats and uncertainty about their own survival, could not have even wept. They had been merely witnessing the ghastly events with broken hearts. The survivors were thankful to the fishermen of Uppada who rescued them, but they were plunged in grief following the loss of their dear ones and their uncertain future. According to them, hundreds of people had lost their lives in and around Mullaithivu and others could only flee for safety as guns were rumbling from all sides. Ms. Benny had said, "The plight of those stuck in the actual battle zone is heart–rending but no one has the time to even think of it". One can learn from Indian history that after 'Kalinga War', the triumphant King Ashoka displayed his repentance for having waged the war, shed tears on seeing the gruesome scenes on the battle field, and embraced Buddhism. But the Sri Lankan Government, its authorities and many people–most of whom are stated to be Buddhists didn't seem to have felt any remorse for the death and exodus of lakhs of their own countrymen. Is it not a wonder that the so-called Buddhists could rejoice at the bloodbath executed by the Sri Lankan army backed by the Government? Is genocide in the name of anti-terrorist action, a matter to relish? Were human rights sent to the grave along with the Tamils? While the nearly 3 lakh refugees in the Government-run camps for the IDPs were struggling for food, water, clothes, medicines, etc, and standing in queues for bathroom in Sri Lanka, the several thousands of refugees in India have nostalgic memories of their motherland. Although the refugee camps in Tamil Nadu provided shelter for them, they could serve their needs only to a limited extent. The Tamil Nadu Cabinet discussed their situation at the end of 2009. A few Ministers visited the camps and made an assessment of the refugees' living conditions. On their reports to the Chief Minister, the State Government decided to provide necessary facilities for the camps and also bring the refugees into the ambit of the Public Distribution System. The Government also recommended to the Government of India to grant citizenship to the refugees. The State Government displayed its interest to improve their living conditions. However, the camp life cannot be equal to their regular life in their native places.

H.M.: Do you think that the military solution to the ethnic conflict is ideal and sustainable?

Ashok: It is an important aspect of pondering over this issue. In this regard, I desire to reflect the views of Mr. Mark Tran expressed in his article published in THE HINDU on 19th May 2009. According to the writer, the military victory was the climax of President Mahinda Rajapaksa's election campaign in November 2005, when he ruled out autonomy for the Tamils. Despite pleas from the US President Mr. Barack Obama and the UN Secretary General Ban Ki-moon, Colombo had zealously pursued it's objective of wiping out the separatist LTTE once and for all. Mr. Rajapaksa was unable to project the offensive as part of the global fight against terrorism. Although the military largely blocked the world's media from covering the carnage in the so-called 'No-Fire-Zone', television images conveyed part of the horror, showing civilians making a desperate attempt across a lagoon to escape the last strip of land controlled by the Tigers. Doctors recounted the cries of the wounded at a makeshift hospital they had to abandon because of continued artillery shelling, despite denials from the Sri Lankan military. The victory for Sri Lankan forces came at a high price in terms of loss of civilian lives and damage to Colombo's international reputation. The Tigers were accused of using human shields. While many Tamils were appalled at the Tigers' tactics, they also had deep grievances about their treatment by the Sinhalese majority. Analysts claimed that the Government's conduct hardened an already humiliated Tamil diaspora, storing trouble for the future. Mr. Mark Tran referred to Robert Templer of the International Crisis Group think tank as having said, "If the Tigers' leadership is removed or killed in a government assault, it is easy to imagine one of the newly energised generation stepping in to fill the void". It was also viewed that although the Sri Lankan Government prevailed militarily, it had a huge humanitarian problem on its hands and would need international aid. I too agree with Mr. Tran's views vis-a-vis the wisdom of military solution. It will be difficult to sustain such solution unless the root cause of the ethnic conflict is eliminated. Mr. Tran also desired Western leaders to call on Mr. Rajapaksa to address the Tamils' demands for devolution of power and language rights. He had deplored "the increasingly authoritarian streak of the Rajapaksa Government, with its crackdown on dissent–particularly in the media" and did not prophesy happy events to happen. To epitomize the whole episode, during the ethnic strife in Sri Lanka spanning three decades, several thousands of LTTE cadres and soldiers were killed. Apart from them, lakhs of Tamil civilians lost their lives. They were made bereft of their rights to live. Several lakhs of Tamils were rendered homeless, forced to starve, and become refugees in India and in their motherland itself. Thus, they were deprived of their rights to food, shelter, livelihood, education and employment. All these situations amounted to gross and utter violation of human rights over half a century in Sri Lanka since its independence.

The ICRC is known for its devotion, sacrifice, and selfless service to the suffering people around the world under distressing conditions. It is constantly demonstrating that humanitarianism is still alive in mankind. In Sri Lanka too the organization served the victims against all odds. But it was not given its due good reputation there. As I told already, its main office in Colombo was attacked in February 2009. The Sri Lankan Government asked the ICRC on 9th July 2009 to scale down its operations following the end of conflicts. Jacques de Maio, the organization's head of operations for South Asia said in a press release in Colombo, "The ICRC is in the process of reviewing its set-up and operational priorities in Sri Lanka. As a first step, it will close its offices and withdraw its expatriate staff from the Eastern Province while winding down its operations in the area. However, the ICRC will continue its dialogue with the Sri Lankan Government on issues of humanitarian concern". It was clear from this statement that a humanitarian crisis continued in Sri Lanka although the Government was celebrating its victory in the war against the LTTE. The presidential poll slated for 26th January 2010 was announced in December 2009. During the same period, the Sri Lankan Government announced lifting of restrictions on the movement of IDPs from the camps. It also claimed to have sent nearly 60,000 IDPs back to their homes. It is anybody's guess as to when the remaining 2.25 lakh IDPs will be resettled. Even when all of them are let out of the camps, they can't be optimistic. On returning back to their war-ravaged towns or villages, most of them may be homeless. They may not have reunion with their dear ones who were either missed or separated from them during the war. As a result of prolonged displacement, restoration of normal life with resurgence of their occupations will not be possible in the near future. The long hiatus will cost them dearly. They have been subjected to a wretched life just because of their belonging to a race which happens to be a minority in the island nation.

H.M.: Okay; I also endorse your notions of this complex issue. Then is there any example of recent genocide in other countries?

Ashok: Yes, of course. A plane carrying Rwanda's then President Juvenal Habyarimana – a 'Hutu' by race, and his Burundian counterpart was downed on 6th April 1994. This incident was believed to have triggered the Rwanda's 1994 genocide in which extremists from Rwanda's 'Hutu' majority slaughtered around 8 lakh minority 'Tutsis' over more than three months. The carnage rocked the entire world and the Western nations were accused of failure to curb the atrocities. On 18th December 2008, a United Nations-backed tribunal convicted the mastermind of 1994 genocide Colonel Theoneste Bagosora and two other ex-military officers of "genocide, crimes against humanity and war crimes" and sentenced the trio to life in prison. In 2003, ethnic minority rebels in Sudan's Western Darfur region took up arms against the Arab-dominated regime for a greater share of power and resources. The Government's efforts to quell them led to an ethnic conflict that took a heavy toll on the people. The Sudanese President Omar al-Beshir was alleged to have committed war crimes and crimes against humanity and the case was heard by the International Criminal Court (ICC). The prosecutor accused Mr. Beshir of having personally instructed his forces to annihilate three ethnic groups–the Fur, the Masalit and the Zaghava. According to him, 2.7 million people were uprooted from their homes, of whom one lakh people died of the consequences of their cruel displacement, especially starvation. The United Nations said that up to 3 lakh people had died since the conflict broke out. In March 2009, the ICC issued an arrest warrant for President Beshir, listing seven counts–five crimes against humanity and two war crimes, however excluding genocide charges though requested by the prosecutor. The President's supporters in Sudan raised a banner of revolt against the proceedings of the ICC. But Darfur's most active rebel group–the Justice and Equality Movement (JEM) threatened to step up efforts to topple Mr. Beshir if he flouted the warrant. Though he was spared from charges of genocide, the occurrence of genocide in Sudan could not be denied by either the ICC or anybody else. The presidential election held on 27th December 2007 in Kenya sparked the worst ever ethnic violence in that country. Mobs of young 'Kalenjin' men were burning the houses of 'Kikuyu' families–the ethnic group of President Mwai Kibaki. The toll was put up at 1300 while more than three lakh people fled their homes. Thenceforth, a peace deal to end the strife achieved by international efforts had been in place and the coalition Government was intact. However, according to a report by the Kenya Human Rights Commission, about 80,000 displaced people were not resettled upto the end of 2008 mainly due to fear and financial problem. Reconciliation meetings between 'Kalenjin' and 'Kikuyu' ethnic groups were under way in certain parts of Kenya, but without focus on the underlying issue of land ownership. The ethnic conflict in Congo created a humanitarian disaster in the region. The UN panel of experts who investigated the crisis had presented substantial evidence, that showed Rwandan and Congolese Governments fuelling the ethnic militias. The Rwandan military was backing 'Tutsi' militia and recruitment of child soldiers while the Congolese military was supporting a rival 'Hutu' faction. The strife had caused an exodus of 2.5 lakh people from their homes in the last quarter of 2008. The report, focusing on the direct government involvement behind the militias had stunned the United Nations Security Council. In such clashes between militias, only the common people are caught in the crossfire. All these ethnic clashes which led to genocide, had violated human rights.

H.M. : You are right indeed. Charli.........What is your opinion about genocide that happened in many countries, especially Sri Lanka?

Charli : I will not air my views on this subject.

H.M. : What is the reason for your aversion to this subject?

Charli : I am not averse to this subject but to your somersault.

H.M. : What do you mean?

Charli : You have unusually asked for my opinion today.

Ashok : He might be discontented with his turn to comment on the subject at the end of the conversation.

Charli : No. Speaking at last is a matter of pride.

Ashok : How could you substantiate your viewpoint?

Charli : My boss has likened me to a VIP or a Chief doctor or the Supreme leader of a political party.

H.M. : Why are you prating like this?

Charli : Shall I refute this charge?

H.M. : Do you want ot waste our time?

Charli : Your question speaks of your reluctance to hear or accept facts.

Ashok : (Towards the H.M.) Let him delineate his reference to VIP, Chief doctor and political leader at the helm.

H.M. : All right; you may go ahead with your ramblings.

Charli : In any function or meeting, the VIP who participates delivers the valedictory speech. In any world-class hospital, the Chief doctor deals with the patient in a serious condition, only at last when the protocol of other physicians have failed. During the executive or general body meetings of political parties, the daylong deliberations become a futile exercise since only the final words of the party leader prevail over them. So, by asking me to speak at last, my boss has elevated my status to that of the trio.

Ashok : That's fine. You may now comment on the Sri Lankan conflict.

Charli : I will not do so.

Sanjay : Why? What does prevent you from giving your opinion?

Charli : When I go to Sri Lanka, I may be deported like Mr. Bob Rae.

Sanjay : Why do you like to visit Sri Lanka?

Charli : I may join the ICRC in their efforts to remove landmines.

H.M. : You may become a victim of landmine blast.

Charli : In that case, I could become a martyr and get an eternal relief from you.

They all go to lunch in a relaxed mood.

7

HUMAN RIGHTS VIOLATIONS DUE TO RACISM

Charli : What is in store for me in the post-lunch session?

H.M. : The glut of lunch may cause stomach ache for you. Don't make a mockery of this session.

Charli : Oh yes, sir. I shall be an amenable child by quietly listening to your discussions.

H.M. : That's good. (Turning to Ashok) You have mentioned racism as one among the causes of human rights violations. How could you substantiate this view?

Ashok. : Racism and its impact on people have been witnessed in many countries. The odious system of slavery existed until the 19th century. Human beings, especially the people of African and Latin American countries were sold for a price like animals. The people of black races were suffering discrimination and humiliation. In the United States, seats in buses were segregated for white and black passengers. In 1955, Ms. Rosa Parks – a black lady, refused to give up her seat for a white passenger in Montgomery, Alabama, for which she was arrested. Her arrest triggered unrest that led to a year-long bus boycott under the leadership of Mr. Martin Luther King. The agitation goaded people on fledgling Civil Rights Movement. Mr. King said, "I have a dream that one day, this nation will rise up." During the civil rights protests, Mr. King was incarcerated in 1963. In the following year, the Civil Rights Act, prohibiting discrimination on the basis of race, colour, religion or national origin was signed by President Lyndon Johnson. However, three civil rights activists were killed by extreme white supremacist organization 'Ku Klux Klan' in that year. Black militant leader Malcolm X, who articulated concepts of race pride and black nationalism, was assassinated in 1965. During the protest march from Selma to Montgomery, the participants were violently beaten by the police. Six days of racial riots in Watts area of Los Angeles left 34 people dead. As a result of protest, Voting Rights Act, enabling Southern blacks to vote was passed in 1965. With a purpose of self-defence from brutality of the police, Black Panther Party was formed by Huey Newton and Bobby Seale in 1966. Mr. Martin Luther King, a Nobel Peace Laureate who advocated non-violent disobedience while spearheading the Civil Rights Movement, was assassinated in 1968 plunging the world in shock and grief. The Equal Employment Opportunity Act enacted in 1972 provided legal protection against racial discrimination in the workplace. A black motorist Rodney King was smitten by four white policemen in 1992. Their acquittal by a jury sparked racial riots in Los Angeles in which 65 persons died. The black people in the United States, despite persistent racial discrimination in all realms, persevered to win equal rights. Their endeavour enabled them scale new heights in prosperity, fame and political power. Many outstanding artistes, athletes, educationists and political leaders have emerged from the black race. In 1984, civil rights leader Jesse Jackson gained 1218 votes at Democratic Convention but failed to win party's nomination for Presidency. In 1989, General Colin powell became the first African-American to head the US military. He became the Secretary of State in 2001. Mr. Douglas Wilder was elected the first black State Governor in the US history to head Virginia in 1990. In 2005, Ms. Condoleezza Rice was appointed Secretary of State. She was the first black woman to hold this reputed post. To a worldwide joy, welcome and approbation, Mr. Barack Obama, the first black presidential nominee won the November 2008 elections and occupied the supreme seat of the country in January 2009. The black people in the US have had a long journey to reach their goals. Mr. Obama himself has recalled an incident in which his father was denied food in a hotel. Mr. Henry Louis Gates Jr., a Harvard University professor returned to his home in Cambridge form China on 16th July 2009. His taxi driver helped him prise open the front door that was stuck shut. Just after his arrival, Sergeant James Crowley, a police officer, reached his home for an investigation of a report of a break-in at Mr. Gate's home. Though Mr. Gates had shown his photo identification, Sgt. Crowley was sceptical of his habitation in that upmarket home and arrested him putting handcuffs. The African-American scholar accused the sergeant of racism. He said, "If it could happen to me, it could happen to anybody–anybody black, but also anybody less fortunate than me of any colour". Harvard's president Ms. Gilpin Faust stated that she was deeply troubled by the incident.

President Mr. Obama accused the police of acting stupidly and said, "It is a sign of how race remains a factor in this society". He called the professor and the police officer to the White House on 30th July and arranged to soothe the irritant and make a reunion between them. This incident is a testament to the fact that even now, the existence of some elements of racism in the US cannot be ruled out.

The apartheid era in South Africa witnessed numerous human rights violations. Crores of aborigines were discriminated, oppressed and denied voting rights by the white minority regime. The black people suffered many problems including obstacles in housing, jobs and trade. Many leaders of the African National Congress (ANC) which spearheaded the anti-apartheid struggle, were lodged in jails. The triumphant hero of the struggle Mr. Nelson Mandela was imprisoned for 27 years. Some white liberals also played a key role in the struggle against 'whites-only' rule. Among them, Ms. Helen Suzman, a Jew, was notable. Her Jewish background had illuminated her and created a sensitivity to the evils of discrimination. All along her career in the legislature between 1953 and 1989, she loudly voiced against apartheid. She was the first Parliamentarian to visit Mr. Nelson Mandela in jail. She brushed aside criticisms including white President P.W. Botha's dubbing her as a 'vicious little cat'. Apartheid came to an end in 1994 and Mr. Nelson Mandela became the first President in the new era of South Africa.

In Italy, there has been a growing incidence of racist violence directed at 'Roma gypsies' and persons of colour. In September 2008, Bharat Gupta, an Indian Ph.D. student was bashed by some youngsters while returning home at night and he was hospitalised. In February 2009, another Indian national Navtej Singh Siddhu who worked as a construction labourer and remained jobless in the wake of winter, was sleeping on a bench in the Nettuno Railway Station. He was beaten, sprayed with metallic paint, sprinkled with petrol and set on fire by three intoxicated youths. His condition was reportedly critical in an Italian hospital. He was first visited by an Indian Embassy official, followed by the Mayor of Rome. The incident described as yet another criminal act with racist overtones had given rise to outrage in Italy. A bomb blast at a 'Shia' mosque in the south-eastern Iranian city of Zahedan killed 25 worshippers and injured 125 others on 28th May 2009. 'Sunny' rebels were suspected of causing the blast. It was a terrorist attack with racial background. Iran's Supreme Leader Ayatollah Ali Khamenei said in a statement that the attack was meant to light "the fire of ethnic and sectarian strife" in order to destabilize the country. Six Indians were playing at a tennis court on the outskirts of Vancouver on 5th June 2009. A group of four Canadian teenagers including a woman approached the players, pushed them into a corner of the court, and hit one of them on the head with a board. The assailants shouted racial slurs at the players and took their belongings away. The police arrested the four offenders and charged them with robbery, assault with a weapon and uttering threats. In Britain, some people had shown racist attitudes towards Asians. Employees of Asian origin in Britain, especially doctors, nurses and teachers often complained of racial discrimination in matters relating to their jobs. In the 1960s and 1970s, white native Britons started to flee areas where they felt "threatened" by an influx of non-white immigrants. It was termed as 'white flight'. After 30 years, there seems to be a revival of the same racist tendencies in Britain. White parents were reportedly withdrawing their children from schools which they believed as having "too many" non-white students. Segregation in schools might sow the seeds of racism at a very young age and also reduce the opportunity for pupils to follow peaceful coexistence with other communities.

Uighurs, a Turkic-speaking ethnic Muslim group, constitutes a majority of the population of Xinjiang region in Western China and is one of 55 minority groups in that country. 'Han Chinese' ethnic group constitutes a majority of China's population. A mass brawl between migrant 'Uighur' workers and 'Han Chinese' workers in a factory at Guangdong in Southern China took place on 26th June 2009, that left 2 Uighurs dead and 118 others injured. In the wake of the incidents, a protest march was carried out by hundreds of native Uighur Muslims in the Western region's capital Urumqi, calling for an investigation into the incidents of racial violence between 'Uighurs' and 'Han Chinese'. In the ensuing mass riots that broke out on 5th July 2009, armed mobs clashed on the city's streets assaulting passers-by including women, torching vehicles and setting buildigs on fire. Heavily armed police swung into action, resorted to firing and rounded up hundreds of suspects. At the hands of the rioters and as a result of police firing, 156 people were killed and more than 1,000 injured. Chinese Government officials blamed an exiled Uighur separatist organization for the violence. They said that 1,434 suspects had been arrested in Urumqi. A group of Uighurs, mostly women, reportedly accused officials of arresting innocent men. There were reports of mobs of several hundred "Han Chinese' organizing themselves 'with sticks and stones'. There were mobs on the streets setting fire to cars and attacking shops as revealed by a college student. Agitations, unrest and police action continued for many days. Racism is the root cause of such troubles causing loss of lives and properties.

H.M. : We hear about racist violence in Australia. What is the actual situation in that country?

Ashok : Around 97,000 Indian students are pursuing their education in Australia. A threat to their security and dignity has been on the rise in the recent past. In the year 2009, many Indians were attacked. An Indian student was attacked on 9th May. After a fortnight, Shravan Kumar, a 25-year-old student from Andhra Pradesh, was stabbed with a screwdriver by a group of teens that also left three of his friends injured on 24th May. He was battling for life in the Intensive Care Unit (ICU) of a hospital in Melbourne. The next day itself, another Indian student Baljinder Singh was stabbed in the abdomen by two armed men. The Federation of Indian Students in Australia held a rally which started from Royal Melbourne Hospital and culminated at the Victorian Parliament House. The rallyists clamoured for swift and stern action against the culprits. But ironically a taxi driver from Hyderabad was assaulted in Melbourne on 31st May by a passenger who was in an inebriated state. He was attacked after he expressed his inability to take the passenger further due to a technical problem in his vehicle. The victim was taken to a hospital in an unconscious state by the police. An Indian community leader claimed that over 20 incidents of "curry bashing" had taken place in Sydney during May 2009. Yadu Singh, a Sydney-based cardiologist and head of a committee that was formed to look after the welfare of Indian students, revealed that the attacks had grown over the last four years and more than 100 attacks on Indian youth had taken place in one year. He stressed the urgent need to address the issue. The Australian Government announced a task force to deal with violence against foreign students. In spite of that, there was a spate of attacks on Indian students. One more student was attacked in broad dayligh in Melbourne on 2nd June 2009. Another 20-year-old Indian student Amrit Pal Singh was beaten up by a group of youths in Melbourne while he was going for part–time work on 5th June. A 23–year–old Indian student was beaten up for the second time in a fortnight on 8th June by a group of youths in Melbourne. A 22–year–old Indian student was allegedly assaulted by a teenager, who hit him on his turban and asked "What's that on your head?" The Indian's nose was broken and his jaw was injured in the attack that happened in Adelaide's busy market area on 11th June. The incident raised a feeling that racial attacks against Indians had spread to Southern Australia. Hardik Bipinbhai Patel (24) who hailed from Surat in Gujarat was attacked by three persons in Melbourne while he was about to enter his car on 12th June. On that date itself, 20-year-old Sunny Bajaj from Delhi was beaten up by two men in Melbourne, leaving him with a fractured finger and a bloody nose. He had to skip an accounts examination at Deakin University. Twenty-year-old M.A. Khan from Hyderabad, pursuing a hospitality course at the Victoria Institute of Technology was punched by two men without any provocation, while he was walking near a Railway Station in the eastern suburb of Melbourne on 22nd June. Khan suffered cuts below his eyes and on the brow, leading to multiple stitches on his face. In another incident, Gulshan Kumar, an Indian taxi driver was attacked by his passengers in the Clayton area in Melbourne. Two men, reported to be Indians, were attacked and struck with a beer bottle by two juveniles on 28th June in Sydney. The next day, a 22-year-old Sikh youth was assaulted at Dandenong Station in Melbourne by six teenagers who tried to remove his turban and cut the hair. Two Indian students were injured in an assault outside a Sydney hotel on 17th July. Another Indian student was attacked in Adelaide after a group of 4 intoxicated locals targeted him the same day. A young Indian woman journalist was assaulted by an unidentified person in Sydney in the last week of July. Gaurav Kakkar, a student from Punjab, and Mohit, a student from Indore in Madhya Pradesh were attacked by violent groups of youths. Both the Indians were attacked in Melbourne on 7th August. In the same city, three Indians-Sukhdip Singh, his brother Gurdeep Singh and uncle Mukhtair Singh were brutally attacked in a bar by 70 youths including women who were attending a birthday party on 12th September. A 28-year-old unidentified Indian student was attacked by 2 men at a train station in Melbourne on 29th September. The victim had 20 sutures on his head. Three Indian students were assaulted and robbed on their way home from Sunshine Station in Melbourne at night on 15th October. An Indian Engineering student was attacked by a group of Australians, including a woman in Melbourne on 3rd November. Unidentified assailants attacked an Indian student by stabbing in his chest. The incident happened in Melbourne on 9th December. The attacks on Indians continued in 2010 also. 21-year-old Nitin Garg, who migrated from Punjab and had permanent residency in Australia, was stabbed to death in Melbourne on 3rd January 2010. A partially-charred body of another Indian youth was found in New South Wales on 5th January. Four men poured an unidentified liquid on 29-year-old Jaspreet Singh and set him afire in a suburb of Melbourne, leaving him with 20 per cent burns on 9th January. But police denied racial motive behind this attack. A 28-year-old man from India was kicked and punched by a group of assailants on a Sydney beach on 11th January. A 25-year-old Indian taxi driver was punched by his passengers in the Victorian city of Ballarat on 15th January. A 25-year-old Indian was assaulted and robbed near his home in south Brisbane on 21st January. In another incident in Brisbane, a taxi driver was attacked that same day. Two Indian students aged 20 and 22, were attacked by members of a large group in Melbourne Central on 25th January. The 20-year-old student sustained an injury on the left ear and the other suffered abrasions on his forearm. Apart from minor incidents that did not come to light, 62 Indians were reportedly subjected to attacks in Australia from 9th May 2009 upto 25th January 2010. The attacks on Indians are likely to continue unless the Australian Government takes stern actions to combat this crime.

H.M.: What action was taken by the concerned authorities to quell the racist violence in Australia?

Ashok: Indian Minister of State for External Affairs Shashi Tharoor said on 23rd June 2009 that it was the duty of the Australian Government to prevent the attacks on Indian students there. Australian High Commissioner in India had assured that the authorities in Canberra were working hard to ensure the safety of Indian students. The Indian Prime Minister Dr. Manmohan Singh took up the issue of racial attacks with his Australian counterpart Mr. Kevin Rudd. The Australian Prime Minister told him that he was appalled by the attacks and assured to bring the perpetrators to justice. He also assured protection for all Indian students. As announced earlier, the Government set up a Task Force to deal with the problem. An awareness exercise for students on security aspects was launched by the Universities across the State of Victoria in Australia from where most of the racist attacks were reported. This was welcomed by Indian students, especially in and around the State's Capital Melbourne. It was decided to conduct a week-long orientation programme for students from abroad who would join in the following academic year. The programme aimed at creating a safety awareness among students, like identifying safe and non-safe areas and hours. The students were to be advised to rent out homes in places generally considered safe. The professors revealed their intention to reschedule classes in such a way that they would end earlier. The Universities stressed the need for a multi-cultural task force to complement the police in dealing with such attacks. A police-student tie-up was also emphasized.

Proceeding on the petition filed by one Ranveer Yadav, a bench of the Supreme Court of India observed, "The safety and security of Indian students in Australia are paramount. We are sure that the Government must be taking all steps but our anxiety is that despite the best efforts on the part of the Government, the incidents of attacks are going on". The Attorney-General told the Bench that the Government of India was extremely concerned over the safety and welfare of Indian students and spared no effort at making sure they were properly protected. The Bench directed the Government at the end of June 2009, to file in two weeks a comprehensive affidavit on the steps taken in this regard, and the contents of the affidavit and the guidelines should be placed on the websites of the Ministries of External Affairs and Overseas Indians Affairs and the Indian High Commission Office in Australia, so that parents and relatives were aware of the situation prevailing in that country. Thus, all possible efforts were made to tackle the problem but the results were not satisfactory.

H.M.: What are the reasons for racist tendencies in Australia?

Ashok: After becoming independent in 1901, Australia adopted 'White Australia' policy for many generations. In the 1970s, Australian authorities felt an absolute need to increase the population. In such context, migrations into Australia began and increased enormously within a decade, especially from the Asia-Pacific region. Besides, migrants from Eurpean countries whose mother tongue was not English, also continued to swell. These developments forced Australia to keep up cultural diversity. Many organizations like the office of Multicultural Affairs, the Australian Ethnic Affairs Council and the Australian Institute of Multicultural Affairs came into existence to step up and safeguard multicultural concept. The process of globalisation has also created the scope for greater migration. With the facilities for education in diverse fields, Australian Universities have attracted several lakhs of students. The intake of students mainly from Asian countries, especially China and India is on the rise every year. As in June 2009, there were 130,000 Chinese and 97,000 Indian students. The migrants from more than 150 countries and the students pursuing studies have contributed much to the economic growth of Australia. However, they sought only Permanent Resident status and got employment in various kinds of jobs. They are prepared to do any type of work. They work hard taking two or three jobs for better earning. It annoys white Australians and makes them develop racist feelings. Then those who enjoyed the benefits of 'White Australia' policy are averse to multiculturalism and even give a political hue to the changes. They always have a latent racist mindset. Another section of people think that the migrants and their employment in all sectors have changed the very fabric of the society. These are considered to be the reasons for racism in Australia. Most of the racist attacks have occured in the State of Victoria. Among the migrants from many countries, Indians are timid and do not repulse the assailants. Further, most of the Indian students work late-night shifts to incur their educational expenses and stay only in less-secure neighbourhoods at less cost. Indians therefore, become the soft target for the racist culprits. The United Nations was called upon to intervene and stop human rights violations in Australia. The boorish attacks on Indians have brought disgrace to the image of Australia as a peaceful multicultural democracy.

H.M.: Are there any steps initiated against racism at international level?

Ashok: There have been longstanding efforts at various levels across the world to eliminate racism. Nevertheless, the malady persists. No society is quite rid of racism. The United Nations anti-racism conference held in Durban, South Africa, in 2001, made some commitments in its final document 'Durban Declaration and Programme of Action (DDPA)' to combat racial discrimination and intolerance all over the world. The follow-up efforts lost glory due to unpleasant actions of some countries. Amid calls for boycott, the UN anti-racism review conference was held in Geneva in April 2009. Ten UN Member States including the United States, Canada, Israel, New Zealand, Australia and five of the European Union nations stayed away from the conference. Regarding the conference, with a courtesy to Mr. Navanethem Pillay, the United Nations High Commissioner for Human Rights, I desire to recount his views expressed in his article published in THE HINDU on 28th April 2009. He has stated, "The conference in Geneva was an opportunity for all nations to come together and agree on a common document enshrining a common aspiration: to defy racism in all its manifestations and work to stamp it out. The conference approved, by consensus, a document. In the document, States undertook to prevent manifestations of racism, racial discrimination and xenophobia, especially in relation to migrants, refugees and asylum seekers. States also agreed to promote greater participation and opportunities for people of African and Asian descent, indigenous people and individuals belonging to national or ethnic, religious and linguistic minorities. They committed to ensure that discrimination would not overtly or covertly hamper access to employment, social services, health care and participation in other spheres of life. Multiple forms of discrimination will also be tackled. The document reaffirms the fundamental importance of freedom of expression and stresses its compatibility with existing international law that prohibits incitement to hatred. Moreover, the document represents an important recognition of the injustice and atrocities of the past and proposes means to prevent their recurrence. These include a commitment to prohibit violent, racist and xenophobic activities by groups that embrace supremacist ideologies.

The review conference has provided a platform for a new beginning. Member States showed their determination, spirit of compromise and respect for diversity to move as one on a common and very urgent cause. This agreement will hopefully have lasting beneficial effects for the countless victims of racism, discrimination and intolerance worldwide. The few States that chose to stay away should now evaluate the outcome document on its own merit and substance. Many of these States participated in its drafting and were part of the emerging consensus until the very eve of the conference. This is why I am hopeful that they will rejoin international efforts to combat racism and intolerance as laid out in this important document. We should not concede ground to those who are intent on stirring controversy that contributes to intolerance. Thus, it is all the more crucial for us–men and women of goodwill, States, international organizations and civil society alike - not to get distracted from the main objective: to nurture discrimination-free societies and a world of equal treatment and opportunity for all of us, or at the very least for our children and our children's children". We can easily understand that the global efforts to counter racism are laudable. As the UN High Commissioner for Human Rights hopes, all the nations should unite for concerted actions on this vital issue. Everyone can be proud of the Geneva document but its fruitful results will largely depend on how far it is implemented in letter and spirit. Racism is a deep-rooted scourge causing severe harm to the people worldwide. Everyone therefore, must strive to bury this evil.

Chandra: Please have some refreshment, sir.

(She provides a snack and coffee to all there.)

8

HUMAN RIGHTS VIOLATIONS DUE TO CRIMES

H.M.: How are human rights violations committed by crimes? Could you identify some of the relevant crimes?

Ashok: The crimes resulting in human rights violations are of many kinds. The causes behind the crimes are also varied such as land grabbing, hatred, vengeance, craze for money or power, lust, suspicion, etc. For instance, the Israeli settlements on Palestinian territory began with about 20 Jewish settlers in 1975 and enhanced gradually. Ofra became the hub of settlements where the present population is more than 4,000. The Israeli human rights group B'tselem had published a report in which it stated that 60 percent of the settlement of Ofra had been built on land which remained in private Palestinian ownership. The group's spokeswoman Sarit Michaeli said that under international law, and in the eyes of the rest of the world, Israeli settlements in occupied territory were illegal. She argued that Ofra did not fulfil certain legal criteria framed by Israel to define a legal settlement. She added that as the occupied land was privately owned by Palestinians, Ofra qualified only as the largest unlawful outpost in the West Bank. But the authorities in the settlement termed the findings as biased and claimed that the land was indeed bought though the sellers had been killed. So, the land dispute is apparent. The United Nations could constitute an expert committee and send it on a fact-finding mission to the West Bank. It may probe and establish the ownership of the occupied land. To achieve this, a consensus among the concerned parties is preferable and if not possible, the UN must force such a move by a fiat.

The Israel-Palestine conflict has destroyed peace in West Asia for more than three decades. During this period, there were many instances of Israeli attack and ceasefire. The late President Yassar Arafat's prolonged struggle could not bring about a permanent settlement. After pulling out in 2005, Israel launched an incursion into Gaza Strip on 20th February 2008. A group of Palestinian boys were playing football on some open ground near their homes in the Gaza Strip on the afternoon of 28th February 2008. Then an Israeli aircraft fired a missile at the boys, killing four of them instantly and seriously injuring another three. Forty six palestinians were killed in the Israeli attacks on 1st March 2008. The next day itself, there was an attack on Gaza's Jabalia refugee camp, killing 120 persons which prompted President Mahmoud Abbas to snap contacts with Israel. Following an international outcry, Israel pulled out its forces from Gaza Strip. In October 2008, the Palestinian Centre for Human Rights reported that 68 children died in Gaza between June 2007 and June 2008. The report highlighted the 'deliberate targeting of civilians including children'. A credible human rights group, then had produced compelling evidence of a persistent pattern of deliberate Israeli targeting of Palestinian civilians, including children. The entire media including the BBC did not fully cover the actual situation in Gaza. Only Al Jazeera aired a three-minute segment that included a moving interview with a bereaved Palestinian mother. Mr. David Cromwell, the co-editor of UK-based 'Media Lens', reported that such silences and omissions in coverage of the Middle East were routine. They were symptoms of a deep-rooted bias that suppressed public awareness of the true gravity of Israel's human rights abuses. He wrote that for those unfortunate individuals caught in the violence, their human aspirations, hopes, dreams, loves and lives were merely of no value.

The Israel-Palestine conflict is perennial. Time and again, Israel had imposed blockades on supplies of food, medicines, cooking gas and fuel to Gaza. The hospitals in Gaza often faced acute dearth of drugs. Frequent power cuts made the incubators for newborn babies unreliable. For want of fuel, generators remained helpless. Keeping 1.5 million Palestinians on life support and then turning the ventilator off time and again was far beyond civilization. A few patients were shifted to Israeli hospitals but none to Egypt. More than 230 patients reportedly died in 2007, waiting for a permit to leave. Most of Gaza's Children showed symptoms of mild or severe post-traumatic stress disorder. About 45 per cent of children under five had iron deficiency and 18 per cent of children had stunted growth due to malnutrition. 71 per cent of children interviewed at a school had revealed their desire to be a martyr. It vividly showed the psychological evolution of Palestinian children.

After a fragile truce ended, Israel resumed its air strikes on Gaza on 27th December 2008. By that time, essential drugs had already run out of stock in hospitals. Medical equipment in every hospital was out of order due to power cut and lack of spare parts. Only very serious patients could get some attention. In Hamas' rocket attacks, the Israeli casualties remained in single digit. An Israeli missile attacked a UN-run school-Asma, located in the Shati refugee camp north of Gaza on 5th January 2009 in which three refugees were killed. The next day, three tank shells exploded inside and around the UN-run school called Fakhura which had been converted into a UN refugee camp as shelter to around 400 displaced Gazans. In this attack, 42 persons were killed. Israel asserted that Palestinian militants were hiding in that school, which was firmly rejected by the UN Relief and Works Agency (UNRWA) which runs the school. There were around 14,000 refugees in 23 schools. In the wake of continuous Israeli bombardment of Gaza for several days, the systems of power and water supply had collapsed, plunging the people in darkness and thirst, according to International Aid Agencies. It rubbed salt into the Gazans' wounds as they were running out of food supplies and medicines, growing the grave humanitarian crisis. The relief works undertaken by the United Nations Relief and Works Agency were hampered by Israeli air raids as revealed by a spokesman of the Agency.

Amid growing international pressure to call a ceasefire and ease the humanitarian crisis, Israel paused its military offensive for three hours on 7th January 2009 to allow in aid. Ambulances were able to drive to some of the most heavily shelled areas in Gaza for the first time to collect the dead and injured. A team of medics and volunteers from the Palestinian Red Crescent took advantage of the lull in attacks to drive to Zeitoun, the scene of an Israeli attack on a house on 5th January 2009 that was known to have killed nine members of the Samouni family. Muhammad Shaheen, a volunteer with the Red Crescent, said that the team found a scene of devastation. They discovered another 10 corpses inside the house and "dozens' more dead lying in the rubble in the area around. "There was a huge number of dead bodies, houses were completely destroyed and many others partially destroyed" he added. Aid workers said that a pause of three hours was not enough to allow sufficient relief into Gaza after months of an Israeli economic blockade. Mr. John Ging, director of operations for the UNRWA in Gaza said, "It is a hell on earth.... Let us stop the fighting, not just for three hours but for 24 hours a day. There is nowhere safe in Gaza. Everyone here is terrorised and traumatised." Journalists were banned from entering Gaza to report on the killings. The World Bank warned that there was a threat of a severe public health crisis because of a shortage of drinking water and the failure of the sewage system. Nearly all sewage and water pumps were out of operation because of a lack of electricity and limited fuel. Sewage had already flooded in some areas and as many as 10,000 Palestinians were at risk of drowning if the Beit Lahiya sewage lake burst.

Since 'Hamas' - considered as a militant organization came to power in Palestine, many countries imposed economic blockade on the country. Israel, viewing 'Hamas' as its foe, began to scale up its offensive against Palestine. But Palestinians elected 'Hamas' to govern, trusting it as their saviour. In the true and unbiased democratic spirit, there is no room for any grudge against the electorate. Palestinian people therefore, should not be persecuted. But Gaza was on the verge of a humanitarian catastrophe. Though Israel's brutal disregard for human lives drew flak from the world community, there was no effective international intervention. Many nations welcomed the France-Egyptian joint effort to halt the diabolic attacks on Gaza Strip and their ceasefire plan. The Palestinian President Mahmoud Abbas reportedly accepted the plan but the ruling 'Hamas' was studying the proposals and remained non-committal with a firm stand that there could be no talks on permanent ceasefire so long as Israeli occupation of Palestinian territory continued. Lebanese 'Hizbollah' leader urged Palestinians to pursue the path of resistance instead of depending on the International community that was incapable of condemning a massacre in a UN institution in Gaza.

Israel's pounding of Gaza Strip was a pogrom rather than a military operation or war. The UN and international pressure notwithstanding, Israel halted its offensive only after inflicting heavy damage on the lives and properties in Palestine. During the 22 days of air strikes, artillery from land and the sea, tank shelling and ground combat from 27th December 2008 to 17th January 2009, more than 1400 Palestinians, most of them unarmed civilians including over 300 children, were killed and around 5,000 were injured. Even the Red Cross was reportedly prevented from reaching the wounded. 25,000 buildings including many public buildings, mosques and government offices were destroyed or damaged. Israel's crime against humanity is ineffable. According to Mr. John Ging, head of the UN relief operations in Gaza, Israeli forces attacked a UN compound with phosphorous explosives despite the presence of the UN Secretary General Ban Ki-moon in the neighbourhood. Mr. John Ging added, "A hospital was also hit on the outskirts of Gaza city. There are phosphorous fires by that are extremely difficult to put out. This is going to burn down the entire warehouse, thousands of tonnes of food, medical supplies and other emergency assistance are there". International law bans the use of white phosphorus against civilians. But doctors in Gaza reported that at least 55 persons were injured on 11th January 2009 due to exposure to burning white phosphorus used in shells fired by the Israeli military forces. Later, after the Israeli troops left the Gaza Strip, Israel admitted that its troops might have used white phosphorous shells in contravention of international law. The Israeli military was alleged to have also used other controversial weapons, namely GPS – guided mortar, depleted uranium – the exposure to which can cause cancer and genetic damage, and cluster bombs that spread over wide area but may fail to explode and lurk as a threat to civilians for years. Palestinian children wer allegedly used as human shields and hospitals were targeted. 'The Guardian' compiled detailed evidence of alleged war crimes committed by Israel. A month-long investigation reportedly obtained evidence of civilians being hit by fire from unmanned drone aircraft at very close range. All that happened in Palestine were crimes against humanity which resulted in utter violation of human rights.

H.M.: How did leaders of other countries and the UN reacted to the inhuman attacks on Palestinians?

Ashok: British Prime Minister Mr. Gordon Brown identified Israels' illegal settlements on the Palestinian territories as the main obstacle to the peace process. In a sharply-worded message to Israel on 15th December 2008, he had called for immediate clearance of the settlements asserting that it was the consistent stand of Britain and he had told this to successive Israeli Presidents and Prime Ministers when he had met them. Just twelve days after his message, Israel resumed its attacks on Gaza. So, viewing his efforts as inert, the frustrated Britons, who in thousands staged a march on Downing Street, hurled shoes at No. 10, the Prime Minister's residence. Nearly 100 British MPs sent a joint letter to the Prime Minister urging him to condemn the Israeli attacks in stong terms and strive for an end to the slaughter in Gaza. They wanted him to halt Britain's arms exports to Israel and persuade other European Union countries to follow suit. The whole world eagerly awaited Mr. Barack Obama's effective intervention for immediate restoration of human rights in Gaza followed by a permanent solution to the Israeli-Palestinian conflict. After taking oath as the US President, Mr. Obama called Palestinian President Mr. Abbas and assured him that he intended to work with him as partners to establish a durable peace in the region. Mr. Obama told Mr. Abbas that he was the first foreign leader he called, since taking office.

Palestinians persistently demanded a complete end to Israeli settlement activity as a prerequisite for a peace treaty. In the first week of May 2009, the US Vice- President Mr. Joe Biden called on Israel to end settlement expansion and dismantle the existing outposts. The president Mr. Obama, during his three hours of talks with the Israeli Prime Minister Mr. Benjamin Netanyahu on 18th May 2009, pushed for a two-State solution, namely a Jewish State and a Palestinian State in which Israelis and Palestinians could live side by side in peace and security. Mr. Obama also said, "Settlements have to be stopped". But 'Peace Now Watchdog' group revealed on the same date that Israel was beginning the construction of the first completely new Jewish settlement in the occupied West Bank in more than a decade. Israel brushed aside the US and European calls to halt its settlement activity. Palestinians described the Israeli move as 'a blunt provocative act'. Despite several requests by the United Nations, Israel denied visas to the group of investigators to prevent their visit to Gaza. Ignoring Israel's opposition, the team led by Justice Richard Goldstone, a legal luminary with his service as chief prosecutor at the International Criminal Tribunals for former Yugoslavia and Rwanda, entered Gaza through the Rafah Crossing from the Egyptian side on 1st June 2009. The purpose of the team's visit was to investigate possible war crimes and other violations of international law during Israel's assault on Gaza with focus on shelling by using phosphorous explosives which could cause severe burns, and targeting residential areas. Israel dubbed the fact-finding UN mission as biased and prejudiced against it. The mission's investigation found deliberate targeting of civilians by the Israeli forces resulting in the death of more than 1,400 Palestinians including women and children who constituted one-third of the toll. The nature of attacks was perceived as the result of the "Dahiya doctrine" which emerged during the Lebanon War of 2006. It involved "application of disproportionate force and the causing of great damage and destruction to civilian property and infrastructure, and suffering of civilian populations". Justice Richard Goldstone's grim findings concluded that "actions amounting to war crimes and possibly, in some respects, crimes against humanity were committed by the Israeli Defence Force". The British-based rights group 'Amnesty International', in a statement in January 2010 said, "Israel's blockade does not target armed groups but rather punishes Gaza's entire population by restricting the entry of food, medical supplies, educational equipment and building materials. The blockade constitutes collective punishment under international law and must be lifted immediately". Thus, Israel's attacks on Palestinians and its disposition to give them every trouble have vividly buried human rights.

H.M.: Do you consider the events in Iraq as human rights violations?

Ashok: Certainly, sir. Many of the prisoners in Abu Graib prison in Iraq were stripped naked and tortured by some members of the US troops. Some soldiers allegedly raped many Muslim women and girls. However, only a few troop members were found guilty of human rights violations and put on trial. In Iraq, criminals and militants held the country to ransom for many years. Many of the gunmen were filling the ranks of the so-called 'Sons of Iraq'- the movement that was steadily growing with a credit of stabilizing Iraqi security. The 'Sons of Iraq' included former Al-Qaeda insurgents. Their names were entered in the US payroll. Captain James Polak was reportedly supervising the handover of responsibilities from his troops to local Iraqis at the Hamani police station. Even the judiciary was cowering in fear from these criminals. Among Iraqi judges and victims, there was a growing sense that justice would never be served. One Iraqi Supreme Court judge who refused to be identified because of a terrorist attack on his home said, "As judges, we are under the most critical of threats". On 30th June 2008, six senior members of the judiciary were targeted by insurgents, who planted explosives in their driveways or shot them on the way to court. The Chief Justice was assassinated at the steering wheel of his car and three other judges were wounded. A judge who was attacked at home said, "We are always stressed and some of us are depressed. We are consulting psychologists, who tell us to go often to wide open places like lakes. We are working beyond our capabilities as human beings". Many lawyers were afraid and had been influenced by different groups in many different ways. One night in March 2008, 21-year-old Nour al-Houda al-Maliki woke up to the gunshots that killed her father while he was sleeping near her. She saw four masked men. Among them, she had known one as a member of the 'Mahdi army', a dreaded group, holding sway over her south

Baghdad area. The next day, she took her mother to the nearby Rashid police station to report her father's murder and identify one of the killers. But she had an execrable experience at the police station. Later she had said, "They said to me, 'You mention the Mahdi army one more time and we will beat you, then jail you,". The police arrested her and after release, she was floundering without a safe place to go. She said amid sob, "I am scared. So scared, but who can I turn to? I don't know what my future is. But if I go back to my neighbourhood or to the court or to the police, they will kill me".The US military had said in a statement, "The Prime Minister's direction is that members of the 'Sons of Iraq' will not be arrested until the warrant is reviewed by an independent joint legal advisory committee". It is quite evident that neither the police nor the US military cared to protect the common people of Iraq. No member of these forces had any humane attitude. Thus, the human rights of the people of Iraq were blown up in the air by criminals, pathetically in collusion with the law enforcement authorities whose cardinal virtue is defence of civilians.

H.M.: Is there any truth in the belief that human rights were violated in the Guantanamo prison?

Ashok: The Guantanamo prison was opened in early 2002 at Guantanamo Bay on the island of Cuba to confine those captured in Afghanistan, Pakistan and elsewhere in the US 'War on Terror'. During the presidential campaign, Mr. Barack Obama consistently called for the closure of Guantanamo prison and for normal rights and protection to the detainees. He dubbed the military tribunals "an enormous failure", and opposed them. When the detainees were tried by the military tribunals, even prosecutors resigned over the biased trial procedures. The Supreme Court criticized the Bush administration for its cruel treatment of the detainees. After election as President, Mr. Obama called the detention and torture centre "a sad chapter in American history", and repeately said that he would close it down. As in November 2008, around 255 detainees continued to be held there for nearly seven years. After being sworn in President on 20th January 2009, Mr. Obama commenced his duties immediately. On the first day itself, he issued an order to the prosecutors at the controversial military tribunals in Guantanamo Bay to halt trial proceedings of the accused. His decision to close the naval detention facility within a year exemplified the new regime's shift in stance. It also raised hopes that the President also intended to end the tribunals and transfer the cases to civilian federal trials within the United States. The Geneva Convention forbids the use of torture against prisoners. During war-crimes trials after the Second World War, the United States condemned as torture, the technique called 'water boarding' by which detainees are half-drowned and half-suffocated in efforts to get them to talk. Anybody therefore, would be startled to know from a memoranda of previous Republican regime's Justice Department made public in April 2009 by President Mr. Obama that the Central Intelligence Agency (CIA) interrogators were authorised to use aggressive investigative techniques against suspects. They used water boarding 266 times on just two of the main Al-Qaeda suspects at Guantanamo. Bay, though it was ineffective to serve the purpose. The CIA's interrogation methods included slamming prisoners against walls, squeezing them into small boxes, and shackling them in standing positions for days. Mr. Obama's unambiguous rejection of the interrogation methods authorised by the Bush administration for use on the prisoners in Guantanamo Bay and his promise never to revive them deserve compliment.

Binyam Mohammed, aged 32-a UK resident, was arrested in Karachi in 2002, and later taken to Morocco, and then sent to Guantanamo Bay. He returned to England in February 2009 and alleged that he was tortured into confession of terror allegations. He also alleged that it was an act of the US Government in collusion with M15. It triggered a campaign by senior British MPs to force the Government to clarify M 15's role in the alleged abduction and torture of terror suspects. The United States, in its so-called 'War on Terror', had repeatedly engaged in the indiscriminate seizure, indefinite detention and torture of perfectly innocent people. Six Algerians were first detained by the Bosnian authorities, but were acquitted in the Bosnian courts, of charges that they were planning to blow up the US Embassy there. Notwithstanding the judgment, they had been seized by the US and taken to Guantanamo, allegedly because they were planning to travel to Afghanistan to fight US forces. They had then been held at the naval detention centre for nearly seven years without the possibility of trial. Judge Richard Leon ruled in a District Court in Washington DC that five of the six Algerians held at Guantanamo must be freed, and there was enough evidence for detention of one among them. A question as to why 400 or more of the 779 Guantanamo detainees were quietly released without charge if they had valid reason to define them as combatants. In the United States, a special prosecutor John Durham called the CIA officials including the former CIA Chief Porter J Gross and the London station Chief before a grand jury in Virginia.

It was as part of an 18-month-long criminal inquiry into the illegal destruction of 92 video tapes. The tapes were evidence of the Agency's interrogators using water boarding and other forms of torture against Abu Zubaydah and Abdal Rahim al Nashiri, described by the Americans as 'high value' detenus held at Guantanamo Bay.

The US Government was serious about closing its notorious detention centre at Guantanamo Bay. Such act could not only eliminate the conspicuous stigma on America's human rights record but also begin the process of ending that country's practice of unlawful indefinite detention policy. In 2002, there were reportedly 779 detainees in Guantanamo Bay prison. They were held on suspicion of links with Al-Qaeda or the Taliban. After release of hundreds, the number of detainees in January 2009 was 245. The Pentagon and the Attorney-General's office believed that about 80 inmates could go on trial and the rest would be released. But many could not be sent to their own countries either because their governments were reluctant to accept them or for fear of execution or torture. Mr. Obama therefore, initiated efforts to persuade the European Union and other countries to take the inmates to be released. But the European Union nations were initially not interested to take them. The widespread opinion in Britain was that the detainees issue was America's own problem and its attempt to pass on the burden to others was ridiculous. In the first week of June 2009, the Interior Ministers of EU nations held a meeting in Luxembourg to discuss the issue of detainees at Guantanamo. The meeting agreed on terms for taking in dozens of detainees and devised security guidelines and a mechanism for sharing information on the detainees. The deal that was reached at the meeting, left it up to individual countries to decide whether to take the inmates. Those who would take them had to furnish all other European Union Governments with intelligence information on the proposed immigrant and pay heed to objections. Martin Pecina, the Czech Interior Minister who chaired the meeting said, "EU States will now be able to accommodate detainees who have been cleared for release but cannot be repatriated for fear that they will be killed, tortured or jailed. They could take in several dozen detainees". But in May 2009, the Obama administration said that it would introduce a number of reforms to the military commissions that were already processing 13 of the most serious cases of terrorist suspects held in the US base in Cuba. The administration insisted that the reforms would make the system fairer and more in line with US justice. The President instructed White House lawers to try and block the release of photographs showing the abuse of prisoners in Iraq and Afghanistan by the US soldiers on the grounds that it would put American personnel at risk of reprisals. These steps were deemed as an intention to continue the trials of Guantanamo detainees under the widely discredited military tribunal system introduced by Congress in 2006 under pressure from Mr. George W. Bush. Though the Obama administration promised to close down Guantanamo, it continued to affirm its intention to retain a number of detainees indefinitely without trial or charge. Such intention was an antithesis of its own objective of closing down the Guantanamo prison. The administration could not adhere to its own deadline of 22nd January 2010 to close it down. So, Mr. Obama drew flak from civil liberty activists. No one could slam any retribution for terrorist outrages. But the prosecutors ought to hold fair trial of the accused and try to impose punishment within the framework of law and the UN convention. The release from prison and even compensation in any form including money, especially to those found not guilty can never retrieve the human rights already violated by the cruel treatment meted out to the detainees. Keeping the suspects in prison for seven years without trial is far beyond civilization. We may hope that the US President will cling on to his original stance on detention of suspects at Guantanamo and release the inmates. Arranging for their safe settlement may be an atonement for the past atrocities on the detainees.

H.M.: People usually talk about Iraq and Guantanamo where the US is involved. Hence I asked you to comment on these issues. Do human rights violations out of crimes, not happen elsewhere?

Ashok: Violations of human rights by crimes are common all over the world. However, depending upon the magnitude of the violations, they become conspicuous. Even civilized Europe can't be spared from the charge of such violations. For instance, the head of the 'European Union Agency for Fundamental Rights' said that Europe had a black market in which migrants, even children, were working in slave-like situations. Somalia was destabilized by anarchy, violence and severe insurgency for the past two decades. Thousands of civilians were killed and lakhs of people fled from machine-gun crossfire, mortar shells and grenades wielded by a powerful insurgent group. The Government had recourse to Ethiopian troops to control the situation but could not achieve tangible results. Ethiopia revealed that its troops couldn't linger in somalia beyond December 2008. However, the insurgents vowed to continue their fight even after the exit of the alien troops. Their sole objective was to herald a rule by Islamic Law. They vowed to fight until implementation of Islamic Law across Somalia. The freedom of religion was under grave threat. The human rights of Somalis were challenged. In India, armed Maoists seized control of Lalgarh and many surrounding villages in the State of West Bengal in June 2009. Central paramilitary forces and the State police launched joint operations that continued for weeks to drive out the Maoists and reclaim the villages. In the crossfire between the joint security forces and the Maoists, many distressing events happened. Godamouli village was an example of the situation that prevailed in the areas under offensive. Most men fled this village apprehensive of both Maoist atrocities and arrest by the police. Only a few women, children and elderly people could be seen in the village. They were hiding in their homes and too terrorised to come out or even speak. Sukalmani Murmu, a woman, fighting back her tears had reportedly narrated how she was tied up, beaten and forcibly paraded through the village by the police. She expressed anguish at the beating up and humiliation of innocent villagers and ransacking their homes by the police who had gone there to restore peace. Many women had told that the villagers were not supporting the Maoists though they were threatened to provide food and support for them. Ms. Sukhi had said that her husband had been arrested for no offence and she was starving with her five children, yearning for his return, being ignorant of the fact that he had been taken into custody. Many women and children were suffering in the absence of their breadwinners. The acts of the police amounted to violation of human rights.

The toxic gas leak in 1984 in Bhopal from the plant of 'Union Carbide', an American company, killed over 20,000 people and maimed several thousands of others permanently. It has plagued the next generation too. A large number of people are still suffering from many diseases and physical disorders. Those responsible for the tragedy had safely escaped. Only after 25 years seven of the accused were sentenced to a mere two-year jail term in June 2010 by a court in Bhopal. But Mr. Warren Anderson, former head of the plant has faced no legal action. The Central Government provided Rs. 1,500- crore package for the victims which was considered inadequate. But the victims, in spite of a plethora of representations, agitations, legal proceedings and struggles, have not been adequately compensated nor any concrete measures taken to mitigate their woes. The apathy on the part of the concerned authorities in safeguarding human rights is deplorable. In December 2008, 30 officials in the State of Tamil Nadu, were slapped a fine of Rs. 25,000 each by the National Human Rights Commission (NHRC) for their failure to give information under the 'Right to Information Act'.

H.M.: What is your perception of the state of human rights in respect of convicts in general?

Ashok: Charles Dickens in his novel 'Great Expectations', has thrown l ght on the horrible life and conditions in prisons. The impetus behind h s focus on this topic is believed to be his father's languishing in 'Debtors' Prison, for several years. The jail conditions being such even in advanced countries, it is needless to narrate much on the ground realities in prisons of developing and undeveloped countries. The pathetic conditions of inmates amount to near-total violation of human rights. They are deprived of proper food and timely medical aid. They are forced to live in congested and unhygienic conditions. They are often subjected to harassment and sometimes torture. In this context, the Director-General of Prisons, Tamil Nadu, after attending the five-day 'Asian Pacific Conference of Correctional Administrators–2008' in Malaysia in November, proposed changes in the law-enforcing mechanism to facilitate deferment of incarceration of pregnant convicts by at least three years. This scheme, emulating Thailand, will ensure every pregnant woman convict's safety, health and peaceful environment for her delivery. She can provide maximum care for her child in its infancy, avoiding disgrace. The DGP proposed among other things, the launch of an in-house journal in Tamil Nadu prisons to bring out the literary skills of inmates. These measures apparently aim to reform the prisoners and raise their status. Such protection of human rights deserves to be hailed, provided the proposals are implemented heartily, encouraging other states to follow suit.

H.M.: At times, individuals are also subjected to sufferings which amount to human rights violations. Why do such events happen? Why is the law silent on these matters?

Ashok: No law of any country does permit human rights violations. Any law can act and serve its purpose if it is judiciously exercised by concerned authorities. But nowadays, the law-enforcing agencies have been manned by many personnel with rude and extravagant behaviour. They brush aside any law and act as they like for their own interests or profit. The true spirit of law remains fettered in the books, as the law-protectors have transformed themselves into law-breakers. By violating the law, these people violate human rights. Arrest without evidence or even at somebody's behest, illegal and indefinite detention without filing a charge sheet, torture of the suspects, taking women to police station at night and humiliating or molesting them, custodial deaths and deliberate encounter deaths are often reported from somewhere in India. But most of the victims do not get justice in time. For instance, a woman of Nagal Kulam village in Tirunelveli district of Tamil Nadu had gone along with her husband to the residence-cum–office of Mr. Mangala Dhanaraj, Inspector of Police to make a complaint on 7th June 1984. The police officer had subtly sent her husband away and raped her thereafter. At the time of the incident, the petitioner was only 28 years old. The victim went to the court for justice and sold her house and property to meet the expenses for legal proceedings. The Sessions Court convicted the police officer to 11 years imprisonment. The Madras High Court rejected his appeal and also directed the State Government to pay the victim Rs. 8 lakh as compensation. The order was issued on 18th November 2009, i.e. 25 years after the crime.

A 14-year-old girl was molested in 1990 by former Haryana Director-General of Police S.P.S. Rathore. The victim committed suicide in 1993 following the harassment her family faced after she lodged a complaint against Mr. Rathore. The official was sentenced to six-month imprisonment. The Union Home Ministry issued show cause notice to him asking him why his police medal should not be withdrawn and pension reduced for abusing power, since he was retired. The Communist Party of India (Marxist) demanded an independent probe into the alleged political shelter the former DGP enjoyed at the hands of successive governments. He was later stripped of his medal.

Since inception of the National Human Rights Commission (NHRC) in 1993, 1502 encounter cases were reported to it up to September 2009. But only in 12 cases, the police claims were detected as false and compensation was awarded to the families of the victims. Further, the Commission received from the public, 1,262 complaints of fake encounters but it found substance only in 11 complaints as revealed by the 'Campaign for Custodial Justice and Abolition of Torture (CCJAT)'. It suggests inept or apathetic functioning of the NHRC. The Law Commission made recommendations regarding custodial violence and called for appropriate provisions in the Indian Penal Code, the Code of Criminal Procedure 1973 and the Indian Evidence Act to prevent torture in custody and to protect the interests of victims of custodial crimes. The CCJAT urged the Government of India to implement the recommendations of the Law Commission to check custodial violence and award punishment for custodial killings and fake encounter deaths. All these crimes against individuals speak of human rights violations.

Very important and dignified persons also become victims of human rights violations. For example, the 63-year-old Nobel Peace Laureate and pro-democracy leader of Myanmar Ms. Aung san suu kyi was arrested in May 2003. Her arrest followed a pro-junta mob attack on her motorcade that left about 70 people dead. Since then, she was held under house arrest. But she was moved to a prison in May 2009 following fresh charges against her of breaking the conditions of her house arrest after a bizarre incident in which an eccentric American Mormon John Yettaw swam to her lakeside prison home in Yangon in early May 2009. Then Ms. Suu Kyi was put on trial. After a six-week adjournment, the trial was resumed on 10th July 2009. The fresh trial found her guilty and the court sentenced her to undergo three-year imprisonment. The junta commuted the sentence to an 18-month house arrest, as if it was helping her. Terming it as an 'outrageous verdict', British Prime Minister Gordon Brown appealed to the international community to react strongly against the happenings in Myanmar. The ruling junta was callous towards Ms. Suu Kyi though she has spent 13 of the past 19 years in detention. Even the United Nations Secretary General Ban Ki-moon was denied permission to meet her in July 2009. The international community ought to have stepped up pressure on Myanmar junta to get the leader released and restore human rights in that country. Her release after election in November-2010 was reportedly expected, but without participation of herself and her 'National League for Democracy' party in the poll.

Mr. Alam Ghafoor, a British Muslim businessman from West Yorkshire and his business partner Rafique Siddique were dragged out of a restaurant in Dubai on 21st July 2005. He was accused of involvement in London bombings on 7th July 2005 and arrested. He was reportedly told that he resembled one of the London bombers and hailed from the same town. One police officer allegedly threatened Mr. Alam, "In the morning, you will be thrown into a pit and dogs will tear you to bits and I will watch and enjoy it". Mr. Alam claimed that he had to sign a false confession under duress. He was released at the end of July 2009 without charges. He alleged that British Intelligence agencies had known what was happening to him. Mr. Alam said that he wanted to know why he was 'put through this hell'.

Dr. Binayak Sen is a paediatrician and human rights activist in India. He has earned international reputation by his health services to the poor masses in the country. He was awarded the 2008 Jonathan Mann Award for Global Health and Human Rights. All these made him popular worldwide. Narayan Sanyal, a senior Maoist leader was in Raipur jail in the State of Chhattisgarh. Dr. Sen was visiting Sanyal in his capacity as a physician treating him for health problems and as a human rights activist. Following this, Dr. Sen was accused of having links with Maoist groups. He was arrested probably in June 2007 and charged with "treason and waging war against the State". The Bilaspur High Court refused to grant him bail in September 2007 and December 2008. A Raipur Sessions Court which began the trial of Dr. Sen in April 2008, could not find any evidence in support of the charges levelled against him. Later, by March 2009, more than 60 witnesses didn't testify against him. With no grounds for the accusations, Dr. Sen was languishing in jail for nearly 2 years. A public statement signed by 22 Nobel Laureates in May 2008 asking for his release was ignored. Former Indian Supreme Court Judge and an eminent personality, Justice V. R. Krishna Iyer, in his letter dated 17th April 2009 to Prime Minister Dr. Manmohan Singh, propounded his legal contention that Dr. Sen deserved release besides pointing out his exacerbated ailments such as diabetes and cardiac problem, and reproached the Indian State for "wrongly branding Dr. Sen and many other human rights defenders like him as terrorists", terming it as a "complete mockery of not just democratic norms and fair governance but its entire anti-terrorist strategy and operations". By May 2009, a group of British MPs signed a parliamentary motion expressing concern over the continued detention of Dr. Sen. They called for Prime Minister Dr. Manmohan Singh's intervention to release him early. As the Supreme Court granted bail, Dr. Sen was released on 26th May 2009. But a Chhattisgarh trial court handed down life sentence to him on 24th December 2010 on charges of sedition, astounding the entire nation. The sentence was deplored by several intellectuals including Justice V.R. Krishna Iyer and Nobel laureate Amartya Sen. 'Amnesty International' said that the sentence had violated international standards of fair trial and the trial itself was "Politically motivated" and also wanted the State and federal authorities in India to immediately drop the charges against Dr. Sen and release him. Following the lead of Mr. Amartya Sen, a group of 40

Nobel laureates from 12 countries expressed their support for Dr. Sen and signed a petition in February 2011, appealing for his release on bail. Human rights activists must be protected and encouraged so that human rights violations could be curbed.

Dr. Haneef, on a work visa in Queensland, Australia, was arrested in July 2007 on suspicion of links to the terrorist plot in the United Kingdom a month earlier. He was disabled to leave for Bangalore in India for a family re-union. After a detention without charges for 12 days, he faced charges that centred on a mobile- phone SIM card which he had allegedly given to his cousins in the UK. On being granted judicial bail, his work-visa was cancelled and a criminal-justice stay-certificate was issued. After undergoing prolonged ordeal, he was allowed to leave Australia mainly due to the lapse on the part of the prosecution. Justice John Clarke who probed the allegation, submitted his report in December 2008. His enquiry report revealed that there was no evidence to show Dr. Haneef's association with, or foreknowledge of the terrorist events in the UK in June 2007. The report further enlightened that the SIM card-transfer had happened 12 months before the terrorist attack and the card could have been bought for a small sum of money, even with a false name. Its conclusion was that Dr. Haneef was wrongly charged by the Australian authorities. The accused found light at the end of the tunnel. But could an apology or even compensation to him reverse the violation of human rights?

During a news conference of the United States President George W. Bush in Baghdad on 14th December 2008, Muntader al-Zaidi, a television reporter hurled his shoes at Mr. Bush, who leaned and avoided being hit. Mr. Zaidi's act symbolized his anger at the US invasion of his motherland. He was arrested and lodged in jail. His brother Uday, who visited him in jail, said that Mr. Zaidi had been stripped to his underwear before being placed in a cell and tortured during the 24 hour period after his arrest. He was so brutally beaten by several men that one of his teeth was knocked out and his right ear was burnt by a cigarette. A corpulent man dumped cold water on Mr. Zaidi and began to smite him with a thick cable.

In February 2009, a six-year-old Dalit girl was brutally beaten up in Uttar Pradesh by a sub-inspector of police and another policeman for allegedly stealing Rs. 280 from a woman. The girl's mother stated that her daughter had seen someone running away with a wallet in the market, but the police had caught her daughter. The SI who grabbed the girl by her ears and hair and forced her to admit the crime was sacked. The other policeman was suspended and criminal cases were filed against both of them. In another incident, eleven-year-old girl Salam Bidyarani was arrested and detained for four days in the cell that was used as a cloakroom of the constables at the Mayang Imphal police station in Manipur in August 2009. The reason for her arrest was only the inability of the police to nab her parents in connection with a stash of weapons kept around their house by a militant group. During her detention, the girl suffered without toilet facility and privacy. Her maternal and paternal grandmothers had to bring water and food for her. The National Commission for Protection of Child Rights reportedly sought a reply from the Manipur Government on the unlawful arrest and detention of the girl who was rattled.

Eighteen-year-old I. Vivek was studying first year Mechanical Engineering in St Joseph's Engineering College in Chennai. According to the police, the student had allegedly indulged in a malpractice while attending the Computer Science practical examination. Vivek was asked to report to the Director and give his explanation. But he could not meet the Director though he waited in front of his room for three days during working hours. Obviously, the student should have been distressed. The college authorities barred him from attending the model examinations that commenced on 29th May 2009. Being unable to face the situation and losing hope in life, Vivek committed suicide by hanging himself in his hostel room on 1st June 2009. The college authorities had shown harsh attitude towards an immature first year student that ultimately cost his life. Instances of violation of individuals' human rights happen very often. I have pointed out only a few examples.

H.M.: What do you think about the overall human rights situation in South Asia?

Ashok: Generally, the situation in this region is not satisfactory because human rights are in poor state. 'Amnesty International' slammed many nations including India, Pakistan and Sri Lanka in its annual report on the state of human rights released in London on 27th May 2009. The report attacked India's new anti-terror legislation for including "sweeping and broad definitions" of acts of terrorism besides extending the minimum pre-charge detention periods for alleged terror suspects. It said that after bomb blasts in several States in 2008, more than 70 suspects were detained without charges for periods ranging from one week to two months and there were reports of torture and other ill-treatment of suspects. The report also highlighted "Violence against minorities"– citing attacks on Christians in Orissa- and forced evictions of marginalised communities in rural areas to locate industries. It pointed out that most of those responsible for communal violence and killing of thousands of Muslims in Gujarat in 2002 evaded justice. As for Pakistan, the report underscored condemnable human rights violations, namely torture, deaths in custody, honour killings, domestic violence and the elected Pakistan Government's failure to ensure human rights protection as promised before the polls. The Sri Lankan Government was accused of ignoring the plight of lakhs of civilians displaced in the war against the LTTE. The report painted a grim picture of the state of human rights around the world.

H.M.: How could human rights be protected?

Ashok: It is not an easy goal to reach. In the first instance, the causes of human rights violations must be eliminated with the wholehearted support and cooperation of concerned authorities. The Human Rights organizations and activists need to be encouraged with moral support and financial assistance for innovative approach to this critical issue. The Governments of all the countries must unite and embark on concerted efforts to protect human rights in every nook and cranny of the globe. In the United States, the Obama administration has taken bold and constructive initiatives by its decision to join the United Nations Human Rights Council (UNHRC) and getting the US elected to the Geneva- based 47-member body. This move demonstrates the US intention to be a part of the global forum for protection of human rights. It will give new impetus to the efforts of the UNHRC. Creation of awareness of human rights among all sections of people is essential. The media's contribution to the campaign on human rights is vital for its success. Rallies highlighting the human rights may be held in towns and villages with the active involvement of students, self-help groups, villages committees, social service organizations, etc. The district collectors may be requested to hold periodical review meetings with the participation of officials, legislators of the area, representative from the State Human Rights Commission (SHRC), educationists and others connected to this subject, to protect human rights and take stern action against the violators. The Social Welfare Department could arrange for cultural programmes projecting human rights.

Talented film directors, photographers, and video artistes from all around the world have produced 22 three-minute films on the six themes of the Universal Declaration of Human Rights, namely culture, development, dignity and justice, environment, gender and participation. Many of them are award winners in contemporary art and cinema. Many of the shorts deal with the subject of terrorism and how it dismally affects young children. One of them portrays a shocking statistic that more than two lakh kids serve as soldiers in many parts of the world. A film deals with domestic violence and another portrays an old-age home. There are some interesting films on the 'Environment'. Another film depicts the unique case of disposed garbage being recycled into a musical instrument 'djembe'. 2,000 such instruments are stated to be produced from 20 tonnes of recycled rubbish. The films were screened at some Human Rights festivals and the United Nations/European Union events in Europe. The shorts graced the 60th anniversary of the Universal Declaration of Human Rights at Bangkok. These short films can be screened at festivals around the world and desirably at cultural and academic institutions also. EU could make available 'Stories on Human Rights' to cultural institutes around the world.

H.M.: That's fine. I have consumed much of your time. Thank you very much.

Ashok: Not at all, sir. I am really moved by your fervour in human rights.

H.M.: Charli...... Shall we go home?

Charli: Your action is in contrast to your ideals.

H.M.: Your retort is an enigma to me.

Charli: What I say is, you have violated human rights by disturbing my sleep.

H.M.: Sleeping by this time is not a human right but a human vice.

Charli: You had caused my sleep.

H.M.: I take exception to your accusation. I didn't give you any soporific.

Charli: I don't blame you but your topic can be likened to a hypnotic.

H.M.: It depends upon how far you savour. Don't try to pick holes in the topic.

Charli: If you feel like that, let your topic not make me fall asleep.

H.M.: I think you were not asleep today.

Charli: Did you not see my eyes closed?

H.M.: Anybody closing his/her eyes can't be regarded as sleeping.

Charli: Do you mean I was feigning to be asleep? I need not eavesdrop on such unworthy topic.

H.M.: If it is so, would you eavesdrop on matters which you consider as worthy?

Charli: If I do so, you can't catch me.

H.M.: You may try that and see what happens.

Charli: There is no scope for it. Since there is no other inmate in our home, I can eavesdrop on you, only if you make a soliloquy.

Sanjay: Do you vie with our headmaster in jesting?

Charli: Yes, of course. But I am always the winner.

After having their evening coffee, the headmaster and Charli leave Sanjay's home.

9

RELIGIOUS INTOLERANCE

The headmaster and Charli arrive at Anand's home.

Anand: Good evening, sir.

H.M.: Good evening, Anand.

Anand: (Turning to his father Nagesh) This is our headmaster, Dad.

Nagesh: Hello, welcome sir. Please take a seat.

H.M.: Thank you. May I know about your family?

Nagesh: By all means, sir.

Anand's mother greets the headmaster and provides tea for all. The headmaster acknowledges her greetings.

Nagesh: She is my wife Jamuna. We have two sons. Our elder son is employed in a textile company in Mumbai. I am an agent for the Life Insurance Corporation of India (LIC).

H.M.: Do you have any other business?

Nagesh: No, sir. My job entails tours at taluk level and meeting many people. So, this facilitates some social work.

H.M.: Is it? What is the nature of your social work?

Nagesh: I am the President of an inter-religious committee functioning here since three years. Our principal objective is to sustain religious harmony.

H.M.: What was the impulse to form this committee and how is it relevant to the present context?

Nagesh: As you are aware, religious intolerance is on the rise nowadays. After usurping the rule in Afghanistan, the Taliban committed many atrocities. While it was at the helm for a short period, its militants had dynamited the world's cultural heritage-the 53 – metre and 35 – metre giant Buddhas in the Bamiyan in March 2001. After one-year feasibility studies, the work for the reconstruction of one of the two Buddhas began in Afghanistan's central Bamiyan Province in June 2009 according to the Director of Cultural Department. A German company had undertaken the reconstruction process.

The Babri Masjid mosque at Ayodhya in India was demolished on 6th December 1992. The Bharatiya Janata Party, the then Chief Minister of Uttar Pradesh Mr. Kalyan Singh and the Hindutva outfits were blamed for the wicked act. The Congress government at the centre was also blamed for not preventing this crime. Mr. K.R. Narayanan, the then Vice-President of India characterised the demolition of the Babri Masjid as the greatest tragedy India had faced, since the assassination of Mahatma Gandhi. In May 2009, Mr. Kalyan Singh stated that he had given an affidavit in the Supreme Court promising to ensure the security of the 16th century monument of the Mughal period, trusting the assurance of two Bharatiya Janata Party (BJP) leaders, whom he did not name. He added that he was misled by them as he was not told that the demolition had been planned well in advance. This revelation came from him after many years. So, one has to think that Mr. Kalyan Singh tried to evade from the evil act by giving political hue to the issue as he had quit the BJP already. A Commission headed by Justice M.S. Liberhan was set up on 16th December 1992 to probe the sequence of events leading to, and all the facts and circumstances relating to the occurrences in the Ram Janmabhoomi- Babri Masjid complex at Ayodhya on 6th December 1992. The Commission submitted its report to Prime Minister Dr. Manmohan Singh on 30th June 2009 after over 16 years that saw 399 sittings and 48 extensions. The report indicted the Sangh Parivar and also viewed the top leaders of the BJP Messrs A.B. Vajpayee, L.K. Advani and M.M. Joshi responsible for the misdeed. In India, any commission of enquiry does not usually serve its purpose. It merely suspends the heat on the issue, diverts public attention and eventually fizzles out. Justice Liberhan Commission report which consumed over 16 years is likewise unlikely to bring the guilty to justice.

On 27th February 2002, some miscreants set fire to S-6 coach of the Sabarmati Express train which was carrying devotees who were returning after 'Kar Seva' (labour service) for the construction of Ram Temple at Ayodhya where the Babri Masjid was demolished by Hindu religious extremists. The crime committed at Godhra in

Gujarat took 59 lives. In the wake of this crime, widespread communal violence erupted in Gujarat in which more than 1100 innocent people were killed and thousands of Muslims fled their homes for safety. Many Muslim women were allegedly raped. It took several months to control the flare-up and restore normality. Investigations failed to produce decisive results. A case of carnage in a bakery in which a young Muslim woman was the key witness, was transferred to Mumbai in view of her safety. But during the trial, she contradicted her earlier deposition for which she was punished by court. The Justice Nanavati and Justice Mehta Commissions which probed the crime till 2008, got one-year extension. There were repeated pleas to reinvestigate the cases relating to the communal violence in Gujarat. As per orders of the Supreme Court, the Special Investigation Team (SIT) was formed with Mr. R.K. Raghavan, former CBI Director as its head. It approached the victims to record their statements for investigating some of the cases afresh. But the victims retracted their charges of rape and bribing of the police by the rioters. They disowned their earlier statements filed in their names stating that they merely signed them unaware of the contents in English. It was apparent how far the victims had been intimidated into changing their previous statements.

During the post-Godhra riots in Gujarat, Bilkis Bano was gang-raped on 3rd March 2002. In this case, a Mumbai court handed down life sentence to eleven persons in January 2008. The Government of India announced a relief package worth more than Rs. 330 crore in May 2008 for the victims of the riots that followed the train burning incident at Godhra. The Supreme Court had stayed the trial of Godhra riots cases. The Special Investigation Team found further materials and identified more accused against whom charges were sought to be brought, and included them in its report. Accepting the report on Ist May 2009, the Supreme Court Bench vacated the stay on trials and requested the Chief Justice of the Gujarat High Court to set up Fast Track Courts (FTCs) to try the cases relating to train-burning in Godhra in 2002 and consequent riots. The Bench advised that senior judicial officers be appointed for satisfactory and expeditious trials that might be concluded soon pointing out the delay of seven years. The Bench also directed to provide security to witnesses wherever necessary to ensure that they depose before the courts freely and fearlessly. As ordered by the Supreme Court, the Gujarat High Court constituted 9 Special Fast Track Courts for trial of 9 cases connected with the communal riots in 2002. A court convicted 31 accused and acquitted 63 others on 22nd February 2011. The court later sentenced 11 convicts to death and 20 others to life imprisonment.

The retired Gujarat Director-General of Police (DGP) Mr. R.B. Sreekumar who was additional DGP in 2004, claimed that the then Home Secretary (Law and Order) had summoned him on 25th August 2004 and said, "If you tell the Commission anything against the State Government, you will not get your promotion." Mr. Sreekumar had covertly recorded the conversation and reportedly submitted the compact disc to the Special Investigation Team. He had also appeared before the Commission for cross-examination during which he had been told by the then DGP that Chief Minister Narendra Modi had asked the police to " allow the Hindus" to give vent to their anger against the alleged killing of 'Kar sevaks' in the train carnage. Political and bureaucratic powers had vividly attempted to bury justice. Many such instances showing hatred and enmity between the people of different religions have happened in some parts of India. Religious extremists misguide the people and cause disunity among them. A desire to avert such abominable scenario in our area was the impetus to form our inter-religious committee. In the context of increasing communal violence, we hope that the committee could curb discriminatory feelings, sustain coordination between people of different religions and strengthen communal harmony.

H.M. : I have known that Christians were attacked in the State of Orissa. What did actually happen there?

Nagesh : In Orissa, there has been an aversion to Christians in the minds of Hindutva extremists. The extremists frequently accuse priests and churches of converting people forcibly from Hinduism to Christianity. But Church authorities deny this charge and term the conversions as 'only voluntary.' The oppressed, having been inspired by the Love and brotherhood of Christians, quit Hinduism and embrace Christianity. But Hindutva extremists are unable to come to terms with conversions. So, they develop acrimony and malice against Christians. On 22nd January 1999, an Australian missionary Mr. Graham Stuart Staines who was serving lepers, and his two minor sons were burnt alive while they were asleep inside a van at Manoharpur in Orissa. The Supreme Court on 21st January 2011, upheld the Orissa High Court judgment in this case, awarding life term to the main accused Dara Singh and the co-accused Mahendra Hembram. Religious intolerance, besides taking a heavy toll on the holy persons, cost the humanity dearly and tarnished the image of the Indian people. A Vishwa Hindu Parishad (VHP) leader Lakshmanananda Saraswati and four disciples were killed by a group of armed men at the Jalespata ashram in Kandhamal district of Orissa on 23rd August 2008. The murders triggered widespread anti-Christian riots and violence in Kandhamal and many other places in the State. About 40 people were killed and thousands of Christian homes, institutions and churches were either destroyed or ransacked. Religious intolerance and communal hatred evolved monsters who smote a priest on 25th August 2008. They crowned their atrocities with a diabolic act of gang rape of a nun in Baliguda church after dragging and parading her nude. Her plea to the bystanding police personnel to protect her went unheeded. The guardians of rule of law had winked at the beastly act. Later, their close dealing with some of the offenders at the police station had shown that the crime was committed with the connivance of the police. The gang rape of a holy sister has left an incurable injury in the hearts of all civilized people around the world. The nun identified two persons during the first Test Identification Parade on 5th January 2009. She identified a third person on 23rd June 2009. The communal violence and unrest in Kandhamal continued for many weeks, forcing thousands of Christians to flee. Around 24,000 men, women and children took shelter in the relief camps within the district. As normality was not restored in the interior areas, thousands of people lingered in relief camps even after one year. The crime branch of Orissa police arrested 4 persons in December 2008 in connection with the murder of the VHP leader. One of them was reported to be a hardcore Maoist and three others were Maoist sympathizers. If the fact of no involvement of any Christian member in the murder is proved, can the religious extremists revive the lost lives? What price will the perpetrators of the crimes pay for the gross violation of human rights committed out of infatuation for their own religion?

In the aftermath of religious violence in Kandhamal, apart from those sheltered in the relief camps, thousands of Christians, mostly 'Adhivasis' (tribes) had left the district. Over 50 of them, who went to Kerala State, were lodged as refugees in homes run by the State Social Welfare Department. They were longing to go back to their native places. Seven months after their displacement, 36 refugees boarded a train for home on 31st May 2009 with nostalgia and hope despite fear and uncertainty over their future and safety. They were accompanied by officials and police personnel from Kerala. The

Director of Social Welfare Department of Kerala had gone to Kandhamal in advance and interacted with the authorities for resettlement of the refugees. He made a formal handover of the refugees to the Collector of Kandhamal after their arrival there. A European Union team visited the rehabilitation camp at Nandagiri in Kandhamal district on 4th February 2010. The camp had 55 families living in tents. They did not want to return to their native village 'Betikala', for fear of attacks by the majority community. While interacting with the team members, the inmates of the camp sought their intervention to ensure work for them and livelihood support. The church and houses in their village were either damaged or burnt down in the violence. So, they reportedly said, "We suffered for our religion. We should be provided (with) a prayer house". Justice S.C. Mohapatra Commission while probing the violence, said in its interim report that conversion and re-conversion were among the major factors which led to the riots in Kandhamal district. It is a pointer to the situation that threatened religious freedom. Religious intolerance wrought havoc on Christians in Kandhamal.

Religious intolerance is so awkward that there was a clash between two groups of Sikh community at a gurdwara in Vienna on 24th May 2009. Eleven persons were injured, nine of them seriously including a preacher of the Dera Sach Khand–Sant Niranjan Das, and his deputy Sant Rama Nand who died later. It happened when a rival group attempted to disrupt a sermon by the 'Dera'.The incident sparked major violence in Punjab State in India on 25th May. The agitators torched two trains and held up 11 trains including long-distance trains at various places. They set fire to many buses. The trouble spread to Haryana State also. Army was called out and curfew was imposed in four cities of Punjab to bring the situation under control. When army personnel opened fire to disperse a mob, one person was killed and four were injured. The root cause of the incident in Vienna was said to be the enmity between two sects of the Sikh religious community.

Muslim-Christian communal violence broke out in Nigeria in the third week of January 2010. According to Red Cross, the four-day religious violence left more than 400 people dead and 18,000 residents were displaced. The northern-Nigerian city of Jos was at the centre of violence where 150 bodies were recovered from a single well. Muslim volunteers were searching for the missing persons among the destroyed buildings and recovered bodies from many wells. Bomb blasts and attacks on churches in Nigeria by suspected members of an Islamist sect on the eve of Christmas in December 2010 left 38 people dead and 74 injured. Such clashes between the people of religions that preach love and compassion, are very distressing.

The desecration of a religious school at Gayathripuram, off Mahadevapura Road near Mysore in Karnataka State where a carcass of a slaughtered animal was found, triggered communal tensions at the beginning of July 2009. An angry mob soon blocked Mahadevapura Road with stones and logs of wood, and another group at the Udaigiri police station demanded action against those who desecrated the place. The police then lobbed teargas shells on the rioting mobs. In the course of time, the police opened fire in the air. Prohibitory orders under section 144 Cr. Pc were imposed in many areas for 4 days as a precautionary measure. According to reports, 3 persons were killed in the mob attacks. Though the police deployed additional forces and brought the situation under control, the trouble-torn areas continued to be tense. In the same State, a 30-year-old Muslim youth was attending a Hindu wedding reception in a restaurant in Mangalore on 15th July 2009. On that occasion, activists of Sri Rama Sena–a Hindutva group, beat him up. Those who flung to the rescue of the guest were also roughed up. An unprovoked attack on the Muslim guest is a testimony to the religious intolerance of the Sri Rama Sena activists.

H.M. : What is the impact of religious intolerance on society?

Nagesh : Religious intolerance often leads to detestation, peevish tendencies, squabbles, wrangles, violence, jihad, internecine riots and perpetual animosity towards the people of other faiths. All these make life rid of security, peace and happiness. Religious violence always violates human rights and destroys lives and properties. Religious tolerance would make people adhere to non-violence. Mahatma Gandhi has enjoined non-violence in our thought, speech and actions. He clung to non–violence all along his personal and political life, advocated this principle to his countrymen, and wielded it as the most effective tool in achieving Independence for India. Thoreau, in his essay 'Civil Disobedience', prescribes only non-violent revolution against an unjust government. Mr. Martin Luther King resorted to a campaign of non-violent resistance to racial discrimination and segregation in America. Islamists say that there is no sentence in the holy Koran advocating jihadi war. In fact, no religion preaches violence. Only the intolerant people who pose themselves as the true loyalists of their religion indulge in violence. The Jain priests Munishree Jinesh Kumarji and Munishree Paramanandji, while visiting Tamil Nadu, said that the objective of their tour was to propagate the importance of non-violence–the strongest weapon for promoting world peace, happiness and brotherhood. They camp at different places throughout their lifetime and take up ‘padayatra’ (journey by walk) for their campaign for non-violence. They preached, “There should be no hatred among the entire mankind in the universe; nor should there be any discrimination between the rich and the poor”. Religious intolerance breeds religious extremism which sows the seeds of violence. So, religious intolerance is an enemy of non-violence. We are, therefore, working to make people cherish religious harmony.

H.M. : Yours is a peerless service. What is the recipe of your inter-religious committee for an enduring unity among different religious people?

Nagesh : Every country is inhabited by people belonging to almost all religions. Each religious group makes its presence felt in most of the nations although with varying percentage of population. Every group therefore, needs to have rapport with all others for peaceful life. Hence, religious harmony is essential for happiness of the world. As for India, there are people of many faiths with diverse cultures and languages.Religious harmony therefore, is a must for India. The overall situation in the country is satisfactory barring a few pockets. The areas prone to religious violence need to be constantly monitored. The Government and the people need to be vigilant to rule out spread of religious hatred to other areas. Our committee’s area of functioning spans our taluk. Our motto is: ‘Unity in diversity’. If there is room for any row between people of different religions, it will jeopardize the mutual relationship. When enmity between them grows, the Government’s action, though necessary, won’t yield a stable solution, nor could it change anyone’s bitter mindset. Our strategy is therefore, to pre-empt even an altercation. If there is a quarrel between two boys belonging to different religions, elders from either side would not interfere in the matter but would bring it to the notice of the committee. The committee would call the boys and put them on right track. Feeling embarrassed at facing the committee, such quarrels are avoided. Any dispute between elders is settled amicably. Transcending its purpose, the committee resolves family problems and also deals with civil cases on request. Although these functions are outside the purview of the committee, they earn good reputation to it because the beneficiaries could save their time and money to be spent in courts. Every decision is taken in an unbiased manner with no tinge of religious sentiment. Our approach to any issue is based on convincing, compromise, reconciliation and guidance. People trust us since we never demand or accept money for any service. All these have become possible mainly because our 15-member-committee consists of representatives from all religious people in our taluk, who are selfless, dedicated to people's welfare and known for probity sans political or exploiting traits. The committee has resolved to send any case of felony for legal action. But in such a balanced and civilized social set-up, there has been no instance of felony. The coordination and bonding between the members are so robust that every religious fete or function is organized with the active participation of other religious members as well as the people. We have made the people of various religions realize that though their ways of seeking God are different, convergence of all religious people and ideals is not inimical to society. Here the people of one religion are not only the special guests to, but also the organizers of family functions of other religious people. The people celebrating a religious festival invite people of other religions. Our committee arranges feasts on all festival days and the members rejoice together. Last year we completed construction of a new building for mosque. Now, we are planning for renovation of an ancient church in the near future. We are also pondering over diversification of our activities by virtue of foray into development works in coordination with government departments and other aid agencies. Thus, the people of different religions in our taluk behave as a clan of relatives in their daily life.

H.M. : Had the religions not emerged, the mankind could have been a single unit. But unfortunately many religions have come into existence in the world. As long as they do exist, religious tolerance and unity are paramount.

In my previous station, I have seen many Muslims voluntarily engaging themselves in conducting the annual festival of a Hindu temple. Muslim youths would decorate the chariot with enthusiasm. One Mr. Samsudeen, a senior Muslim citizen, would illuminate the temple and its precinct at his expense. Muslim and Christian people would come out of their homes and enjoy the chariot procession along the main streets. I have seen thousands of Hindus from all over India and even from abroad worshipping at the same time at Velankanni Church and Nagore Dargah (mosque) in Tamil Nadu. In all these occasions, I was thrilled to see the union of different religious people at holy places of worship. In fact, the people of various religions across the world desire only peaceful coexistence. Only the powerful vested interests disrupt religious unity. Such forces need to be eliminated at all cost. I am much delighted at your assorted services to the society, and the religious harmony in our taluk and wish the same to prevail among the people all over the world. Thank you for giving me so much information about an important subject.

Nagesh : Not at all, sir.

H.M. : Charli...........

Charli : (Hiding behind a curtain) Present, sir.

H.M. : When did you join the school?

Charli : I have already left the school after completing my academic studies there. Now I am studying in a religious school.

H.M. : Whose school is that?

Charli : It is managed by two persons by me.

H.M. : I am bewildered by your absurd reply.

Nagesh: Perhaps, it is an allusion to both of us.

Charli: You are really sagacious.

H.M.: Don't think that you are very clever by viewing this place as a school. No class would be concluded after about two hours.

Charli: A philosopher has said, "Precious metals weigh much in little bulk".

H.M.: So, do you spell out a new philosophy that a subject could be grasped in a couple of hours?

Charli: Why not? It is enough for a genius.

H.M.: Do you consider yourself a genius?

Charli: Why do you doubt my intelligence and skill?

H.M.: What creed have you learnt here?

Charli: I have not only learnt the nucleus of your talks but also begun to practise it at once.

Nagesh: You are here with us. How could you practise anything?

Charli: Did you not watch me while playing truant since half an hour ahead of your closing bell?

Nagesh: Is it true? I didn't notice your prank. Whither did you go?

Charli: I went to the church, mosque and a Hindu temple, and worshipped. The priest of the church gave me some snacks. The priest of the Hindu temple gave me sweet pongal (cooked rice with jaggery added to it). A helper in the mosque provided tea for me in a nearby tea shop. Buddhist and Sikh temples are not available here.

H.M.: You have visited these holy places only to fill up your belly.

Charli: Don't ridicule a pious man.

H.M.: Are you pious? Why are you standing behind the screen? Come out.

(Charli comes out and appears before all of them in the guise of a mini-saint. His brow wears three parallel streaks of sacred ash with a small circular mark of vermilion at the centre which is flanked by the crescent on one side and the cross on the other).

Charli: Am I not showing the way for religious harmony?

All those present are laughing at him. After having tiffin, the headmaster and Charli leave for home.

10

SOCIAL EVILS AFFECTING CHILDREN/DOWRY

The headmaster and Charli arrive at Sofia's home.

Sofia: Good evening, sir.

H.M.: Good evening, Sofia.

Sofia: (Turning to her father Richard) Please meet our headmaster, Dad.

Richard: Hello, sir. Please be seated.

H.M.: Thank you. I find only father and daughter. What about others?

Richard: I have a son who is elder than Sofia. He has accompanied my wife to attend a function at a relative's home today.

H.M.: So, I have to miss them today. However, I shall have an opportunity to meet them soon. By the way, may I know about your occupation?

Richard: I am an Assistant Director in the Women and Child Welfare Department.

H.M.: That's good. Could you please expound the problems faced by children?

Richard: Among the social evils, the suffering of children is foremost. The threat to a child begins while it grows as a foetus in the womb, i.e. even before being called a 'child'. Many people, especially in some pockets of a number of states began to hate female children, mainly because of poverty, previous possession of female children and the impending high cost of rearing, education and marriage that entails dowry. There is a tendency to perceive a female child as a burden in life. So, some people are eager to know the sex of the growing embryo. Medical advancements including scan are helpful to them. Though the Pre-Natal Diagnostic Techniques Act of 1996 is in force, it is often flouted and misused for determination of the sex of child during pregnancy. Such offence facilitates female foeticide. The evils of foeticide, infanticide and abandonment of newborns were on the rise in the districts of Salem, Namakkal, Dharmapuri, Theni and Madurai in Tamil Nadu and some other parts of India. It is very distressing to note that pregnant and suckling mothers and grandmothers of babies, who are all women grown up from the stage of female babies, play an active role to eliminate female babies. They induce and convince other family members for their consent to commit the crime. In most cases, they themselves carry out abortion or killing of babies using herbal methods. In some cases, they just encourage others to do the cruel act. These evils have changed the balanced sex ratio of children in several states in India, threatening with harmful social implications for the future. In order to curb this dismal trend and save the surrendered and trashed children, the 'Cradle Baby Scheme' was launched in Tamil Nadu. Till January 2009, 1,144 babies were abandoned and brought into the scheme in Dharmapuri district alone. According to officials, surrender or abandonment of children-mostly female children, has increased by 20 per cent every year in Madurai and Theni districts alone. Babies from remote villages in Virudhunagar and Sivaganga districts were also brought to Madurai for surrender to orphanages. The children are usually surrendered within 15 days of birth. From 2005 to 2008, around 300 babies were either surrendered or found abandoned on road in four southern districts alone in Tamil Nadu. Among those children, there were cases of physical deformity or mental retardation. Non-Governmental Organizations recognized by the Government have been taking care of the rejected babies. Poverty and more number of female babies at home were among the reasons for surrender or abandonment of babies.

Sometimes, sales of children have been reported. In February 2009, a newborn female child was sold by her mother to a woman engaged in child trade. This incident happened in Cuddalore district of Tamil Nadu. Police enquiry found that she had sold the infant because she already had three female children following which her husband had deserted her. In this case, the couple's failure to adopt family planning methods, and the man's irresponsible character are to be blamed for the abominable sale of child. A five-month-old girl child was found abandoned in the Government Hospital complex at Mannargudi in Tamil Nadu on 13th November 2009. The baby was initially admitted to the children's ward and later handed over to a non-governmental organization by the Collector.

An orphanage was run for several years at Valliyoor in Tirunelveli district of Tamil Nadu, by one M. Rajan. In June 2009, child kidnapping and selling from this orphanage came to light. Rajan had sold the children who were kidnapped by a woman named R. Dhanam. He used her for transit of the infants to two men- A. Paramasivam and S. Muthusamy for selling them. The Tiruchy city police first arrested the trio except Rajan, and after interrogation, rescued seven infants aged between 20 days and 18 months. Five kids were restored to their parents. Rajan was arrested later on 9th June 2009. The police constituted three special teams to probe further into the case. Such sort of child abuse is often committed by criminals to make money.

Children are abused in many ways. As part of a daredevil show at a primary school at Keezhperumpakkam near Villupuram in Tamil Nadu, a motorcyclist rode over he outstretched hands of school children on 15th July 2009. In another incident, a motorcyclist rode over a wooden plank placed on the stomach of a girl student. A State Minister's wife who was present there had seen the plight of children and stopped the show. The National Human Rights Commission raised a serious issue of violation of human rights and sought a factual report from the Chief Secretary of Tamil Nadu Government within four weeks. Child rights activists and parents across India condemned the show. In the guise of taking measurements for the school uniform, a male teacher allegedly misbehaved with tribal girls studying in classes III, IV and V by stripping them. This incident happened in a school in Vidisha district of Madhya Pradesh in July 2009. The National Commisson for Women (NCW) sought a report on this incident from the State Government and the Education Department as well. Misbehaviour of a teacher towards children deserves condemnation and severe punishment.

There were allegations that the Liberation Tigers of Tamil Eelam (LTTE) had recruited young boys and girls and trained them to fight against the Sri Lankan army. Congolese militia leader Thomas Lubanga allegedly forced recruitment of child soldiers who were part of a rebel army responsible for mass killings, rape and torture of civilians. Mr. Lubanga was charged with conscripting children under 15years and sending them into combat. The International Criminal Court in The Hague began trial of the accused in the last week of January 2009.

Several children in Pakistan were forcibly recruited by the Taliban allegedly to be used as fighters or suicide bombers. Lt General Nadeem Ahmed said on 28th July 2009 that he had met nine boys rescued from the Taliban. According to him, the boys had sometimes been lured by offers of food, but they had been underfed and some had fallen ill. He added, "They have been brainwashed and trained as suicide bombers, but the nine whom I met seemed willing to get back to normal life. It seems that there are some 300 to 400 such children whom the Taliban had taken forcibly or whom they were training". North West Frontier Province Senior Minister Bashir Ahmad Bilour said that security forces had rescued dozens of children aged 6 to 15. He added, "They are propared mentally. They say that Islam is everything for them. They say, they are doing it for Islam. They say, they have to carry out suicide attacks for the sake of Islam". This kind of abuse of children not only deprives them of their education, proper food, health, playful activities, peace of mind and happy childhood, but also instil wicked ideas into them, groom them for militancy and invite their premature death.

(Sofia provides coffee for them.)

H.M.: Are children sexually abused?

Richard: Yes, of course. It is a shameful aspect of child abuse. A teacher's act of taking measurements for uniform in a school in Madhya Pradesh which I have explained, was obviously in a manner of sexual abuse of children. In February 2008, a 19-year-old Dalit girl student of the Patan Government Women's Teacher Training College in North Gujarat, fell unconscious in the college. Later she reported to the authorities and the police that six teachers had sexually assaulted her repeatedly between November 2007 and February 2008. The girl ascribed her inhibition of the traumatic incidents to the intimidation of the wicked teachers who allegedly threatened to fail her in the internal assessment and ruin her career if she didn't submit to their lascivity. A Fast Track Court sentenced all the six felons to life imprisonment in March 2009. Another case of sexual abuse of pupils at St George's School in Chennai by a British national was investigated by a UK-based investigation team in June 2009. After the investigation, Detective Inspector Mr. Mark Little of Gloucestershire police who led the team to Chennai, stated in a press release: "During our investigations in Tamil Nadu, we have interviewed 14 children and 16 adults. Our investigations are now concluding and evidence has been obtained that identifies at least 9 pupils and former pupils of St George's

School who were subjected to various incidents of sexual abuse within the school boarding home by a UK suspect when he was a volunteer of 'Batemans Trust'. Further enquiries will now be undertaken in the UK before a file of evidence is submitted to the Crown Prosecution Service who have the responsibility of reviewing evidence and making decisions regarding criminal prosecutions". He underscored the need of the school and the boarding home to understand their duties to prevent abuse and immediately report incidents of abuse to parents and authorities when allegations were made. He emphasized on staff training and adoption of clear child protection policies by organizations working with children.

A member of the Andhra Pradesh Legislative Assembly T.V. Rama Rao is the Chairman and Managing Director of Spruha College of Nursing, Nidadavole. Five girls, all belonging to Kerala, pursuing B.Sc. Nursing Course, accused the MLA of having made attempts to outrage their modesty. They submitted a detailed written complaint that was also signed by their parents, to the State Home Minister. When they met the Minister, some parents were also present. The girls broke down before the Minister while narrating how the MLA made overtures to them in the college hostel. The Minister assured them that she would refer their complaint to the Crime Investigation Department. The Kerala Government wrote to the Prime Minister and the Chief Minister of Andhra Pradesh seeking a detailed probe into the allegations. The MLA T.V. Rama Rao was arrested on 20th July 2009 on the charge of sexual harassment of girls. The Crime Investigation Department (CID) of police arrested him and he was remanded to judicial custody.

Ireland's commission to enquire into child abuses investigated more than 100 schools run by Catholic Religious Orders - the majority by the Christian Brothers and Sisters of Mercy, and prepared a 2,600-page report. The five-volume report confirmed allegations from thousands of former pupils from the institutions. It found that for decades, rape was "endemic" in more than 250 Irish Catholic Care institutions from the 1930s to the 1990s. Rape was particularly common in boys' homes and industrial schools run by the Christian Brothers. More than 100 priests are facing allegations and 400 people have been identified as victims. Children in industrial schools and reformatories were treated more like convicts and slaves than people with human rights. Children lived with the daily terror of not knowing where the next beating was coming from. In some schools, a high level of ritualised beating was routine. Girls were struck with implements designed to maximise pain and were struck on all parts of the body. The Education Department inspectors were "infrequent and toothless". The inspections even failed to ensure that children were adequately fed, clothed and educated. The church in Ireland protected paedophiles in its ranks from arrest. The report criticized the failure of the Irish State, notably the Department of Education for allowing the abuse and exploitation to continue for decades. Irish Justice Minister Dermot Ahern published on 26th November 2009, a three-volume report on the sexual and physical abuse of children by the clergy from 1975 to 2004. The report accused four former archbishops in Dublin, a host of clergy and senior members of the police force of covering up the scandal involving more than 170 paedophile priests. The vast majority of priests had turned a "blind eye" to abuse, though some individuals did bring complaints to their superiors, which were not acted upon. The State authorities had facilitated the cover-up by allowing the church to be beyond the reach of the Law. In the wake of the report, two Roman Catholic bishops, Donal Murray of Limerick and Jim Moriarty of Kildare quit in early December 2009. Two other Dublin Bishops, Eamonn Walsh and Ray Field offered an apology to child-abuse victims and announced their resignations during Christmas Mass on 25th December 2009. Sexual abuse of children mars their career. The offenders in schools botch up the Educational System and tarnish the image of the institutions. The holy adult-child relationship based on pure affection is tainted with libido. The guardians of children at times turn worse than animals which never approach their young ones with lust.

Besides sexual abuse of children in educational institutions, we are often perturbed at reports of girls-trafficking. The Central Bureau of Investigation (CBI) detected trafficking in minor girls bought from Kolkata, Assam, Uttar Pradesh and a neighbouring country after raiding various places in Mumbai. The 34 rescued girls including eight minors were rehabilitated in an observation home. Eight persons were arrested and a sum of Rs. 4.79 lakh was recovered from them. Such girls-trafficking happens often in India.

H.M. : Are there any steps taken to root out sexual abuse of children in schools?

Richard : In Tamil Nadu, the Directorate of School Education embarked on organizing awareness programmes for District Educational Officers on 'Prevention of Child Sexual Abuse'. Addressing the first programme in Madurai on 4th July 2009, the Director of School Education said that all teachers must be vigilant against child abuse. He added that as sexual abuse of children might happen not only in schools but also on the way to school and at any other place, schools must have a mechanism to address the issue. He stressed that headmasters must immediately approach the police in case of any complaint of sexual abuse and the school must not try to cover up the issue. A complaint cell was functioning at the Directorate in Chennai. The Director, terming the issue as 'sensitive', told that teachers and headmasters in all schools would have to be sensitised to prevent incidents of sexual abuse of child. Tackling child sexual abuse would be made a component of adolescent education and counselling, he said. These measures are appreciable and could be followed by all the States. Besides, Parent-Teacher Association is functioning in every school. The association should act as a watchdog to find out child abuse if any, and if it has any inkling of such crime, it must nip the crime in the bud and banish the wretch.

H.M. : Corporal punishment in educational institutions also amount to abuse of children. Could you please comment on this problem?

Richard : We find corporal punishment of children and widespread apathy among teachers in caring for them in educational institutions. Eleven-year-old girl Shanno was studying in a school run by the Delhi Municipal Corporation. After she failed to recite the full English alphabet string on 15th April 2009, a teacher named Manju punished her by making her stand in a crouching position in the hot sun for two hours and even loaded seven bricks on her back. When Shanno asked for water, the teacher kicked her. As her head hit a wall, she began to bleed from the nose. Later she fell unconscious, slipped into coma and died in a government hospital on 17th April 2009. The National Commission for Protection of Child Rights (NCPCR) ordered an enquiry into the shocking indident. A departmental enquiry into the incident was also held. The principal of the school and teacher Manju were suspended. The Police registered a case against the teacher for causing death by negligence. In April 2009, Aakriti Bhatia, a teenage girl student of Modern School in New Delhi, died after she reportedly suffered an asthma attack. Her parents alleged that the school management had failed to arrange for immediate treatment. The NCPCR sought reports from the Delhi Government and The Delhi Commission on Protection of Child rights. The NCPCR chairperson Ms. Shantha Sinha told that on getting the reports, a long-term policy on child care in schools would be formulated. Ms. Renuka Chowdhury, Minister of State for Women and Child Development said, "It is not about one individual or one school principal. We have to look at this as a systemic failure at several levels."

The Supreme Court of India banned corporal punishment on 1st December 2000 and directed the States to ensure that children were not subjected to corporal punishment in schools and they could get education in an environment of freedom and dignity, free from fear. In the same month, the Delhi High Court, on a public interest litigation, directed the Delhi State Government to ban corporal punishment in schools and ensure that children get education in an environment of protection and dignity without any fear. In spite of all these directions, reports of violence on children in the form of corporal punishment are continuing to pour in from schools across the country. The NCPCR therefore, has written to the States in June 2009 to take severe action against those found guilty of the offence and prevent such punishment. Expressing concern over the violence on children in schools, the Commission has written to Collectors, District Magistrates and Deputy Commissioners warning that action would be taken against the school as a whole on any act of violence on children. In order to put an end to corporal punishment of children once and for all and enable school teachers to treat children as equal human beings with respect and dignity, the chairperson of the Commission Ms. Shantha Sinha has asked the District Collectors to organize block-wise meetings for all school headmasters to make them wake up to the guidelines on corporal punishment and convey to them that they are answerable for any act of violence in their schools. The state should conduct meetings of District Educational Officers, Block Educational Officers as well as the staff on the importance of protection of children's rights and action against corporal punishment in schools and issue instructions that they would be held accountable for any instances of violation of children's rights and corporal punishment in schools. The Commission had issued guidelines in this regard on 9th August 2007, asking the States to inform children about their rights through campaigns and publicity drives. The purpose of such steps was to enable children have a right to speak against corporal punishment and bring it to the notice of the authorities. The Commission sought an 'action taken report' with regard to the guidelines on the issue. Based on the orders of courts and the NCPCR, the Central and State Governments also issued necessary instructions to schools to desist from corporal punishment. Notwithstanding so much directions and warning, the evil continues in some schools. For instance, Sree Manaswini, a four-year-old LKG girl student of Akshara Public School in West Godavari district of Andhra Pradesh, was beaten by her teacher Ms. Y. Sridevi in December 2009. The child's left eye was badly damaged due to caning. Following a complaint by her mother, the police registered a case against the teacher. The child underwent an operation in a eye hospital and an artificial lens was implanted in her eye, replacing the damaged natural lens. The Child had told that her teacher had beaten her saying that her handwriting was poor. Even after two months, the child was in the grip of fear. Will it not affect her mind, health and studies?A class VII student of a private school at Mirza in Assam died in June 2010 after beating by his teachers. Apart from the reported incidents, many instances of corporal punishment do not come to light. They usually lurk because most children inhibit the cruelties inflicted on them and suffer silently. So, any form of punishment including smacking and spanking must be ruled out. Corporal punishment can be eliminated only if the guilty parties are harshly punished even by making necessary amendments to the relevant laws.

H.M. : 'Child marriage' is an old practice and one among the social evils. How does it affect children and does it still continue in India and elsewhere?

Richard : The UNICEF's latest "State of the World's Children-2009" report highlights the child marriages in India that accounts for 40 percent of the world figures. This vice results in gender discrimination, illiteracy and high maternal and infant mortality rates. Discrimination on the basis of gender denies girls and women access to education and has a direct impact on maternity health by preventing them from seeking or getting enough health care and disabling them from making crucial decisions on health matters of mothers and children. Saving the lives of mothers and their newborns require more attention than routine medical treatment. To fulfil this, the medical personnel and the family members must follow an ideal approach that ensures high regard for the rights of women and children.

Three teenage girls–Afsana Khatun, Sunita Mahato and Rekha Kalindi in the backward and poverty-stricken Purulia district of West Bengal State showed courage in firmly resisting their impending marriages. All these three girls had seen the sufferings of their siblings who were married off earlier at young age. Their elder sisters' dreary experiences haunted them. Besides, they were resolute in pursuing their studies. They therefore, rejected the marriages arranged by their parents. Parents are forced to marry off their minor children by societal pressure and the usual practice prevalent in some areas. These three girls approached Mr. Prosenjit Kundu, the Project Director of the National Child Labour Project (NCLP) and requested to save them from being married off. Mr. Kundu ascertained that the girls' mothers too were subjected to early marriage, and had known its consequences. So, he along with teachers and friends, first convincingly spoke to their mothers who helped to bring the rest of each family around, and accept their advice. He bailed the three girls out of marriage and enrolled them in the school run by the NCLP. President Pratibha Patil was impressed by their courage to confront social evils. She had an audience with the girls and rewarded them with compliment and a cash purse of Rs. 10,000 each to help them pursue their education. Expressing happiness at their courage, the President observed that the girls' act had a positive effect on their communities. Child marriages still continue in many parts of India. This evil is prevalent among some tribal communities in many other countries also. All young girls who are forced for marriage, could emulate the trio and fight to eliminate the age-old practice of child marriage. The Government officials' role in curbing this evil is very important. For instance, the marriages of six children were scheduled to be performed on 2nd September 2009 in Dharmapuri district in Tamil Nadu. Acting on an information, the Collector instructed the concerned Tahsildars and the police officials to visit the villages and prevent the evil. Accordingly, the marriages were stopped a day in advance. In the same district, three child marriages were scheduled for 22nd January 2010. On a tip-off received from the public, the Collector instructed the officials of the Revenue Department to stop the marriages. Accordingly, the officials prevented the marriages on 21st January. In the same manner, six child marriages scheduled for 27th January 2010 in the district were also prevented by officials.

President Mrs. Pratibha Patil, during her conversation with Mr. N. Ram, the Chief Editor of 'The Hindu' on 4th January 2009, mentioned 'child marriage' among many social evils. According to Mr. N. Ram, the President had pointed out that girls were being married at the age of 10-13 and this evil was prevalent in Madhya Pradesh, Rajasthan and Bihar, and perhaps to a small extent elsewhere in India. Such girls had their first child when they reached puberty, had five or six children in many cases, and were crushed by family worries and chores. Maternal and infant mortality rates continued to be high. Such circumstances led to malnutrition and illness. The President had observed poignantly, “They can never come out of poverty.” She had even coined a slogan: “One child marriage has ten ill effects.”

A child marriage not only wrecks the education and health of the couple in general and of the girl in particular, but also derails their natural course of life. Mutual understanding, judgement, love and liking for each other between spouses are possible only at a matured age. A wedding at an immature age blocks all these foundations that are vital for conjugal felicity. So, the children entangled in such wedding, later become a mismatched couple and lead a miserable life. Whenever they see any other couple leading a happy life, they feel disgruntled at their marriage. Due to living in the grip of apathy, they fail either to prosper or even to manage their basic needs. Such a situation often results in the breakdown of their marriage. Their children if any, have to suffer much amidst the separation of parents. In some cases, teenage girls are married off to their maternal uncles. These grooms are usually either elders or widowers. For instance, if a twelve-year-old girl is united with her uncle who is aged 35, she flounders for about 8 years. When she reaches an ideal age for matrimonial life, her husband’s youthhood is past. If he dies before 50 years of age, she becomes a young window. Having lost her health due to early marriage, deliveries of babies, malnutrition and anguish, she is emaciated. Still, she has to toil alone for several years to bring up her children and get them married. If she lacks mettle or falls sick for a long time, the only option before her is to kill her children and commit suicide. Under Indian culture and traditions, a widow, irrespective of her age, cannot remarry in most of the communities. Remarriage is quite rare, especially in rural areas. The life therefore, becomes a hell for many women married in their childhood. Some States in India have made registration of marriages compulsory. It must be strictly enforced in all the states and also other countries which do not have such law, so that age specifications could be followed without any deviation. If any marriage is performed without registration or against the law, it must be declared null and void and those responsible for an illegal marriage must be prosecuted. Besides, an awareness must be created among the people, especially in areas that are prone to child marriage, to avoid this practice. All village committees need to be alerted to prevent child marriage. Only then our children can be protected from treading a perilous path.

H.M. : What is the present trend of child labour?

Richard : Child labour is a widespread problem in India and the steps taken to curb it are inadequate. For instance, 143 child workers were rescued from carpet looms in Uttar Pradesh, where they were working from 1993 to 2003. As the authorities of seven districts of Bihar, the home state of the workers, didn't take action to rehabilitate them, they were forced to live in miserable conditions. Two of them had passed away. Following the intervention by the National Human Rights Commission (NHRC) the Bihar Government rehabilitated 81 child workers. The NHRC directed the district authorities in December 2009 to complete rehabilitation of the remaining 60 persons and submit a report. The police conducted a raid at Jamia Nagar in Delhi on 15th February 2011 and rescued 26 child labourers, aged 8-15, trafficked from Bihar. Eight employers were arrested. India has the largest number of child labourers in the world. According to the National Sample Survey Organization, nearly 16.4 million Indian children aged 5-14 are engaged in various works. The Principal Secretary, Labour Department, Tamil Nadu, has stated that there were 56,589 child labourers in the State in 2004 alone. Under the INDUS Project, a joint venture of Labour Departments of India and the USA, 7,855 child labourers were admitted to regular and special schools. The Employment and Training Department provided skill training to 5,195 child labourers. Efforts need to be taken to ensure employment for all the rehabilitated child labourers after their studies or skill training. The most recent global estimate has revealed that more than 10 crore girls are involved in child labour and many of them are exposed to some of its worst forms. Girls face a lot of problems. They are exposed to danger since much of the work they undertake is hidden from public view. For example Ayesha, a fourteen-year-old girl from Sirsi in Uttara Kannada district of Karnataka State, was allegedly brought to Mangalore against her will and entrusted to one Abdul Salam in an apartment by an agent to serve as domestic help in August 2009. The girl's employers had not allowed her to leave the house and locked her inside whenever they went out of home. After working in the house for 8 days, the girl tried to escape from there on 26th August 2009 when her employers had gone out after locking her inside. In her bid to climb down the balcony of 4th floor apartment, she slipped down and sustained injuries with dislocation of pelvic bone. She was admitted to a hospital where Mr. Geo D' Silva, a member of the District Child Welfare Committee visited her. After ascertaining the facts from the severely traumatised girl, he issued a notice to her employer.

Girls make up the overwhelming number of children engaged in domestic work in the households of other people. Their circumstances make them soft targets for abuse and such reports have become common. Another factor that has emerged now to aggravate the problem is, 'the global financial crisis'. According to a new report- "Give Girls a Chance : Tackling Child Labour- a key to the Future", released on 12th June 2009 by the International Labour Office to mark the 'World Day Against Child Labour', the financial crisis could push an increasing number of children, particularly girls, into child labour. The recent estimates indicate a decrease in the number of children involved in child labour.

But this trend is likely to be reversed by the financial crisis. Because of the increase in poverty as a result of the crisis, poor families with many children may have to choose which children need to stay at home, discontinuing their education. Then they are likely to enter the workforce at an early age. While making decisions on children's education, giving preference to boys is usual in many countries, thereby forcing the girls into the danger of child labour. Other factors that enhance child labour include cuts in the national budgets for education, and a decline in migrant labourers' remittances which often helped to keep children in schools.

H.M. : What are the initiatives taken at international level to forbid child labour?

Richard : The International Labour Organization Convention 182, which addressed the need to prohibit and eliminate the worst forms of child labour, came into existence on 12th June 1999. This day is observed as the 'World Day Against Child Labour'. The Governments worldwide hold some campaigns on this day to focus on the issue but fail to sustain their efforts. The ineptitude of governments and apathy of society have provided a favourable climate for child labour to rise steadily, even ten years after the ILO Convention came into force. The United Nations Convention on the Rights of the Child, to which India is a signatory, was aimed at overall development of children.

H.M. : Is there any law in India to prohibit child labour?

Richard : The Children (Pledging of Labour) Act of February 1933 and Employment of Children Act of 1938 and many legislations against child labour are in place. The Ministry of Labour in New Delhi issued a notification on 10th October 2006 for banning Child Labour and it warned those employing children, of imprisonment. But it has not produced any significant change in the situation of child employment.

H.M. : What are the measures necessary to eradicate child labour?

Richard : The true situation is that the conditions of poverty and lack of awareness impel many parents to prefer child labour to child education. They desire to make money through their children depriving them of their rights to education, play and an amusing childhood. The children therefore, become labourers. To safeguard child rights, the efforts of the Government, judiciary and the police would not be sufficient. The masses need to be sensitised and awareness created in their minds regarding child rights with special focus on their education that will decide their livelihood and path of life. To achieve this, parents having a tendency to divert their children from schools must be personally illuminated and encouraged not to expect any income from their growing children but to educate them at any cost, bearing their future in mind. It could be successfully done by teachers, volunteers of service organizations and members of Women Self-Help Groups. Their persuation by interaction with parents could play a positive role in protection of child rights and elimination of child labour. Children born in rich families could enjoy all comforts even if they are lacking in studies. But those born in poor families are wretched even if they excel in studies. Once a child becomes a dropout, he/she is either forced to seek some work or falls into the trap set by employers who are on the lookout for child labourers. They prefer them because they can extract maximum work from children for 12-16 hours daily for paltry wages. The children who seek work, are usually employed in agricultural farms, livestock units, brick kilns, liquor shops, grocery shops, apparel stores, tea shops, hotels, lodges, cracker units, match units and other small industries. They are treated as slaves, often humiliated and even beaten. Being young and born in poverty-stricken families, the pathetic children have to tolerate any aggressive or even offensive treatment.

Child labour is a national shame. Amassing of wealth constantly by rich people creates more poor people. When common people face unemployment, they are pushed into poverty and in turn, poverty drives them to child labour. Alcoholism, lack of awareness and irresponsible way of living on the part of parents also generate child labour. This social evil cannot be eliminated unless every child gets access to school.

A majority of developed countries have made education compulsory.Universalisation of education is a must. In India, the laws prohibiting child labour are not implemented effectively and rehabilitation of rescued child labourers is not monitored well. The employers and parents of children are insensitive to the laws and government instructions on child labour and brush them aside. The Government authorities are also lax in penalizing the offenders and eradicating child labour. The attention of officials to this social evil is quite rare. In February 2010, a special surprise squad inspected some brick industries in Chengalpat taluk of Kanjeepuram district in Tamil Nadu and identified two child labourers working there. Action was taken against the employers under the Child Labour (Abolition and Prohibition) Act. The squad headed by Mr. M.C. Sampandham, Deputy Inspector of Factories deserves praise. Such action needs to be intensified.

The political will to tackle this problem is not encouraging. The international conventions and existing laws in affected countries must be given more teeth to forbid child labour of any kind. Trade unions must be strengthened to be a watchdog against employment of children in workplaces. Abolition of child labour warrants a multi-dimensional approach. The law on right to education enacted by Indian Parliament is expected to greatly serve to protect children from child labour. Compulsory education will be useful for this purpose. A mechanism must be evolved to watch truants, long absence and part-time employment of school children and ensure that no pupil becomes a dropout. The National Commission for Protection of Child Rights (NCPCR), the most important body to tackle the problem of child labour, is expected to exercise zeal in eradicating this social stigma.

H.M.: The general notion is that prevention of child labour and education of children would make them civilized and prosperous. But a number of teenagers misbehave in spite of education. Will this character have any impact on their later life?

Richard: You might have studied and understood human psychology better than me, especially in respect of students. As I know, the mental qualities in terms of wisdom, listening, grasping, tolerance, response and attitude vastly differ among individuals naturally. Education, though intended to inculcate virtues in children, the syllabi are not designed to suit this purpose. Nowadays the sole aim of parents and teachers is to make students score high marks and become doctors, engineers or bureaucrats. They have little concern about children's growing as good human beings. Preceptors and the culture of paying heed to precepts have almost vanished from educational institutions. Some rare focus on morals by anyone does not reach all children uniformly nor is imbibed well. Misbehaviour of teenagers therefore, is not a matter of surprise. But it is likely to affect their life someway. A British study on the link between adolescent behaviour and the standard of life later, was led by Ian Colman of the University of Alberta, Canada, and the findings were published online by the 'British Medical Journal' on 9th January 2009. The study launched a long-term investigation among 3,652 Britons, who were born in 1946. With their consent, these volunteers were monitored at occasional intervals since their birth, filling in questionnaires about their health, family and professional life. This group was assessed by their teachers at the ages of 13 and 15 and their behaviour graded as having 'severe', 'mild' or 'no' conduct problems. In this group of teenagers, 9.5 per cent had severe problems; 28.8 per cent had mild problems; and 61.7 percent had no problems. Forty years later, the follow-up enquiry found an obvious link between misbehaviour at school and difficulties in adult life. Compared with those without conduct problems, persons having mild form of misbehaviour had problems in life. However, their problems were limited to a lesser degree vis-a-vis those classified as 'severe' who suffered more problems such as leaving school unqualified, doing manual job or remaining unemployed, premature parenthood, strained relationship with spouses, children or friends and divorce. The study therefore, suggested, "adolescent misconduct might adversely affect developing social behaviours and result in pervasive social and mental health difficulties throughout adult life". So, every student must be conscious of good conduct and behaviour and no one should turn naughty.

H.M. : Is there any link between child labour and bonded labour?

Richard : In case of bonded labour, the labourers are caught in the clutches of their employers, who at times obtain written agreements to work permanently under them. To facilitate this, employers lend money to poor labourers and entangle them in debt trap. Then the labourers are drawn to work on the pretext of helping them to clear their loans. But in fact, they are deliberately disabled to repay their loans so that they would toil under their employers for ever. The labourers' wages are too meagre to save money. They always struggle to make both ends meet. They are engaged in hard works in brick kilns, stone quarries, agricultural farms, livestock and poultry units, etc. As their places of work are usually secluded, their contact with the general public is not easy. Further, the employers happen to be criminals with money and muscle power. Under the circumstances, the labourers can't get relieved or escape from them. They are unable even to look after their infants properly. They also grow half-fed to become future child labourers at the same place. In certain cases, parents get money from such employers and send their boys or girls, who become bonded labourers in the course of time. So, the category of 'bonded labourers' includes adults and children of both the sex.

H.M. : Bonded labour is illegal as per law. Does it still continue in India?

Richard : Laws prohibit bonded labour. Nevertheless, this evil continues in many parts of India. In many cases, this offence continues to happen silently. Due to apt locations, it remains inconspicuous. Further, it does not come to light because of the bonded labourers' lack of awareness or fear to make any complaint. Moreover, they are unable to think about an alternative livelihood. The National Human Rights Commission received complaints that bonded labourers were toiling at brick kilns in Ghaziabad district of Uttar Pradesh state. Its investigation team joined by local officials, held an enquiry on the spot and found that 21 members of 3 families were engaged as bonded labourers. The labourers reportedly told the enquiry team that they were paid an advance by a contractor and since then they were being forced to work in lieu of that advance. One family of seven members preferred to continue at the kiln. Other 14 persons were rescued in June 2009 and sent to their native place as they desired.

A petition was filed in the Madras High Court by one Lakshmanan Gounder stating that he and 35 others had been employed in stone-crushing units in Karur district of Tamil Nadu. The employers had allegedly forced them to remain in a shed and paid them only a pittance, threatening to "crush them in the crusher" if they attempted to leave. The complaints made to the South India Cell for protection of human rights and consumer rights, and subsequent orders by the Collector and the Sub-Collector concerned, directions to rehabilitate the labourers and provide them relief did not help them, as they had no effect. The court directed the Collector to "ensure sufficient rehabilitation measures" for the affected labourers to be settled in their native places. It also directed the police officers to ensure sufficient protection for the detenus to go to the crushing units and take back their belongings and to protect their life and freedom. As only 32 of the detenus were produced, the court directed the Police Inspector to produce the four missing persons within four weeks. The High Court gave all the directions in this case in August 2009.

In a moving instance, adolescent Dalit girls in some villages near Madurai in Tamil Nadu, moved to cities and towns such as Coimbatore, Tiruppur, Dindigul, etc. to work in spinning mills. After discontinuing studies, they were pushed into the web of bonded labour. Poor economic conditions, inability of parents to manage, educate and get them married, and social discrimination are the factors that make the girls soft targets for agents. The agents allegedly collect Rs. 2,000 for each girl for placement as a labourer. The girls are toiling in the mills which extract high level of labour from them and pay daily wages ranging from Rs. 35 to Rs. 45. Many mills provide jobs to young unmarried girls for three years under what they call 'Sumangali Thittam' (Scheme to make Mrs.). Many girls fall sick and are unable to complete three years of service. Poverty and caste discrimination, alas, drive the Dalit school girls into bonded labour. The State and Central Governments need to take more steps to identify the bonded labourers. After rescue, the labourers must be properly rehabilitated with job security, so that they can lead a free life and avoid starvation without any inclination to return back to their former employers who had held them for years with no compunction.

H.M.: What is your opinion about the dowry system that plays havoc with the lives of women?

Richard: The dowry system in society very often takes its toll on women. One Sangeetha was married to Senthil Kumar of Veerarakkiam village in Tiruchy district of Tamil Nadu in 1999. Since their marriage, Senthil Kumar and his parents were allegedly harassing Sangeetha, demanding dowry. Being unable to withstand their harassment, Sangeetha committed self-immolation in 2001. The youth and his parents were sentenced to seven-year rigorous imprisonment in July 2009. In another case, a woman named Padmavathi threw her two children into a well and committed suicide by jumping into it in a village near Papparapatti in Dharmapuri district of Tamil Nadu on 10th June 2009. Padmavathi took the extreme step following pressure from her in-laws to bring gold ornaments for the children from her parents. Her in-laws were arrested. These are only examples of hundreds of deaths connected with dowry, happening every year in India. Such deaths are caused not only by suicides but also by murders mostly in the form of burning alive. Since the beginning of the 21st century, the demand of dowry has been modernised in some so-called civilized families. For instance, the parents of a youth tell the parents of the damsel who is sought for marriage, "You need not give jewels or cash as dowry, since we do not expect them. It is enough if you just provide a house and a car for the comfort of your daughter". We also find some parents saying, "We don't want any dowry. But we have already spent a lot of money to educate our son. He now desires to pursue his higher education abroad. If you (the girl's parents) can arrange to fulfil his ambition and settle them abroad, we shall agree to their marriage". Do such parents educate their son for the welfare of his future wife?

A software engineer in Bangalore who was given the pseudonym 'Vijayalakshmi' for reporting, was married in 2008. Vijayalakshmi's husband and his parents were not asking her parents for cash or jewellery. There was no demand for dowry. But the educated upper middle class family of Vijayalakshmi's husband was forcing her to do a Hotel Management Course in Australia against her will. The expenses reckoned at Rs. 20 lakh was to be thrust upon her father. This case exemplifies subtle attempts to innovate and adopt modern means of extracting dowry.

The dowry system is an age-old practice in almost all communities. Formerly it was regarded just as a presentation to the groom. But in recent years, the dowry system has escalated into a lucrative business involving the holy marriage. It has spread its cruel wings to annex castes and religions which traditionally remained outside its ambit, and stimulate them to embrace the evil practice (of dowry). The system has assumed monstrous proportions. By virtue of engaging brokers, parents of youths trawl through a state or more for rich and employed girls. Many parents prefer girls with no siblings in order to enable their sons inherit the property of the girls' parents. In the families of low-income groups, the dowry-related problems are found less vis-a-vis the families of middle or higher income groups. A youth's parents of middle or upper middle class fleece as much dowry as they can before marriage, making the bride's parents financially weak and exhausted. Out of ardour and necessity to get the girl's marriage done, her parents allow their resources dwindle away. They even sell their property to meet the marriage expenses including dowry. After the weeding is solemnized, they heave a sigh of relief. But the post-marriage scenario astounds them. The groom's parents persistently demand various things, jewellery or money for their own purpose. Besides, on every occasion such as festival, delivery of baby, ceremony connected with it, etc., the woman's parents are subjected to extreme hardship. If they fail to meet even a single demand, it sows the seeds for harassment of the young woman. Eventually, the woman's husband and in-laws pour hatred on her. As her parents struggle to manage their family and look after the other children, she becomes a helpless victim. Being unable to withstand mounting pressure and harassment, she either eommits suicide or quits the family and returns back to her parents seeking divorce. If she is mollified and convinced to reunite with her husband, such compromise does not endure in the absence of love and liking for her in the hearts of her spouse and in-laws. They view her as a junk, and a resoluteness to eliminate her at all cost is implanted in their minds. They therefore, resort to domestic violence either to drive her out or set her ablaze. They don't hesitate to commit any crime against her. For example, a young woman who hailed from Tiruchi in Tamil Nadu, was married to a professional in the United States. One day, she was pushed out of the running car by her husband in 2007. She sustained grievous injuries and was admitted to a hospital. Anyone can imagine the magnitude of her parents' misery on hearing this information. The victim's father rushed to the US, stayed at her bedside for a week and brought her to India for further treatment. Her affliction made her parents melancholic.

Dowry has become a daily affair among the people. Harassment based on regular or frequent demand of dowry is quite common. But many events are ignored or suppressed. Barring them, thousands of cases of dowry harassment are dealt with by courts. It is a matter of grave concern that women with the title of 'mother-in-law' spearhead the harassment of young women who are married to their sons. It is they who even propose another marriage for their sons by terminating the first marriage aiming to collect dowry once again. They are not even conscious of their daughters either married off to somebody else or waiting for marriage. Most of the mothers-in-law adopt only double standard towards their daughters and daughters-in-law. Some social activists think that more laws are necessary to curb the practice of dowry. But I feel that it won't solve the problem. The present Dowry Prohibition Act in India, though regarded as stringent, has not proved to be an effective deterrent to the offenders. Many people don't make a complaint about dowry because both giving and accepting dowry are punishable.

The Joint Committee of Indian Parliament on the Dowry Prohibition Bill recommended in 1959, deterrent punishment for persons offering or receiving dowry. It recommeded that both fine and imprisonment be inflicted on the offenders. The laws against dowry were enacted with high spirit. But the laws are not fully fruitful due to non-cooperation of people and occasional misuse by some women to settle their score. It is enough if the authorities take steps for effective implementation of the existing laws regarding dowry and also prevent any misuse. Justice Markandey Katju observed that those burning women for dowry deserved to be hanged. Though such remark of a Supreme Court Judge seems to be passionate, it is logical and sensible. The dowry system has marred the peace of several young women and destroyed some of them. It has not only forced many to remain spinsters but also taken a heavy toll on married women. In this context, the village Panchayat of Nilambur in Kerala State has embarked on a unique project against dowry in January 2009. It has resolved to eliminate this social barrier in a year and become India's first dowry-free village. This is a highly commendable move which can surely usher in a revolution in that village, and is worthy of emulation by all people in India and elsewhere to get rid of this social stigma.

H.M.: Thank you very much for giving me so much information on this important topic.

Richard: Not at all, sir. I must be thankful to you for your enthusiasm in such societal issues.

H.M.: Charli........

Charli: Yes, boss. What can I do for you?

H.M.: You can do nothing but suspend your loquacity and come with me. Let us go home.

Charli: I shall come with you, provided you make a promise to help me by giving Rs. 500.

H.M.: Why do you need money now?

Charli: I have to meet some personal expense.

H.M.: What is your covert expense? Don't keep me in suspense.

Charli: After your terming it as 'covert', how can I reveal my purpose?

Richard: (Towards the H.M.) Is he your jester?

H.M.: No, I am not a king or duke to have a jester. He is merely a Chatterbox.

Charli: It is a half lie, which I can't agree with.

Richard: Is there any percentage in lie? Your retort is implicit.

Charli: Yes, of course. Lying is not always complete. Sometimes it is partial. That's what my boss has done.

Richard: I am still perplexed by your contention.

Charli: To be honest, he may not be a king or duke. But I am not only his jester but also his extraofficial assistant, room-mate, friend, guide, messenger, escort, bodyguard, cook, sweeper and so on. But in spite of my holding so many posts, he is paying me only a single salary.

H.M.: You are getting from me, one salary in cash and many salaries in kind.

Sofia: How is it possible, sir? What does he get in kind?

H.M.: It is only food. His diet is worth five times the value of his salary in cash.

Charli: Please don't imitate me to jest.

Richard: The denouement regarding your need of money is yet to be exposed.

Charli: Oh! It is just that I must pay for an advertisement in the media projecting myself as one seeking a girl to marry without dowry.

All are laughing at him.

Sofia: I have prepared dinner, sir. Please have it for our pleasure.

After dinner, the headmaster and Charli return home.

11

RAGGING IN EDUCATIONAL INSTITUTIONS

The headmaster and Charli arrive at Akash's home.

Akash: Good evening, sir.

H.M.: Good evening, Akash.

Akash: (Turning to his father Devaraj) This is our headmaster, Dad.

Devaraj: Hello, welcome sir. Please take a seat.

H.M.: Thank you. How many children do you have?

Devaraj: We have two daughters and a son. Akash's elder sister has been married off recently. His younger sister is studying 8th standard. She has now gone to a friend's home.

Akash's mother greets the headmaster and provides a cool drink for all those present.

H.M.: May I know about your occupation?

Devaraj: I am a lecturer in social science.

H.M.: That's nice. I would like to hear from you about an important aspect of students' activities in colleges.

Devaraj: Oh, yes; by all means, sir.

H.M.: Could you please give me an account of ragging incidents in your college and elsewhere in the recent past?

Devaraj: There was only one ragging incident in our college last year. A first year student was forced by three of his seniors to drink water added with salt. When the matter was brought to the knowledge of our principal, he convened a meeting of our college teachers and discussed the problem. Though the offence was mild in nature, we didn't like to condone it. We resolved to avoid laxity and nip ragging in the bud. So, all the three senior students who indulged in ragging were dismissed from the college. This ruthless action was notified to the parents of all other students with a caution to discipline their sons or daughters. Since then there was no more incident of ragging in our college. However, this abominable culture is widely found in most of the educational institutions above high school level.

Nadiminti Triveni was a student of the Government Agricultural Engineering College at Bapatla town in Andhra Pradesh. She attempted suicide citing ragging by her seniors in the hostel over a period of time. Following a complaint by her parents, four girl students named by her as the offenders were arrested by the police on 14th March 2009. The Revenue Divisional Officer and Tahsildar at Tenali met Triveni in the Intensive Care Unit of a private hospital at Guntur where she was recovering, and questioned her about the episode.

P.S. Akhil Dev, a 19-year-old first year student at the PSG Arts and Science College at Coimbatore in Tamil Nadu, was brutally ragged by five of his senior collegemates on 7th March 2009. With serious injuries to eyes and ears, the victim was battling trauma. His parents didn't wish to send him back to the college, nor the student had the courage to step into the campus. The student's father, a novelist who had respect for the institution, expressed displeasure that the college authorities felt it imperative to safeguard its name instead of bringing the offenders to book. He added that his son was beaten in earlier occasions also and alleged that snatching money from and committing atrocities to the juniors were the habits of some senior students which warranted immediate action. He wanted to ensure that such harassment would never happen to anyone else in the future. But R.P. Kumar, a B.Com. student was ragged in the same college on 13th July 2009.

In a ragging incident at a residential school in Himachal Pradesh in the first week of May 2009, many junior students were brutally beaten up by their seniors. Seven seniors who committed the crime were sent back home. The State Government ordered a magisterial enquiry into the incident. In another ragging incident at a medical college in the same State, a first year student was horrified by a senior in September 2009. The victim's complaint to the principal proved futile. As there was no action, the mischievous senior student felt no deterrent to his misdeed and beat his junior to death. In another case, a first year Engineering student of an institute at Noida near Delhi, was beaten up badly with iron rods by his seniors when he tried to prevent them from ragging his batchmate in the hostel on 26th May 2009. The college authorities, after an enquiry, found ten students guilty and expelled nine of them. One student was suspended from the college for six months.

In his writ petition submitted to the Madras High Court, Mr. Abdul Kareem hailing from Ernakulam district of Kerala, stated that his son Mahin Sha who was enrolled for B.Tech. in Mechanical Engineering at the Bharathiyar College of Engineering and Technology at Karaikal in Puducherry State and stayed in the hostel on the college campus, was tortured in the guise of ragging by some seniors, who also extracted money from him. When Mahin Sha withdrew money from an ATM in December 2008 and was on his way to the college counter to pay uniform fees, he was kidnapped by two students who tortured him using an iron box, burning cigarettes and a blade. When he fell unconscious, the sadists took his money and fled. Apprehensive of further assault, Mohin Sha later returned home leaving his paraphernalia behind in the hostel. The college authorities paid no heed to Mr. Kareem's request for return of his donation of Rs. 1.75 lakh and action against the culprits nor did they forward his complaint to the police, he alleged. Mr. Kareem sought a direction to the college authorities to forward his complaint of ragging of his son to the police and pay him a compensation of Rs. 5 lakh for the mental agony suffered besides issue of Transfer certificate and return of all original documents of his son. The court ordered notice of motion.

On a complaint lodged by Ramakrishna, a junior student of Sri Venkateswara University at Tirupati in Andhra Pradesh, police arrested eight M.Com. final year students on 18th July 2009 on charges of ragging under Andhra Pradesh Prohibition of Ragging Act 1987. Eighteen-year-old Bhagath, a first year student in a private college at Coimbatore allegedly sustained injuries in ragging and assault on 13th August 2009. The city police arrested four students who were remanded to judicial custody. The Dibrugarh University in the state of Assam slapped punishments on 10 students including two girls on 14th August 2009 for allegedly ragging their juniors. The punishments included expulsion, rustication for two semesters, fines to the tune of Rs. 20,000, withholding scholarship, etc. Four students of the Medical College at Coimbatore ragged three juniors on 19th and eleven on 21st October 2009 in the college hostel. The victims were reportedly injured. After enquiries by the hostel warden and the Ragging Monitoring Committee, the Dean preferred a complaint. The city police arrested 4 offenders and remanded them to custody. They were also suspended from the college.

Three senior students of Government Physiotherapy College at Tiruchi in Tamil Nadu, ragged their juniors. One of the affected students was represented by his father by making a complaint to the college authorities. Following this, an enquiry into the affair was held by a committee. After the enquiry, the college principal placed the three senior students under suspension on 26th October 2009. On getting information about the incident, the police arrested the trio and registered a case against them. In another incident, three students of the Siddhartha Medical College at Vijayawada in Andhra Pradesh who were pursuing MBBS final year in 2007, ragged and harassed two students of BDS first year on 19th June 2007, besides threatening G. Satish Kumar, a student of BDS final year then, who went to the rescue of the duo, with dire consequences. Mr. Satish Kumar lodged a complaint with the police stating what actually happened. A magistrate court awarded one-year imprisonment and a fine of Rs.1,000 each to the three offenders on 12th November 2009, while they were house-surgeons in the medical college.

One Shoban Babu of Melur in Madurai district was doing first year in Mechanical Engineering at the Hindustan College of Engineering at Ottahakaal Mandapam, Coimbatore and staying in the hostel. Some senior students had demanded money from him for a party on 22nd October 2009. Following Babu's refusal, they reportedly ragged and threatened him. In the wake of his complaint to the hostel warden, the seniors took him to the fourth floor and allegedly threw him from there. He became unconscious with injured spinal cord and fractured leg. He regained consciousness only after two and a half months. He then moved the Madras High Court seeking a direction to the State Government to pay an interim compensation of Rs. 5 lakh for treatment. In another shocking case, K. Sridhar, a first year student of a private arts college at Bommaiyarpalayam near villupuram in Tamil Nadu, died on 5th February 2010 following self-immolation that he committed the previous day after allegedly being ragged.

In spite of stringent laws, firm steps and the heightened media focus, the menace of ragging in educational institutions across the country (India) has increased in 2009. The number of ragging cases reported in the media in a year from July 2008 to June 2009 was 88.

There were 12 ragging deaths and 5 attempted suicides. In the previous year, there were 11 deaths and 5 attempted suicides out of 89 cases reported. Between July 2003 and June 2008, there were 28 ragging-related deaths and 11 attempted suicides. An analysis of the last five years' reports indicates that the States of Andhra Pradesh, West Bengal and Uttar Pradesh are the worst hit.

H.M.: What are the steps taken to contain this evil practice?

Devaraj: Ragging is an 'imported culture'. Perhaps, this practice was started in colleges and institutes with a sensible idea of making the juniors shed their bashfulness and feel comfortable in the midst of moving with their seniors. But ironically, it has transgressed the bounds of decency and become an evil. Ragging is now a sort of human rights violation in the name of fun and college tradition. Ms. Pratibha Patil, the President of India has said, "I saw the agony of parents who lost their child in a ragging incident. These are intelligent and brilliant students. Those new students who are subjected to ragging can go through a range of emotions from fear to humiliation. It is a crime against humanity". She added that ragging was emerging as a major problem on campuses. Expressing deep concern over the spate of ragging incidents in the country, she called for a comprehensive legislation to end the menace.

The Supreme Court of India appointed a committee against ragging headed by Mr. R.K. Raghavan, former director of the Central Bureau of Investigation. Two cases of ragging-one in the Dr. Rajendra Prasad Government Medical College in Himachal Pradesh, and the other in the Bapatla Agricultural Engineering College in Andhra Pradesh came before the Supreme Court. These two cases were referred to the R.K. Raghavan committee, which submitted its report to the court after an enquiry. The committee wanted tough action to be taken against those indulging in ragging. Any lenience or misplaced sympathy would only lead to its aggravation. At the same time, Mr. R.K. Raghavan felt that a psychological approach combining 'deterrence with rehabilitation' was desirable in handling the menace. Based on the report, the court issued a series of directions and guidelines to deal with the menace of ragging in educational institutions, on 8th May 2009. The court asked all states to set up two committees on campuses–one on ragging and the other on alcoholism. The first committee consisting of mental health specialists and educationists will examine the impact of ragging on young students as well as the reason why seniors torment their juniors. It also recommended urgent and mandatory mental health measures to be implemented in, and practised by schools, colleges and all educational and vocational institutions. A close link between serious cases of ragging and alcohol consumption was detected during the investigation of certain cases. So, the second committee was meant for dealing with cases of alcoholism. The Bench directed that every college should have a psychiatrist to provide counselling to students who indulge in ragging and take de-addiction measures in cases of alcoholism and there must be monitoring cells at the university level. A proposal submitted by the Ministry of Human Resource Development to set up a toll-free helpline to enable ragging victims across the country to seek immediate help was endorsed by the court. The Bench asked the HRD Ministry to set up a central crisis-hotline and anti-ragging database saying, "Once the database/crisis-hotline is operative, State Governments should amend their anti-ragging statutes to include provisions that place penal consequences on institutional heads who do not take timely steps in the prevention of ragging and punishing of those who rag." The court's view that the primary responsibility of curbing ragging rests with the educational institutions themselves, has been made clear. The court's directions are very appropriate to tackle the social evil of ragging.

'THE HINDU' organized a round table on "Beyond Raghavan Committee Report: How to stop ragging" at the Administrative Staff College of India at Hyderabad on 18th July 2009. Mentoring the juniors, addressing the deviant behaviour of seniors and mercilessly applying the law of the land were among some of the suggestions made to check the growing menace of ragging in educational institutions. The University Grants Commission was poised to implement tough anti-ragging rules. The penalty proposed to entail a fine of upto Rs. 2.5 lakh, expulsion from the institution and a bar on future admission of those who indulge in ragging.

Prof. Raj Kachroo, founder of 'Aman Satya Kachroo Trust', has been playing an active role in spreading awareness about ragging after losing his son to a ragging incident. He said that the recent Supreme court judgement placed the onus on the principals and administrators of colleges to prevent ragging in their campuses. College administration authorities had been framing regulations for some time, but there was very little communication from students and others to officials. To facilitate easy communication, a website was made available for students of Tamil Nadu colleges to allow them provide information on ragging in their colleges to an independent body, which would alert the college administration without revealing the student's identity. It was desired to extend this strategy to other states. In Tamil Nadu, the Police Department set up anti-ragging cells in all districts in June 2009. It was in a bid to contain ragging. The strategy was to deploy police personnel in plain clothes in the close vicinity of colleges as part of a statewide exercise ahead of admissions to professional and other courses. The Additional Director General of Police (Law and Order) said, " Besides making discreet enquiries, we will maintain close vigil and interact with students, teachers and the management periodically. Where instances of teasing or mischief come to light, the police will inform the college authorities for appropriate action. If cognizable, we will arrest those involved". This kind of effort by the police deserves compliment. While taking action against the offenders, there should be no discrimination on the grounds of sex because girls also indulge in ragging. The punishment therefore, must be equal to boys and girls who rag their juniors. In addition to all these steps, anti-ragging awareness meetings may be held in colleges with the participation of VIPs, actors, singers, players, etc. The ill-effects of ragging could be explained to the students in a smooth and convincing manner. It could be a deterrent to the students indulging in this uncivilized evil.

H.M.: Thank you very much. Charli......

Charli does not respond to his call. He is sitting morosely in a corner and contemplating.

H.M.: Charli ..... Charli .....

Charli wakes up to his call now but has a mute look at him.

H.M.: What is amiss? Are you not well?

Charli: I am all right, sir. But I feel nostalgic for the college where I studied.

H.M.: You ought to have continued in the college.

Charli: It was not my fault. I was forced to quit the college by the brutal act of four persons.

Devaraj: What is the use of thinking about it now?

Charli: I am seriously thinking about rejoining the college.

Devaraj: Do you desire to continue your studies?

Charli: It is not my aim because I am already pursuing my degree course under Distance Education'. In fact, I want to attend the college at least for a month.

Devaraj: What is your purpose of one-month learning?

Charli: I was subjected to ragging by four senior students. In the wake of that incident, I left the college. I want revenge for the humiliation I suffered, by paying them in their own coin now.

H.M.: Those particular students might have been either relieved from the college or promoted to higher classes. How can you rag them now?

Charli: In that case, I will rag the junior students as it usually happens.

H.M.: If you do so, how can you perceive it as a revenge?

Charli: I can at least mollify myself by such action.

H.M.: It is a stupid idea. In fact, it will rebound on you because if you join the college again, you will be treated as a fresher and subjected to ragging once again.

Charli is startled by this presage and makes no reply.

Devaraj: How did your seniors rag you?

Charli: It was an embarrassing event.

Akash: You may share your experience with us so that I can learn to escape ragging menace in the future.

Charli: As I was a day student, my seniors struggled to have access to me. Time and again, they were at my heels. one day, they overpowered me near the college gate-stripped me naked and bade me to run away. I was running in the street like an insane boy.

Akash: What did happen after that incident?

Charli: Nothing happened because thenceforth I never returned to the college for class, but only once to get my Transfer Certificate.

After dinner, the headmaster and Charli return home.

12

CORRUPTION AMONG OFFICIALS/POLITICIANS

The headmaster and Charli arrive at Ajit's home.

Ajit: Good morning, sir.

H.M.: Good morning, Ajit.

Ajit: I am happy at your early visit since I expected you to be here only in the evening.

H.M.: As I am free today, I chose to come here now itself.

Ajit: It's nice, sir. (Turning to his brother Gopinath) Please meet our headmater. (Towards the H.M.) He is my elder brother, sir.

Gopinath: Hello, sir. Please be seated.

H.M.: Thank you. Could I know about your family?

Ajit's mother welcomes the headmaster and provides coffee.

Gopinath: She is our mother, sir. We have a sister who is elder than Ajit. She is pursuing B.Sc. degree. She has gone to a relative's home today along with my wife.

H.M.: Are you employed or engaged in business?

Gopinath: I am an Inspector in the Directorate of Vigilance and Anti-Corruption (DVAC).

H.M.: That's fine. You are holding a vital job. May I hear from you about the problems you are dealing with?

Gopinath: Certainly, sir. I can explain whatever I know.

H.M.: In spite of anti-corruption establishments functioning at Cental and State levels, there is a general public perception that corruption is prevalent in all government departments. Do you agree with this view? If so, can you give some examples?

Gopinath: Nobody can deny this perception. Corruption cases are dealt with by the designated law-enforcing agencies only on some clues or information about the happening or impending offence. The bribe-takers are very discreet in their dealings while the givers feel complacency, unmindful of the law and the disastrous consequences of their misdeed. Owing to mutual understanding or agreement, bribery is usally clandestine. It comes to our notice only when we get some clue about a suspicious situation or if the aggrieved party makes a complaint about the corrupt official following some disagreement between them. In such circumstances, corruption is rampant in all the Government depatments. Besides, irregularities and malpractices have become common. It is not possible to analyse the events of all bribery cases that came to light. However, I shall give you a few examples of corruption cases that happened in the recent past.

The Regional Passport Officer of Chennai-Sumathi Ravichandran, her husband who is a Medical Officer in the Chennai Corporation and two travel agents were arrested on 25th April 2009 on charges of corruption for issue of passport. Further, the Central Bureau of Investigation searched the residence of the RPO and the clinic of her husband. It unearthed a racket and seized cash and documents. In another case, Dr. M. Ezhilarasi, Director of Medical and Rural Health Services (Employees State Insurance) was arrested by Anti-Corruption officials on 6th August 2009, while receiving Rs. 8.53 lakh as bribe in connection with a Rs.15 crore contract for durg supply. Five employees of different drug companies were also arrested. In yet another incident, Dr. K. Senthilvel Murugan, Deputy Director (Tuberculosis), Kanyakumari district, data entry operator Balamurugan and Ravindra of Madurai had collected huge sums as bribe from candidates intending to appear for an interview for the posts of laboratory technician and laboratory supervisor. They boarded the 'Kanyakumari Express' train to Chennai for delivering the money to Dr. Subburam, Additional Director of Medical and Rural Health Services/ State Tuberculosis Officer of Tamil Nadu. On a tip-off, the Joint Director, Directorate of Vigilance and Anti-Corruption (DVAC) swung into action and instructed to form two teams to investigate the complaint. The accused were intercepted on the train and Rs. 17.13 lakh was recovered from them on 9th September 2009. As they pointed the finger at Dr. Subburam, the police searched his room in an official guesthouse and seized Rs. 3.2 lakh. Preliminary enquiries revealed that the accused had demanded a minimum of Rs. 1.5 lakh from each aspiring candidate and the money was collected one week before the date of interview. Though Balamurugan was not aware of the conspiracy, some money was recovered from his bag. So, he was arrested and let on bail. All others were arrested and remanded to judicial custody.

The Joint Commissioner of Hindu Religious and Charitable Endowments (HRCE) Department of Tamil Nadu, Mr. Sundaram heard a revision petition filed by one D. Sekar to restore the first honours and rights of a temple to his community people. He allegedly demanded Rs. 2 lakh as bribe to deliver a judgement in favour of the petitioner. When his Bench clerk N. Sivaraj took Rs. 50,000 as first instalment of the bribe on his behalf on 26th June 2009, officials of the DVAC arrested both of them. Besides searching the official chambers of the accused, the DVAC official scoured their houses too. An Assistant Commissioner of the same HRCE department at Salem had allegedly demanded Rs. 10,000 to permit a few 'archakas' (temple priests) to perforem 'poojas' (rituals) in a temple. Following a complaint, the DVAC laid a trap and apprehended the official on 10th September 2009. An Inspector of the Central Crime Branch (Land Grabbing Wing) Mr. T.C. Ruskin and Head Constable S. Mohan were caught redhanded while taking a bribe of Rs. 2 lakh from an accused and arrested by the DVAC police in Chennai on 17th December 2008.

The officials working in the Baggage-Unit of the Air Cargo complex in Chennai were allegedly taking bribes from passengers for charging less or no duty at all. G. Kumar, an outsider, acted as mediator. A special team of the CBI conducted a series of raids and seizures on 23rd November 2009. A total of Rs. 59,400 was seized from customs officials on duty at the complex and Rs. 16 lakh in unaccounted cash and 2 kg of gold were detected on their premises. G. Kumar and nine customs officials, including four Superintendents were arrested on 24th November. All the nine officials were placed under suspension by their authorities.

Corruption among high officials is quite common nowadays. For instance, a middleman had demanded Rs. 20 lakh from the owner of an Engineering College in Andhra Pradesh on behalf of a Member-Secretary of the All India Council for Technical Education (AICTE) for inspection and approval of his college. While accepting the first instalment of Rs. 5 lakh on 16th July 2009, both of them were arrested by the Central Bureau of Investigation (CBI). A search operation was conducted at the Delhi office and Hyderabad residence of the official and the middleman's residence at Ongole in Andhra Pradesh. A sum of Rs. 9 lakh in cash and documents relating to bank accounts and properties were recovered. In another case, the owner of an Engineering College in Faridabad in Haryana alleged that the Regional Officer of the AICTE had demanded money for processing an increase in the intake of seats. The complainant was reportedly harassed and forced to give money. He brought this to the knowledge of the chairman, Adviser and Deputy Director, but no action was taken by them. The CBI registered a case against all the accused under the Prevention of Corruption Act, 1988. The residences and official premises of all the accused were being searched. The AICTE Chairman R.A.Yadav was placed under suspension to ensure that he did not influence the investigation in the bribery case registered against him. Mr Ketan Desai, President of the Medical Council of India (MCI) and three others were arrested by the CBI in a Rs. 2-crore bribery case on 23rd April 2010. The CBI Director pointed out large-scale systemic corruption in the MCI. The tainted MCI was dissolved on 15th May 2010. The Chairman and Managing Director of National Aluminium Company (NALCO), Abhay Kumar Srivastava, who was found receiving bribes from bidders and suppliers of the Public Sector Undertaking, his wife and two accomplices were arrested by the CBI on 25th February 2011. About 10kg of gold bricks, jewellery valued at around Rs. 2.13 crore and Rs. 30 lakh in cash were recovered from them. The Government later suspended Mr. Srivastava from his post. Mr. Ratan Pal Singh Bhatia, an executive of a company was also arrested subsequently on charge of a payment of Rs. 20 lakh as bribe to Mr. Srivastava.

Dr. R. Radha krishnan, vice-chancellor of Anna University-Coimbatore, was suspended in a case of alleged corruption against him. A review meeting of officials of the Food Corporation of India (FCI) was held in Chennai on 18th September 2009. Following a tip-off that Area Managers who came from differnt parts of the state, had brought money to be given as bribe to the General Manager and Deputy General Manager, the CBI's Anti-Corruption Branch raided the venue of the meeting and seized the alleged bribe money of Rs. 1.5 lakh. After recording statements from the accused and witnesses, the agency registered cases against the GM, DGM and six Area Managers. The FCI placed all the eight officials under suspension on 24th September 2009. The Anti-Corruption Bureau (ACB) of Andhra Pradesh had kept close tabs on K. Gopalakrishna, Special Secretary in the Legislative Assembly for many weeks. Finally, teams of the ACB swooped on seven premises, four in Hyderabad city and three in Nellore, pertaining to him and conducted simultaneous searches on 11th February 2010. The teams found that the official who had started his career as typist in 1978 and risen to higher position, held various assets amassed during his service that were worth over Rs. 15 crore.

Corruption in judiciary is an abominable offence that takes place often covertly but seldom comes to light. Justice Nirmal Yadav of the Punjab and Haryana High Court, for example was subjected to a probe in January 2009 by a three-member in house committee into the alleged delivery of Rs. 15 lakh in cash by a person named Prakash Ram. In her appeal to the Chief Justice of India against the manner and scope of the probe, the judge categorically stated that the cash that was delivered at the residence of Justice Nirmaljit Kaur as deposed by Prakash Ram, was not meant for her and that she was targeted due to similarity in their first names. Though it is a controversy to be dealt with by a competent court, it is a matter to worry about. Justice P.D. Dinakaran, Chief Justice of the Karnataka High Court was one among the five persons recommended for elevation as judges of the Supreme Court of India. It was alleged that the extent of land possessed by him was approximately 500 acres and there had been vast encroachment of Government land in Tamil Nadu. The Chief Justice of India had requested the State Government to look into the allegations and send a report. Based on the findings of the District Collector that there had been an encroachment of 197 acres, the Tamil Nadu Government sent an adverse report. Consequently, the Supreme Court Collegium headed by the Chief Justice of India decided on 10th October 2009 to put on hold, the elevation of Justice P.D. Dinakaran, that was recommended on 27th August 2009. The Cental Government later refused in early December 2009 to elevate him as a judge of the Supreme Court. Happening of such allegations against judges in the venerable judiciary is a matter of grave concern for all the people who trust the courts as guardians of unbiased justice.

Corruption in the banking sector is a young malady. It has infected some personnel in recent years. Former Chairman and Managing Director of the Indian Bank M. Gopalakrishnan and a former Assistant General Manager of the Bank A.V. Shanmugasundaram were accused of conspiracy and misuse of their official positions to sanction credit facilities to a company, flouting the regulations. After trial, the additional judge for the CBI cases in Chennai found that they had cheated the bank and caused a loss of Rs. 8.67 crore to the bank. The judge ordered M. Gopalakrishnan and A.V. Shanmugasundaram to pay a fine of Rs. 70 lakh and Rs. 80 lakh respectively and sentenced both the accused to undergo 14 years rigorous imprisonment. In another case in the banking sector, one Bhoomi Kumaran, manager of Kuravupulam branch of Canara Bank in Nagapattinam district of Tamil Nadu, was arrested while taking a bribe of Rs. 5,000 from a farmer on 20th January 2010 for sanctioning crop loan to him. Such instances exemplify prevalence of corruption in the banking sector. Corruption is plaguing the Public Sector Undertakings too. For instance, P. Kirupanandan, General Manager of the Neyveli Lignite Corporation was arrested in his official chamber by officials of the Anti-Corruption Branch of the CBI, soon after he took a bribe of Rs. 50,000 from a contractor on 25th February 2010. During searches at his residence in Chennai, investigators seized Rs. 22 lakh, bank passbooks showing a balance of Rs. 16 lakh and movable/immovable property totally worth about Rs. 1 Crore. The accused was remanded to judicial custody.

As for Information Technology Sector, though there is no report of bribery, it has not been spared by scandal. The embezzlement in 'Satyam Computers' - India's fourth largest Information Technology company, was far beyond anybody's belief. The accounts of the company were fudged to the tune of Rs. 7,106 crore over a period of several years. The company's Chairman B. Ramalinga Raju admitted the gigantic fraud and resigned. As Serious Fraud Investigation Office (SFIO) and Securities and Exchange Board of India (SEBI) embarked on probe and strigent action against him was imminent, he surrendered to the police. All opposition political parties reproached the Andhra Pradesh Government of having prior knowledge of the crime. The British international business newspaper 'Financial Times' said, "The $ 1 billion fraud perpetrated by Satyam Computer Services will not only throw the $ 40 billion software and outsourcing industry into a tailspin, but also raise disturbing questions about the risks of doing business in India - and even the sustainability of the country's much-vaunted growth miracle". As I told you a little while ago, I have recounted only a few instances of corruption. Since you are on the verge of retirement from government service and much elder than me, you might have known about various aspects of bribery and corruption in government departments better than me. Hence I should like to hear your views on this issue.

H.M.: Mr. Gulzarilal Nanda, a former Prime Minister of India, during his previous tenure as Home Minister, vowed early in the 1960s to root out corruption. But after about two years, he confessed his inability to succeed in accomplishing his goal. However, corruption cases were rare and at a low ebb in his day. His sensitivity to and concern about corruption symbolized the honesty of political leaders of his period and how seriously they viewed this evil. But this situation has now become a thing of the past. Corruption and bribery began to spread over all government departments and take root like a banyan tree around 1970. Within two decades, the evil permeated the entire government machinery. Since 1990, corruption has reached monstrous proportions. It has now become a 'culture' and routine affair since neither the bribe-giver nor the taker is scrupulous in their dealing. As you said, only when there is a row between them, their misdeed leaks out. These days, no government department functions with a clean slate. But there are honest officials in every department whose percentage is unfortunately very low.

In the Education Department, teachers are not involved in corruption perhaps because of having no scope to take bribes as they are dealing with only pupils. But they have to give bribes to the officers and staff of the same department for taking action on any personal application for transfer, sanction of loan, etc., which they are legally entitled to. Such intra-departmental bribery is happening in all departments. This activity is the epitome of the vile trait of corrupt officials. It also vividly shows how far they would coerce the staff of other departments and the public into giving bribe. In the Department of Employment and Training, the candidates have to pay money for registration of name, renewal of registration, etc. There are high 'special rates' for manipulation of seniority in the records, interview call and selection for vacant posts.

Once upon a time i.e. upto the 1960s, the Department of Medical and Health Service was very honest. Drugs and equipment were supplied to all government hospitals by the government-owned Medical Stores Depot (MSD) as per the indents placed by the institutions. Medicines and equipment were acquired from reputable companies and storage and distribution were done at State level. There was no personal contact or link between the officials of the department and manufacturers. Nobody thought of any malpractice. The quality of the products were maintained at high standards. But eventually the system was changed. Officers at regional level were authorised to choose the drugs and equipment for their areas and place orders to the pharmaceutical companies. This is where the trouble started. As the companies mushroomed, their representatives began to call on the higher authorities in the depatment first to get their products approved and then to get orders for supplies. The agents of companies vying with each other for getting bulk orders, coaxed the top officials into placing their indents by virtue of bribery. This malpractice has been growing constantly. It has encouraged the manufacturers to compromise on quality standards of their products, putting the lives of patients at risk. They feel very comfortable in the absence of strict quality control measures and laws like those in China under which a head of the concerned department was executed for laxity in enforcement of quality control on food items and medicines, and amassing of wealth disproportionate to his legitimate income. Besides, the drugs supplied to government hospitals are not fully dispensed to genuine patients. A part of the supplied products is often misued. Until the middle of the 20th century, medical services were regarded as a holy profession and doctors as proxies for God. They lived up to peoples' expectations and displayed compassion for patients with selfless service. With the depletion of such doctors, the situation began to change in the 1970s. Getting treatment for almost all ailments from a single doctor at cheap cost was also phased out by the growing number of specialists whose treatment at times clashes with that of some other doctor for a different problem and leads to complications, The doctors from the next generation are greedy for money. They want to become rich at all cost. So, they get bribes from inpatients and motivate outpatients to visit their private clinics. In their clinics, they prescribe unwanted investigations and insist to get the results from particular laboratories. The reason for such attitude is obvious to anyone. Often they prescribe drugs of unpopular brands othat are not dependable, to please the company representatives who woo them with free samples of drugs and gifts. Some doctors have their own medical shops managed by proxy. Others guide their patients, especially in rural and semi-urban areas to patronize particular medical shops for their personal gains. Thus modern doctors leave no stone unturned to boost their income. If doctors behave like this, how can we expect honesty from nurses and paramedics? There were reports of kidney-theft from patients by some doctors in Bangalore, Mumbai and Tamil Nadu. People who trusted doctors were startled by their heinous crime and became victims whose grievance can never be redressed. A kingpin of Kidney trade was nabbed in Nepal and brought back to India for trial. The fact that he is a specialist doctor has broken the hearts of people. What else could be more disgraceful than theft of human organs by doctors? Some sincere and perfect doctors have been hurt by this malpractice.

The care and attention of patients in government hospitals are inadequate though they are well equipped for treating all kinds of cases. This trend has paved the way for private hospitals to flourish and collect exorbitant charges which are not affordable for the common people. Though world-class treatment is available in India, it is accessible to only the elite. The low and middle class people can never avail themselves of the advanced medical facilities because they are already grappling with the problem of inflated cost of treatment even from a consultant physician. The consultation fee and charges for laboratory analyses are often raised. The cost of drugs faces an upward revision every 3 to 6 months. The manufacturers increase the prices whenever they want to do so with no proper regulations or control over fixation of prices. Corruption plays an effective role at all levels. Nobody cares about the hardship and inability of poor consumers to tackle their medical expenses. Soaring costs are not a matter of concern for the rich. The quality treatment therefore, is akin to a product of auction sale that goes to the highest bidder. The Health Insurance Scheme for people below the poverty line, launched by the Tamil Nadu Chief Minister Mr. M. Karunanidhi in August 2009 is a laudable step in the right direction to protect the health of the poor. But the Government must ensure that the benefits of this noble scheme fully reach the targeted group of people in an unbiased manner and without any erosion or exploitation by the implementing personnel, as it usually happens in the case of government schemes.

A public awareness programme telecast in 2007 by the popular 'Sun TV' focused on the Government depatments actively involved in corruption. A list of departments in an order of rank showing the proportion of corruption had been prepared on the basis of a survey. As per the list, the Regional Transport Offices clinched the first rank. In the wake of steady and enormous increase in the number of all kinds of vehicles owned by people, there are registrations galore. Consequently, the situation entails issue of driving licences to a lot of applicants and subsequent renewal of licences on or before the specified dates. Besides, the purchase of new mopeds, cars, vans, buses, lorries, trucks, etc. growing at rapid pace, involves numerous registrations and issue of certificates. So, the Regional Transport Offices are always thronged with applicants and their vehicles, and look like large business enterprises. Such conditions are propitious for the officials. They are so honest that they don't receive any bribe from the applicants with their hands. Adopting a subtle approach, they fix rates for every official action they take and collect bribes only through their agents, especially those who run driving schools. As for private buses, the officials do much favours to the bus owners and take huge bribes. For instance, while fixing the bus timings the owners' wishes are fulfilled, making their buses ply with overloads of passengers while the Government buses follow them carrying only a few passengers. The RTOs do not care about the poor revenues of and losses incurred by the Government Transport Corporations. Are they loyal to the Government which pay their salary? There are rumours of misuse of materials and spare parts supplied to the State owned Transport Corporation depots. In view of all these facts, giving first rank to the Regional Transport Offices is very apt.

The Department of Registration has won the second rank in the magnitude of bribery. In the registration offices of this department, it has been customary to put cash on the face of each document while presenting it to the registration authority as prescribed by the concerned document writer who tells the amount of bribe according to the value of the property to be registered. Apart from this, collection of bribes, for issue of copies of registered documents, encumbrance certificates, etc. and furnishing other information, is made and the consolidated bribe is divided among the officer and staff. Everyone's share is proportionate to the individual's position in the office so that there is no room for any altercation. The officials are very happy with their daily collection. The bribe-giver is always satisfied with the registration of his document. He feels no compunction about bribing the officials against the law and encouraging the evil. Thus corruption is a smooth-going affair in this department. The DVAC officials raided some offices of this department in the recent past (2009). But this action was not a deterrent to the illegal act of officials in the Registration Department. They have now changed their modus operandi by making the document writers their sole agents to collect bribes on their behalf and give the money to them at a safe moment of every day, totally avoiding contact with the concerned parties who are called in by a Last Grade Servant only to obtain signatures and fingerprints in the office records. The officials do not even speak to the parties as if they are gentle and honest. Their strategy is similar to that of thieves who find out ways to escape instead of desisting from theft when safety measures are adopted. It is appropriate that this department has been ranked second.

The Revenue Department is an important one in the Government's administration of a state. It is carrying out a wide range of duties including land tax collection, issue of 'patta' (an official authorization for ownership of land), patta transfer, issue of solvency/ community/ income/ nativity certificates, implementation of most of the welfare schemes, emergency services like flood relief, drought relief , cyclone relief, quake relief, coordination with fire service personnel in case of fire mishap, supporting the police to maintain law and order during riots, road/ train blockade, conduct of statistical surveys, dealing with Old Age Pension Scheme, playing the leading role in the conduct of elections and so on. Having various functions under its control, the department gives ample scope for its officials to get bribes. All their duties are connected with the public but most of the duties are carried out only after taking bribes. Many officials of the Revenue Department at various levels faced arrest across the country on charges of corruption but nobody fears about such action. Barring a very few perfect personnel, all are continuing their usual practice of corruption.

The Police Department has been vested with powers and responsibilities to maintain law and order and safeguard people. Until 1960, policemen were the true guardians of people. In spite of their low salary and poor living conditions, they didn't demand bribes. Whenever they visited villages, the President of panchayat (a unit of villages for local administration) or the village munsif would provide food and drinks for them. But those policemen would not accept even a cup of tea from anyone involved in a case. They were impartial, equitable and justified in dealing with the cases. They therefore, were revered by people. The true nature of a policeman was depicted in a Tamil movie- 'Policekaran Magal' (Daughter of a policeman) released in the late 1950s. Everyone, especially the police personnel needs to view that film now.

Corruption is the root cause of all malpractices committed by policemen. It impels many of them to collude with criminals and bootleggers in their unlawful activities. So, the moral fear for the police that had existed for centuries has now vanished. This factor has given room for a steep hike in crimes, namely theft, drug/child trafficking, arrack trade, rape, murder, etc. The culprits have been emboldened to feel that they can commit any offence and pay the policemen of their area. In other words the criminals take it for granted that the policemen would always defend them at any cost. They even consider crimes as their purchased rights. A Prohibition Wing of the police is functioning in States having district level units to eliminate illicit liquor. But there are frequent incidents of spurious-liquor tragedies causing loss of many lives and making many people blind or disabled. In some places, bootleggers were allegedly called to the police stations and the disputes between them over their area of operation were settled by policemen in their own interest. The more interesting matter is, policemen are posted to the Prohibition Wings for a period of probably two years in rotation, i.e. a team of policemen would be replaced by another team after the said period. Policemen vie with their colleagues to get transfer to this wing and spend huge amount of money to succeed in their bid. Those who get posting to this wing become rich after their tenure. The very purpose of formation of this wing has been defeated. Once the Tamil Nadu Chief Minister Mr. M. Karunanidhi wound up this wing. But the policemen rose in revolt and successfully forced him to revive the wing because most of them are always zeroing in on posting to the Prohibition Wing. The more disturbing factor is that many policemen commit crimes themselves as often reported. The crimes include illegal detention of suspects, harassement and torture of suspects and even innocents as instigated by their opponents, taking women to police stations at night-time against the law, molestation, rape, murder and fabrication as suicide, fake encounter and so on. A traveller was robbed of huge money by a trio at Koyambedu Bus Terminal in Chennai probably in 2007. The robbers were caught and handed over to the police. An enquiry distressingly revealed that all the three fellows were policemen in service in Tutucorin district of Tamil Nadu and had come to the State Capital on leave. Who can imagine or believe that policemen would stoop to robbery? The age-old eulogistic image of the police has been shattered. A former Director-General of Police in Tamil Nadu, Mr. Nailval stressed the need to 'bolster the saggy image of the Police Force'.

The Hindu Religious and Charitable Endowment Department is responsible for administration of temples. Immovable properties such as lands and buildings are owned by all major temples in India. Executive officers have been posted to manage the affairs of temples. With his cooperation, the temple trustees and those involved in the religious services of temples usually hide the income from temple properties and swallow it up themselves. In several places, they have gradually become the owners of the properties because of longstanding enjoyment. As the properties had been endowed by rich devotees of the previous generations, people of our times have no precise knowledge about the source or legal ownership of any particular property held and enjoyed by hereditary rights. Further, people have no inclination to probe the matters of persons connected with temples. So, such persons face no problems in this regard. 'Dheekshidars' (a class of votaries), who were managing the affairs of the 'Natarajar Temple' at Chidambaram in Tamil Nadu had reporteldy stated that there was no immovable property for the temple but enquiries revealed the temple's ownership of about 1,000 acres of land. Apart from many irregularities vis-a-vis property dealings, there are allegations of misuse of cash income of temples from service charges, donations, hundi (a box for offerings) collections, etc. The officials of the Government department condone all the malpractices in temples allegedly because of being beneficiaries. The holy temples have been converted into unholy collection centres.

The Public Works Department carries out all kinds of civil engineering works such as construction of government buildings, bridges, laying new roads in rural areas, maintenance of such infrastructure and irrigation tanks, etc. So, engineers and contractors call the shots in all activities of this department. They carry out works throughout the year. Most of the contractors save as much money as possible from the sum allotted by the Government for every work as per the approved estimate or tender, by using sub-standard materials and poor execution of work, neglecting the technical specifications. They bribe the concerned engineers to make them wink at the shortfall in the standard of their works. A share of the bribe goes to the superiors. While the cash component of cyclone/ flood/tsunami/ earthquake/ drought relief is handled by the Revenue Department, a huge allotment of money is provided for the Public Works Department to carry out reconstruction works that leads to an escalation in corruption. A catastrophe which is a bane of the people is a boon for contractors and engineers. At times, certain special works are entrusted to this department. For instance, sale of sand from quarries in the dried-up river beds and other sites was made by this department in Tamil Nadu. It was authorized to sell sand at the rate fixed by the Government. But there were constant and widespread allegations that the department officials had sold sand without bills but taken money from lorry drivers. They had also sold sand at higher rates. This evidently shows that officials are not prepared or willing to discharge their duties without cheating the public and the Government. The Highways Department makes no difference from the Public Works

Department in matters relating to engineers and contractors, their corrupt practices etc. The only difference between them is that the former's job is limited to the main roads classified as 'highways'. However, the allotment of money to the Highways Deparment is also huge as the roads are fairly long and most of them are connecting towns and cities. The scope for bribes therefore, is not low.

Cities are served by corporations of different grades. Towns are managed by municipalities that are also graded; small towns and villages by town panchayats and village panchayats respectively. These are all called 'local bodies'. Their primary responsibility is to provide people with basic amenities such as drinking water, street lights, roads, sanitary facilities, parks, playgrounds, drainage, garbage disposal, etc. In urban areas, they are running schools also. They construct shopping malls and the rights of occupation are auctioned to traders periodically. Vehicle stands are also auctioned. The rights of toll collections in bus stations, weekly markets, parks, etc. are also auctioned. In all the activities save education, the officials take bribes. The most important avenue to get huge bribes from a large number of people is approval of building plans by civic bodies. There are many other departments including the Department of Cooperation, Agriculture Department and Social Welfare Department which are not conspicuous in corruption. However, some officials of these departments take bribes whenever it is possible.

The State Electricity Board is partly involved in power generation and fully involved in power distribution, installation of power stations and electrical lines, maintenance of the whole electrical network in the State, assessment of power tariff and collections. Various kinds of materials are puchased-distributed-and stocked in the storerooms and office precincts. Often some employees talk about theft of materials. The officials of the Electricity Board demand and take hefty bribe for every power connection. Even for maintenance and repair of supply lines, the consumers are forced to give money. Power theft from high tension lines are common which allegedly happens with the knowledge of the concerned officials who are tight-lipped becaused they are offered huge bribes. As a result of administrative flaws and corruption, Electricity Boards are running at loss.

Banking was a reputable sector from day one. In the 1970s, Integrated Rural Development Project (IRDP) was launched across the country by the Government of India. The Project Offices, with heads and many officers representing various departments and administrative staff, were established in district headquarters. The projects implemented Central Government's schemes which focused on development of agriculture, animal husbandry, rural industries, etc., and training of artisans. The beneficiaries under various schemes were to be sanctioned subsidy-linked loans. This factor entailed a constant connection between the nationalised banks and the loan applicants. After a few years, the IRDP was renamed as District Rural Development Agency (DRDA) and the banks' additional workload was on the rise. Banks were unable to deal with a deluge of loan applications and the beneficiaries. In order to cope with the situation, some officials from out of the banking sector were appointed in banks. As I remember, agricultural officers were first posted to banks as Assistant Managers (Credit). In addition to the credits under DRDA schemes, grant of personal loans also gathered momentum. Thenceforth the evil of corruption in banks has been talked about. I don't know who exactly are involved in corruption in banks. But the present image of the banks is not as good as it was until 1980 in the matter of honesty.

The Indian Railways having about 11 lakh personnel and divided into many regions, is the largest department in the country. It is a department of the Central Government having its own annual budget which provides it with stupendous allocations of money. Among the various functions of Indian Railways, building of coaches and laying rail tracks are the foremost. As all the Railway Engineering works are done by engineers and contractors, corruption has become a part of the process. Purchase of various materials in bulk by the department enables the top officials to take huge bribes. Besides, a few officials indulge in odious acts. For instance, some shopping malls were found to exist at Chennai Central Railway Station, flouting the rules. Some high railway officials had owned many shops and managed them with benami. When the offence was unearthed in September 2009, they fled. The CBI bust 8 persons for multicrore railway recruitment scam in June 2010. Apart from bribery, scam is another problem found in the Government sector. The Comptroller and Auditor General of India has on many occasions pointed out overspending and irregularities in some government departments. Does it not indicate the existence of scam? In the fodder scam in Bihar State involving about Rs. 10 crore, the CBI named the then Chief Minister Mr. Lalu Prasad Yadav also as an accused. Some senior Indian army officers allegedly played a major role in issuing a 'No-objection Certificate' to a property developer in buying a 70-acre plot near the military establishment in Darjeeling, West Bengal. The Defence Minister Mr. A.K. Antony asked the Chief of the Army Staff General Deepak Kapoor to take disciplinary action against lieutenant General Avadesh Prakash, for his alleged involvement in the land scam. Accepting the Minister's advice, the army chief ordered court martial proceedings against him (Lt Gen. Prakash) and issued show-cause notices to other officers for administrative action. A court martial found Lt.Gen.P.K.Rath, Deputy chief of Army Staff-designate, guilty in the Sukna land scam and ordered a two-year seniority loss, 15 years of loss of service for pension and a severe reprimand in January 2011.

An Indian Police Service (IPS) officer Mr. A.K.Viswanathan's property statement filed by him at the time of joining government service had shown the value of his properties only in thousands of rupees. But a copy of Property Valuation record given to him by an auditor in 2007 had shown his possession of 8,400 square feet of house site and 29 arces of farm land, totally valued at Rs. 18 crore in the vicinity of Chennai. Besides, 5.24 acres of land valued at Rs. 5 crore in 2007 had been purchased in the name of his wife. Thus the police officer has amassed wealth to the tune of Rs. 23 crore. Apart from this, more than 500 acres of land were allegedly purchased by him in the names of his close relatives in Kallikudi area near Madurai in Tamil Nadu. All these details have been furnished in the biweekly Tamil magazine 'Junior Vikatan' dated 16th September 2009. A thorough investigation into any such case of possession of wealth disproportionate to one's known sources of income, could elicit something wrong such as corruption, scam or malpractice.

Transcending the Government sector, scam has infected the Information Technology sector too. The chairman of Hyderabad-based Satyam Computer Services Mr. B. Ramalinga Raju has manipulated the company's accounts to the tune of Rs. 7,106 crore as you have said. It is astonishing how such a magnitude of fudging the accounts could have escaped the notice of auditors. It is the biggest scam in Indian Corporate history. The Satyam fiasco cast a shadow over the quatily of corporate management in India. If we speak about every incident of bribery, corruption and scam in various government departments, boards and government undertakings in detail, it will be an infinite discourse. So, I have given just an outline of the subject with reference to a few instances.

Gopinath: That's true, sir. The known cases of corruption all over the country may be in several thousands. The lurking cases could be many times the number of known cases.

H.M.: By the by, what do you say about corruption in politics?

Gopinath: Nowadays politics has become the most lucrative business without any capital investment. There is no probity in public life of politicians. Their sole trait is avarice. With the purpose of amassing wealth and leading a luxurious life, about 90 per cent of the politicians lead themselves astray. They are always unscrupulous and brushing aside their oath of allegiance to the constitution of the country taken at the time of swearing-in, if they become Ministers, MPs or MLAs. They are prepared to commit any offence for money. Some members of Indian Parliament, for example were found involved in the 'cash for questions' scam. The Speaker Mr. Somnath Chatterjee had shown them the door. Later under usual political compulsions, the action against them was withdrawn. Three Bharatiya Janata Party members of Parliament waved wads of banknotes in the House on 22nd July 2008 and whined that the cash was given to bribe them to vote in favour of the motion of confidence in the Government headed by Dr. Manmohan Singh, defying their party whip. A 7- member Parliamentary Committee was constituted to enquire into the reproach. The main recommedation of the panel in its report was that the matter should be further investigated by an agency like the police. Finally, no concrete action on the allegation was taken.

The 'Volker Committee' report on the oil-for-food programme of the United Nations in Iraq named Mr. K. Natwar Singh, former Indian Minister of External Affairs as a beneficiary. The charge evoked wide condemnation and the Government of India appointed the Justice Pathak Committee to probe the report's contents. In August 2006, the Committee's findings were accepted and a notice was issued to Mr. K. Natwar Singh and his son alleging violation of the provisions of the Foreign Exchange Management Act (FEMA). Mr. Singh had to resign as Minister and then forced out of his Congress Party. The Enforcement Directorate initiated proceedings against him under the FEMA and the case was heard by the Supreme Court.

The Central Minister for Communications and Information Technology Mr. A. Raja was accused of having caused a loss of about Rs. 60,000 crore to the national exchequer by allocation of 2G Spectrum at prices lower than prevailing market rates. The reproach initially came from the Union of Employees of his own department, followed by opposition political parties. The Minister justified the allocation adopting the principle of 'first come first served'. The Communist Party of India (Marxist), terming it 'the worst-ever financial scam in the country', insisted in the Lok Sabha (the Lower House of Indian Parliament) that only a detailed discussion in Parliament and an enquiry by a 'House Committee' would be able to bring out the truth. The comptroller and Auditor General later in his report, reckoned the loss to the exchequer as a result of the 2G-Spectrum scam at Rs. 1.76 lakh crore. The entire opposition was up in arms over this issue and demanded probe by a Joint Parliamentary Committee. After resistance and reluctance for over three months, the Government conceded the demand in February 2011. Mr. A. Raja was arrested by the CBI. A leading think tank in washington stated that the Indian State was the "biggest culprit" for rampant corruption with reference to the 2G-Spectrum allocation and the scandal in 2010 Commonwealth Games.

A criminal case against the former Rajasthan Chief Minister Ms. Vasundhara Raje and five others was registered by the police as per the court directive in January 2009 in connection with the Deendayal Upadhyay Trust land scam. The trust headed by her was allegedly allotted land, valued at Rs. 50 crore for just Rs. 65 lakh and registered on 20th August 2006. She and her aides were accused of cheating, criminal conspiracy and breach of trust. In another case, the Enforcement Directorate registered a case on 9th October 2009 against former Jharkhand State Chief Minister Madhu Koda and his associates Sanjay Choudhary and Vinod Kumar Sinha on charges of making huge illegal investments abroad. Following this action, the Income Tax Department carried out nationwide searches on at least 70 premises associated with Mr. Koda on 31st October and seized voluminous documents, computer peripherals and other records pertaining to bank details and investments. The Income Tax Department claimed that they had found evidence of hawala transaction and investments to the tune of Rs. 2,000 crore after searches were conducted at Delhi, Mumbai, Kolkata, Ranchi, Jamshedpur, Lucknow and Nasik.The department sealed the properties of Mr. Koda and his associates in the first week of November 2009. Whatever may be the outcome of the legal proceedings and judgement, giving room for such grave charges against the Chief Ministers highly pollutes the Indian polity.

Corruption among politicians is rampant in India. Since it is unfeasible to tell about all the cases, I have mentioned only a few, pertaining to politicians. A former Tamil Nadu Chief Minister Mr. C.N. Annadurai–popularly called 'Anna' or 'CNA', who is known for his simplicity and real concern for the poor, advised his colleagues at the first Cabinet meeting after assuming office in 1967 thus: "People have reposed great faith in our party and it is our bounden duty to live up to their expectations. Your attitude must be positive. You must act fairly and according to your conscience". Has anyone of the politicians who claim to be CNA's disciples and following in his footsteps, sincerely adhered to his advice? In fact, they have buried their conscience and become corrupt multimillionaires but subtly display their hypocrisy on the anniversaries of Anna's birth or demise.

H.M.: It is said that corruption is prevalent in foreign countries also. Is it true? If so, could you point out some instances?

Gopinath: Yes, of course. Corruption is found in many countries but India is one among the few, where its magnitude is alarming. A former Prime Minister of Thailand Mr. Thaksin Shinawatra was toppled in a military coup when he was abroad in September 2006. While living in self-imposed exile, he was convicted and sentenced to jail in 2008 in a conflict-of-interest case relating to his tenure as Prime Minister. Thailand's Supreme Court ordered seizure of Mr. Thaksin's assets amassed while he was holding the highest political office.The court ruled on 26th February 2010 that his frozen assets worth nearly $ 1.4 billion, would "become property of the State". Another former Prime Minister of Thailand Mr. Somchai Wongsawat's associate was found guilty of electoral malpractice. The court held that the disqualification of any member of a party for poll irregularities of any kind would warrant the dissolution of the party itself under the Constitution in force. Accordingly, Thailand's Constitutional Court unseated politically beleaguered Prime Minister Mr. Somchai on 2nd December 2008 by ordering that his People's Power Party be disbanded for electoral fraud. He was disqualified to contest elections for five years. Along with Mr. Somchai's party, two of its coalition partners in government were also dissolved. In Taiwan, former President Chen Shui-bian and top officials were allegedly involved in high-profile corruption scandals in 2008.

In the 1990s, a cash-for-questions scandal blighted the conservative government of John Major in Britain. The Government headed by Mr. Tony Blair was hit by cash-for-peerages row that led to arrests of high-profile Labour Party figures and police interrogation of the Prime Minister. This issue demoralized the Labour Party. In

January 2009, four Labour peers including two former Ministers were facing allegations of offering to help amend legislation for fees of up to 1.2 lakh pounds. British Prime Minister Gordon Brown announced wide-ranging plans for constitutional reforms on 10th June 2009 that included the voters' right to recall MPs. He also proposed to include a legally binding code of conduct for MPs and rules to make it easier to expel those found guilty of corruption. As of now, members of Parliament could be imprisoned for up to a year without any condition to give up their parliamentary seat. The sanctions available against financial misconduct or corruption have not been updated to meet the needs of the times, Mr. Brown said. He also referred to the allegations that peers were abusing their position for monetary benefits, citing the suspension of two labour peers for demanding money to influence amendments to legislation and proposed a crackdown on members of the House of Lords.

In December 2008, the Governor of Illinois in the United States of America Mr. Rod Blagojevich was found indulged in corruption spree and arrested. He was slapped with many federal corruption charges for trying to sell Mr. Obama's vacated Senate seat to the highest bidder in return for kickbacks. Within hours, he was released by a judge for a fine of $ 4,500. After a four-day trial, the Illinois Senate voted 59-0 to convict him and he was thrown out of office on 29th January 2009. He was the first Governor to be banished by impeachment in 20 years.

The US Attorney's office in Newark, New Jersey said that the 10-year investigation "Operation Bid Rig" exposed influence-peddling and bribe-taking among a network of public officials and a separate multi-million dollar money-laundering ring that funnelled funds through charities operated by local rabbis. Forty four persons including three Mayors, officials, New Jersey politicians and prominent rabbis were arrested on 23rd July 2009 in a sweeping federal probe that detected human organ sales apart from corruption and money-laundering. Ed Kahrer, an agent in charge of the FBI's white collar crime and public corruption programme in New Jersey said, "New Jersey's corruption problem is one of the worst, if not the worst, in the nation".

Eleven French engineers had been killed in a bomb blast in Karachi (Pakistan) in 2002. Mr. Olivier Morice, a lawyer close to the investigation revealed in Paris in June 2009 that the crime was an act of retaliation at the French State's failure to pay Pakistani officials $ 33 million in promised kickbacks for a 1994 submarine contract.

Pakistani officials kept asking for the unpaid bribes for several years. Prosecuters were also looking into the possibility of 'reverse-kickbacks' or a repatriation to France, as part of the promised commisions to finance the 1995 presidential campaign of the then Prime Minister Edouard Balladur who lost his bid to Mr. Jacques Chirac.

After the Taliban was knocked out of power in 2001, Mr. Hamid Karzai became the President of Afghanistan and an elected government was subsequently installed, raising hopes and aspirations of the people. Since then American and other foreign aid in billions of dollars continued to pour in to make the country stable. But ironically, the politicians and bureaucrats have vigorously embarked in enrichment of themselves, brushing aside the welfare of the country and its people. Shamefully, every job from the bottom to top was sold for a price that ranged according to the position. Dominant officials owned gorgeous edifices and led an ostentatious life. Mr. Ashraf Ghani, a former Afghan Finance Minister branded the Government as 'shadowy and incapable' and attributed his resignation in 2004 to 'the narco-mafia's reign of State'. The President Mr. Hamid Karzai himself said, "The banks of the world are full of the money of our statesmen". Mr. Karzai's vow to combat corruption, while being sworn in as President for a second term on 19th November 2009, can be perceived as an acknowledgement of sheer corruption prevailing in that country. It is a pathetic situation for the Afghan people passing through tunnel but with a bleak prospect of seeing the light.

A former South Korean President Mr. Roh Moo-hyun had earned a credit of making his country more democratic and less authoritarian. But his image was tarnished when he was questioned in the corruption probe that centred around a payment worth $ 1 million to his wife and another worth $5 million to the husband of a niece by a shoe manufacturer. Mr. Roh plunged to his death off a mountainside on 23rd May 2009 in an apparent suicide. A suicide note he left reportedly said, "I caused so much trouble to many people. Please cremate my body. Please erect a small tombstone for me at the village". Mr. Roh had apologised for his family's involvement in the corruption case without admitting any guilt on his part. Whatever may be the fact, the multi-million dollar corruption had led him to death by committing suicide.

The Italian Prime Minister Mr. Silvio Berlusconi was accused of having paid his former British tax lawyer Mr. David Mills, $ 6 lakh to give false evidence in two trials in the 1990s. As a High Court stripped the Prime Minister of his immunity, the corruption trial against him was scheduled to take place by the end of 2009. In China, Justice Huang Songyou aged 52, who served as the vice-president of the country's Supreme Court was dimissed from service for taking a hefty sum of bribe. He was convicted on corruption charges on 19th January 2010 and sentenced to life in jail. Corruption is prevalent in many other countries also.

H.M.: What are the steps under way to weed out corruption?

Gopinath: There is no dearth of anti-corruption laws and enforcement agencies in India. Notwithstanding the functioning of the Central Vigilance Commission (CVC), Central Bureau of Investigation (CBI), Directorate of Vigilance and Anti-Corruption (DVAC) and Economic Offences Wing, the malady of corruption has flourished to monstrous proportions. The Government and the agencies have woken up to the alarming levels of this evil throughout India. A two-day biennial conferece of the CBI, state anti-corruption bureaus and other agencies was held in New Delhi in August 2009. The conference resolved to set up a national mission against corruption that will focus on the preventive and punitive aspects of the menace.

It was decided to make the Ministry of Personnel, the nodal agency for formulating recommendations of the mission and modernisation of the State anti-corruption bureaus and other vigilance agencies. The conference urged the Union Government to take steps to ratify the United Nations Convention against Corruption and also get parliamentary approval for the whistle- blower legislation as recommended by the UN Convention and directed by the Supreme Court. The Indian Prime Minister Dr. Manmohan Singh urged the anti-corruption agencies to set their trap for corrupt people at high levels.

The CBI and the National Institute of Criminology and Forensic Science jointly organized a two-day national seminar on "Fighting Crimes Related to Corruption" in New Delhi. The Chief Justice of India Hon K.G. Balakrishnan, while addressing the seminar on 12th September 2009, favoured a statutory provision for confiscation of assets of persons convicted of offences under the Prevention of Corruption Act. He said, "The rationale behind the same is that if a public official amasses wealth at the cost of the public, then the State is justified in seizing such assets". An investigation agency needs to obtain prior sanction from the competent authority before initiating prosecution against a public servant. But the sanction is usually delayed or denied. Pointing out this problem, the Chief Justice said, "It is necessary there should be a speedy manner of granting sanction. The prosecution becomes ineffective if the sanction is granted after 6-7 years". He also focused on the shortage of designated courts that had led to pendency of 9000 corruption-related cases. The obstacles pointed out by the Chief Justice need to be overcome by establishing more courts and expediting sanctions for prosecution of the offenders. While delivering the valedictory address at the seminar on 13th September 2009, the Union Minister for Law and Justice Mr. Veerappa Moily said, "Corruption discourages investment (foreign/domestic), harnessing of best technologies, resources, etc., that require transparency and fair play, and is an impediment for integration with global economy. The issue of fighting corruption and building good governance are of paramount importance for achieving rapid economic development". The Minister suggested wide-ranging reforms to curb corruption- "The scope of Prevention of Corruption Act should be widened to include gross perversion of the constitution and democratic institutions amounting to wilful violation of the oath of office, abuse of authority by unduly favouring or harming someone, obstruction of justice, squandering public money and collusive bribery". Mr. Moily expressed his view that prior sanction should not be necessary for prosecuting a public servant who has been trapped redhanded or found in possession of assets disproportionate to his known sources of income. He said that the Government of India would consider amending Articles 309, 310 and 311 of the Constitution, thus removing protection and safeguards that impede prosecution of corrupt public servants. He added that the Corrupt Public Servants (Forfeiture of Property) Bill as suggested by the Law Commission should be enacted without further delay.

Addressing the Valedictory function of the two-day International Conference of Jurists on International Terrorism in New Delhi on 22nd November 2009, the vice-president of India Mr. Mohammad Hamid Ansari said, "Corruption is an ailment that is pervasive, cancerous and multi-dimensional. In moral terms, it corrodes the social and political fabric of society and increases injustice; in its legal implications, it results in disregard for the rule of law; in its developmental aspect, it tends to distort the decision-making processes, shakes the legitimacy of the State, erodes sovereignty of the State and its capacity to exercise sovereign functions including ensuring law and order for the citizens. It has emerged as a significant threat to national security. National and international media is full of reports of how the elite are able to subvert the rule of law with money or influence". (After having lunch and taking a siesta, the headmaster and Mr. Gopinath resume their conversation.)

H.M.: What are the other remedies that you consider as suitable to annihilate corruption?

Gopinath: If we go to a doctor to cure an ailment, an efficient professional would first focus his attention on the aetiology. Otherwise, the treatment rendered cannot cure the disease though it may produce some symptomatic relief. Similarly, the causes of corruption need to be probed and traced out to facilitate remedial measures. Until two decades from India's independence in 1947, about 95 per cent of the political leaders and their party cadres were honest and service-minded. They had true concern for the difficulties faced by the common people. They regarded their political or government positions as opportunities to serve the masses but never as a means of earning money. Ministers and other elected representatives had their income only form their family properties and the Government salary but not from any illegal source. There were instances of some Ministers losing their family assets, being unable to balance their legitimate income and their additional expenditure that was entailed by their political commitments, for example electioneering. Some of them had no own house at the time of their demise. They served as politicians only for their pleasure, good reputaion and fame among the people. The remaining 5 per cent of the politicians might have committed some petty offences but were not involved in major corruption cases. The great advantage of the situation was that the same was reflected by the official machinery. The officials did not demand any bribe for their service. Ministers, Members of Parliament (MPs), Members of Legislative Assemblies (MLAs) and heads of civic bodies did not interfere in the office administration to get favour for any individual. They did not intercede with the authorities on behalf of either their relatives or their party men. Their interference in administrative matters was limited to either a common public cause or redressal of some individual's valid grievances. So, there was no illegal nexus between politicians and officials. Whenever somebody offered a paltry sum to a government official as a token of gratitude for timely service, the latter would neither receive it nor encourage such practice. Almost all the Government officials except a very few possessed this trait. Even those officials at low percentage having the foible to enjoy side income, did not demand bribe. Whenever money was offered to them, they accepted it covertly with nervousness being conscious of wrong-doing. Corruption therefore, was not a conspicuous problem in India until the 1960s.

In the following years, politicians and officials began to make a U-turn in their moral standards, attitude and behaviour. The previous generation of honest politicians were gradually replaced by the next generation of unscrupulous persons. In the 1980s, the number of dignified political leaders was depleted to single digit. Since then the virtues and values of politicians have turned from bad to worse. Most of the senior citizens and a few surviving freedom fighters feel quite nostalgic for the noble leaders who were eliminated by, in the words of Shakespeare- 'Time's scythe' and 'his cruel hand'. Former Indian President Dr. S. Radhakrishnan has said, "A politician thinks of the next election but a statesman thinks of the next generation". Most of the former leaders were in fact 'statesmen' wearing the coat of 'politicians'. The word 'corruption' itself was out of their thought. They were quite content with the salary and facilities provided by the Government. They expected nothing beyond that.They therefore, had absolutely no necessity to commit any crime or indulge in malpractice and unlawful activities. But how many statesmen can we find now in India? Does a septuagenarian or an octogenarian who has amassed wealth by misusing his/her official position, and is crazy about clinging on to power, deserve to be called a statesman? Is there any political leader who is ready to reject power but for Mrs. Sonia Gandhi? She displayed her unique quality by declining the position of Prime Minister in spite of pressures to accept it. Is any politician who eulogized her as a selfless leader, ready to follow suit?

The present political leaders, their aides and partymen are quite opposite to their honourable predecessors in all respects. They have no concern for the do's and don'ts in politics. They vie with each other for party's nomination when elections are announced. In order to succeed in this bid, they pay huge bribes to their own party district secretaries and some powerful functionaries to influence the party high command. Such inner party corruption speaks of the nasty situation in electoral politics. Even a party man who makes his debut for election reckons his electoral expenditure and the prospective income during his tenure. In order to win the elections, contestants adopt clever tactics and indulge in all sorts of misdeeds, unmindful of the law and the code of conduct for polls. Taking advantage of the people's weakness, poverty, illiteracy and a lack of political wisdom and awareness, the candidates coax them with bribes. It is at this point, the seeds of corruption are sown. Many restrictions imposed on candidates' electoral expenditure and method of campaign are violated. After victory, the successful candidates draw up their strategies to recoup their election expenditure first within a short period of time and then their efforts are in full swing to amass wealth by all available means. Those who become Ministers land in paradise to prosper and are able to do whatever they like. They misuse their positions for selfish gains. They create new opportunities to boost their sources of income, in the name of schemes, projects, transfer of officials, pacts with private or foreign firms, etc. The vast country with a population of 130 crore, which achieved freedom after paying a heavy price in terms of human lives, imprisonment and torture over a span of nearly two centuries, has now fallen into the hands of callous politicians who are not conscious of these painful memories. Fortunately, unlike some other countries, India continues to have honest Presidents and Prime Ministers since independence. But this factor could not be a deterrent to the wicked politicians in the context of Indian laws and system besides some compulsions on the Prime Minister to hold on to power with required majority.

On the other side, the quality of officials also suffered degradation simultaneously. As the honest officials made their exit in a phased manner on retirement or otherwise, the next generation of officials took their positions and emulated politicians as regards corruption and malpractices. They developed nexus with higher officers as well as politicians for collection and sharing of bribes usually in percentage terms. They have fixed rates for various items of work that are hiked while dealing with well-to-do persons.They are not conscious of the fact that they are performing only their duties for which they get salary from the Government. They behave in such a manner that they are doing only private service. In the matter of bribery, officials may be broadly classified into four categories. The first category consists of scrupulous and honest government servants who are unfortunately rare nowadays. The second covers officials who mildly demand bribes and accept whatever is given. The third is comprised of those who bargain with the concerned persons for more than what is given. The fourth category of officials consists of those who adopt coercive measures to extract maximum bribes from the people. Politicians and the Government officials have thus become partners of the large-scale business of corruption.

The bribe giver wants his purpose served earlier than the normal time of action or by violating the law or flouting the prescribed norms. He uses his money power to make some officials fall in with his desire. So, he is equally responsible for corruption as the bribe taker is. If anyone argues that corruption is unavoidable or justifies it, it is an irresponsible,senseless and reckless contention. The Government departments are spending the money provided for various purposes in the annual budget. If the custodians of public funds embezzle the money themselves, the public cannot detect how and when the crime happens. The system of audit is a mere formality. When a team of auditors arrive at any office on the scheduled date, the personnel of the office provide them with all comforts, namely accommodation, food, drinks, entertainment, visit to tourist resorts and anything the auditors may like to do or have. The office personnel are indulgent towards the auditors to delight them during their stay and also give them a handsome money when they leave after finishing the audit. The audit therefore, helps only to fill the auditor's coffers with bribes and safeguard the officials by burying their misuse and misappropriation of government money, thereby making the Government and people the real losers. The officials who spend money for the auditors collect many times the amount spent, from the people citing 'audit', breeding corruption further. The same is the phenomenon during detailed inspection of offices. How ingenious the officials are, in converting expenditure into income with profit! So, audit and inspection in government departments will be a complete farce so long as corrupt officials are engaged in service. People should understand the reality that no one except the poor gives bribe from his legitimate income. The money given as bribe should have been earned or will be recouped by some illegal means. An employee takes it from another bribe giver who in turn repeats the same crime. Thus, one case of corruption multiplies making countless cases that erode entire society like cancer which erodes the patient's tissues. Corruption not only lowers the dignity of the Central and State Governments and society as a whole, but also poses a grave challenge to the economic development of the country. As the poor and underprivileged people are also forced to give bribes even for their trifles, they have to suffer much. Corruption involving policemen weakens maintenance of law and order and paves the way for rise in crimes and scant respect for rule of law which will lead to disastrous consequences for the safety of the people. Communal and social conflicts, and a race to become rich or richer cause abundant problems which warrant a crucial role of the police.

In order to effectively tackle the problems before them, the police should not compromise on honesty and discipline while discharging their duties. As corruption defends and encourages misuse of government funds, it will eventually destabilize the nation's exchequer.

As corruption is a deep-seated problem in all the Government departments, it will be a tough task to weed it out. But in order to protect the honour and welfare of the nation, this evil must be eliminated at all cost. In the first instance, the relevant laws must be made to have teeth. Primarily, the corrupt politicians must be dealt with suitably. The elected representatives of people continue in office for a term of usually five years. So, they are tenacious to fully exploit their official position. The money amassed by means of corruption is stashed in foreign banks and invested in properties after keeping a portion of the illegal income to contest the next election with disbursement of largesse to voters. The most ideal remedy to this problem could be a firm action of every party leader to rein back his party Ministers, MPs and MLAs. But many of the political party leaders are allegedly getting shares from the corrupt Ministers who are purposefully allotted with lucrative portfolios. If the fence itself swallows the crops, what can a farmer do? Democracy is the best and peerless form of rule for a country. But when the Ministers, MPs, MLAs and their partymen abuse it and destroy the interests of the nation, what is the use of democracy? Does any democratic set-up permit immoral acts? Is such behaviour of politicians not abominable? Will it not eventually make the people lose their confidence and hope in the much vaunted democracy itself? The situation is already very distressing. Before it deteriorates and slips out of control, the Hon Prime Minister of India should come forward to give top priority to this burning issue and crush the evil with an iron hand. He may have an exclusive wing consisting of officials and intellectuals well known for their honesty, attached to his own office to deal with corruption in politics. An assessment of properties, bank accounts, etc., owned by present and former Ministers and heads of Government undertakings and boards must be made and action taken fast to confiscate the assets that are disproportionate to their known sources of income with retrospective effect, as suggested by the Chief Justice of India in respect of government officials. The wing must always keep close tabs on suspicious politicians. The corrupt representatives of people should be shown the door and debarred from contesting elections once and for all. He/she should be sent out of the party and disabled to join any party for ever. It must be made mandatory for the Prime Minister and the concerned party leader to take such actions against the offenders. But it will be difficult to enact such laws as most of the MPs won't support them since they are corrupt and averse to mend their ways. In order to overcome such barriers, the Prime Minister and his virtuous aides may arrange to groom the educated youth who are truly zealous for selfless public service, for future ministerial positions and MP or MLA status. At the time of elections, they may be nominated to contest the polls. Other parties including the Opposition may be persuaded to choose their candidates in this manner. If any party does not cooperate, the issue could be taken to people. Only the corrupt leaders and their cadres will oppose such measures. The common people who constitute the major portion of the vote bank will like and welcome the moral people to govern them.To make this possible, good leaders, patriots, educationists, intellectuals, eminent personalities, social organizations, the media and the well-wishers in all walks of life must strive to create political knowledge and awareness among the masses and impress upon them, the need to form a government without corruption. The people must be made to throw away the freebies given by candidates to hoodwink them into casting their ballots in favour of those crooks. Their deceptive wooing must be illuminated to the people who need to be disillusioned. If the voters are up in arms over a candidate's misdeeds, his money and muscle power acquired by corruption will become invalid. They will realize the importance of the evaluation of the candidates before exercising their franchise. They must be encouraged to vote for only good candidates even if they are independents. Though political parties dominate democracy, they are not so important for the common people as they are for the partymen who enjoy benefits in various ways. A political party is a group of persons who work more for their party than for the people, because their aim is always to hold power. As they discuss and decide on important matters themselves, there is no transparency in administration. Such a situation promotes corruption. That's why some party leaders do not like to form coalition government that will have Ministers belonging to other parties. Many politicians across India have criminal background. Even leading political parties in the country had reportedly fielded criminal candidates in the general elections held in 2009. Such persons becoming law makers is detestable. Criminalisation of politics should not be allowed to grow since crime is intertwined with corruption. Most of the huge bribes are stashed abroad. Eminent Lawyer Ram Jethmalani said in the first week of

November 2009 that he had filed a petition in the court on the issue of black money stashed away in Swiss banks but could not secure quick results due to court procedures, accumulation of cases, and the apathy of the Governmnet. Hence he decided to take the issue to 'the court of the people' with the help of yoga expert Ramdev. He intended to launch a mass movement in this regard. Such movement deserves strong support of various sections of the people, intellectuals, thinkers and the media.

As for government officials, it is easier to fight their corruption vis-a-vis that of politicians. If Ministers and other elected representatives function with a clean sheet, they will have the moral courage to instruct the heads of all departments to discipline their officers and staff for corrupt practices. A fiat with stern warning against corruption may be issued to every official. It will have a positive impact on most of the officials. If anyone neglects caution or defies the law, the incumbent must be dismissed from service. Many crores of youths possessing various qualifications remain unemployed. They may be called for counselling and preparation to firmly reject bribes during their career, and then appointed to fill the vacancies created by dismissals. Such actions must be given wide publicity in the media since it will act as a deterrent to those in service. For the first time, the Central Vigilance Commission (CVC) posted on the website in September 2009, the names of 123 corrupt government officials, most of whom were holding high posts. The CVC had suggested prosecution or imposition of penalty for their alleged involvement in corrupt practices. This is a welcome step. There must be a constant fear of severe action for involvement in corruption. Otherwise, officers and staff who are accustomed themselves to taking bribes can't be put on right track though the new incumbents could be edified. The officials holding high posts must be honest and dignified so that they can control their subordinates in all respects. If they are not content with their huge salary and become greedy for more wealth they resort to corruption. Such officials will spoil their departments and staff. So, they deserve retribution for misuse of their position. Political leaders usually advise officials to have close contact with the people. This advice could be wise only if the Government servants are honest and service-minded. But the situation is quite different. Since most of the officials are corrupt, this goodwill advice is always counterproductive. Whenever a member of the public approaches an official in his office, the latter thinks of what he can extract from the gullible former who is drawn to the office many a time at the cost of his time and work, even for minor purpose. The officials-public contact which is vital for development, in fact promotes corruption. So, suitable ways must be found to minimize the contact without affecting the administration, besides protecting the interests of the people. To do this successfully, some innovative measures and administrative reforms will be required. With the advancement of Information Technology, almost all offices have been computerised. This modern system could be utilized to perform all the functions of the Government offices. Every application from the public may be received by registered post and properly entered. There must be a time-bound action on every matter and the applicants may be informed by post. Adherence to this procedure must be closely monitored as delay leads to corruption. For instance, if there is an application for 'patta' transfer, the matter must be examined by the Tahsildar in consultation with the field staff and by getting required information from them. Then the order may be despatched to the applicant. Similarly, all activities in government offices may be regulated in such a manner that the doors for entry of bribes are firmly closed. If some bribe giver is caught and severely punished, others will be discouraged from indulging in this evil. Above all, social organizations and civil society have an important role to play in the fight against corruption. Vigorous anti-corruption campaign must be launched and the people must be made to realize that nobody can prevent or deny their legitimate rights and it is only their haste or hurry that emboldens officials to demand bribes. The bribe givers and takers must be discouraged from even thinking of illegal bribery. The suggestions given by the Chief Justice of India and the Union Minister for Law and Justice which I have cited, must also be enacted and implemented. Russian President Dmitry Medvedev in his address to the Federal Assembly on 30th November 2010 proposed to fine bribe takers 100 times the amount of the bribe. It is a wise suggestion.

H.M. : An incident in the past comes to my mind. One day, while I was waiting at a sub-Treasury, a senior colleague who was retired the previous day, came there. He was speaking so loudly that his words could be heard by all the staff at the Treasury. He said to them, "All the bills to draw my retirement benefits have been presented to you today. If there is any mistake in the bills, please return them to our office for rectification. If you find the bills to be in order, you may pass them for payment at your convenience. I can wait and get the amount whenever it is ready, as I have no urgent need for money". At that moment, I could not understand his thought. When I had an occasion to meet him in the bazaar after five days, he said to me, "The Treasury staff demand huge bribe from retiring officials to pass their bills. If we ask them to pass the bills early, they would further hike their demand. Hearing my words in that manner, they kept silent but passed all my bills the next day itself without demanding bribe. However, I just arranged to provide tiffin and coffee for them".

Gopinath : That incident vindicates the view that if anybody goes to an official and urges him to do something, he is forced to give bribe. The people therefore, must be enlightened and prevented from giving bribes. The corrupt officials should be given harsh punishment. Otherwise, they will empty the nation's coffers and push the country towards bankruptcy. India's dream to develop into a superpower by 2020 will therefore, remain only as a dream.

H.M. : I do agree with your presage. Thank you very much for your information about an important issue and wish your DVAC to succeed in eliminating the perilous evil of corruption.

Gopinath : Thank you, sir.

H.M. : Charli..........Charli...........

Charli : I am here on the veranda, sir.

H.M. : Shall we go home?

Gopinath : Please have your dinner here today, sir.

Ajit : Our dinner is ready, sir. Please come to the dining table along with your PA.

Charli : I don't want dinner.

H.M. : Then what do you want?

Charli : I want a job and you must get me that early.

H.M. : I have already told you that I would try to get a job for you in a company.

Charli : I don't want to serve in any company.

Gopinath : Why do you hate the company job? There are many good companies!

Charli : They always extract maximum work but pay only minimum salary.

H.M.: Where do you want to serve?

Charli : I like only a government post.

Gopinath : Is it your desire to become a teacher?

Charli : No. It is a useless post for the individual in terms of income.

H.M. : What kind of post do you prefer?

Charli : After hearing your conversation, I like to work at a Regional Transport Officer's office or a Sub-Registrar's Office.

Gopinath : What is the reason for your choice?

Charli : It is just because those offices have been ranked first and second respectively.

H.M. : One day, you will be given the first rank in a list.

Charli : Oh! What list is that? I am eager to know about it.

H.M. : It will be the list of convicts behind bars.

Charli : If it so happens, you are here to bail me out of trouble.

H.M. : Never imagine like that. I will not come to the rescue of any corrupt trash.

Charli : Hon C.N. Annadurai (Anna) has said, " The law is like a fishnet. The very small fishes escape out of it, whereas the big ones tear it off". I am not even a small fish but only a fingerling.

After having their dinner at Ajit's home, the H.M. and Charli take leave of them.

13

CRIMES TORMENTING PEOPLE

The headmaster and Charli arrive at Kumar's home.

Kumar: Good evening, sir.

H.M.: Good evening, Kumar.

Kumar: (Turning to his father Balaji) Please meet our headmaster, Dad.

Balaji: Hello, sir. Please take a seat.

H.M.: Thank you. How many children do you have?

Kumar's mother greets the headmaster and provides coffee for all.

Balaji: She is my wife Devika. We have two children. Our daughter is elder than Kumar and she is pursuing B.Com. She is staying in the college hostel.

H.M.: Kumar told me that you were in the Police Department.

Balaji: Yes, sir. I am a police inspector in the crime branch.

H.M.: It is an interesting job despite challenges. Could I know some information pertaining to your job?

Balaji: By all means, sir.

H.M.: There is a perception that crimes are on the rise. Do you agree with that?

Balaji: This view can't be denied. Though the number of medical colleges is increased every year and doctors are produced in plenty, there is a rapid increase in the number of patients suffering from various kinds of ailments and new mysterious diseases also crop up.

Similarly, notwithstanding the expansion and modernisation of the police force, crimes are on the rise. Thousands of crimes are recorded and dealt with every month in each State of India.

H.M.: Which crime is considered as serious? Could you give some examples?

Balaji: As you know, crimes are of various kinds. Among them, murder and rape are obviously treated as serious. For instance, sixteen children were brutally murdered at a house in Noida, near Delhi between 2004 and 2006, and the bodies were disposed of nearby. The owner of the house Moninder Singh Pandher, a businessman and his domestic help Surinder Koli were arrested and put on trial. The CBI Special Court in Ghaziabad in February 2009, convicted and sentenced both the accused to death in the case relating to the rape and murder of 14-year-old girl Rimpa Haldar. But Moninder Singh Pandher was acquitted by the Allahabad High Court in September 2009. The Bench made it clear that it would not affect decisions at the trial court level, in other murder cases, of which Pandher was a co-accused in five.

A freelance journalist came to India from Britain as a tourist. She was raped in Rajasthan's Udaipur district on 23rd December 2007 by Parbat Singh, a guest house owner on the pretext of giving her an extra blanket at his guest house. He was convicted in May 2008 but the High Court suspended the sentence in July 2008 and released him on bail. On the plea by the rape victim challenging the grant of bail, the Supreme Court cancelled the bail. Despite the court proceedings, such felony tarnishes the image of India as a safe tourist destination. In February 2008, Scarlett Keeling, a British teenage girl, was ravished and slain in Goa. Her body was found on a beach. Later it was suspected as a gang rape. A German woman was sexually assaulted on the Kappad beach, a tourist spot near Kozhikode in Kerala state on 14th December 2008. In another incident, a nine-year-old Russian girl was playing on the Arambol beach in North Goa on 26th January 2010. Anil Raghuvanshi, an Indian, struck a conversation with her mother–a doctor, and his companion Aman Bharadwaj sexually abused the child behind a rock. On a complaint by the girl's mother, the police registered a case. The Central Minister for Tourism Ms. Selja called the Goa Chief Minister Mr. Digambar Kamat and asked him to ensure probe into the case and action taken against the culprits. After tracing the identity of the felon as Bharadwaj and his accomplice as Raghuvanshi,employees of a Goan pharmaceutical company, the Goa police arrested the main accused in Mumbai and the other in Panaji on 29th January 2010. Such sexual crimes against our foreign guests make us feel embarrassed

An 18-year-old girl from Bhandarpadar village in Chhattisgarh State was allegedly raped in March 2008. She filed an affidavit before the chief judicial magistrate in Dantewada, naming four persons as her assailants. They were all leaders of the self-styled group 'Salwa Judum' movement that was launched against the naxalites and promoted by the State Government with the backing of the Central Government. A Public Interest Litigation (PIL) Case filed in the Supreme court alleged that the 'Salwa Judum' was guilty of serious crimes against the tribal population of 'Bastar' including murder, rape and arson. As the allegations were corroborated by the National Human Rights Commission (NHRC), the Supreme Court directed the state authorities to investigate and punish the perpetrators. As the Government's 'Action Taken Report' filed in January 2009 was attacked as inadequate, a few weeks time was sought to file a reply. But a deleyed 'Enquiry Report' filed in August 2009 stated that the girl in question had left her village. It also dismissed her complaint of rape as "entirely false", based on the statements given by the accused. Everyone's eyebrows were raised at the acceptance of the statements of the accused without probing the facts and the submission of a report to the Supreme Court in defence of the criminals.

Two young women–Neelofar (22) and Asiya (17) of Shopian, a town in South Kashmir, went missing on 29th May 2009 and their bodies were recovered from a nearby rivulet on the following day with bruises all over. Their mysterious death raised a hue and cry among the people. It triggered violence and unrest in Kashmir. There were suspicion and complaints of conspiracy, rape and murder. Agitations against the incident continued for many days. There was a reproach of involvement of some police or army personnel in the crime. Forensic Sciences Laboratory later confirmed that the two women had been sexually assaulted before they died. The doctors who conducted the autopsy found visible marks of violence. The State Government appointed a Commission of Enquiry headed by Justice Muzafar Jan to probe the crime. The Commission's report was released on 10th July 2009. It found that the media had misrepresented the facts of the case. The charges that:

1. Some Central Reserve Police Force (CRPF) personnel had

chased one of the victims.

2. The local police had sought to hush up the case on the orders of their superiors.

3. The two women were badly beaten up and gang-raped, and

4. One victim's brow was smeared with sindoor (vermilion) suggesting that the rapists were Hindus–were found to be false. But the commission failed to name those responsible for the crime. Following the Commission's report, the State Government suspended 4 policemen including the former Police Superintendent of Shopian. Cases of lying on oath before the Commission and destruction of evidence were also filed against them. Following an order of the Jammu and Kashmir High Court, all the suspended-policemen were arrested on 15th July 2009. The investigation of the case done by the Special Investigation Team of the state police was taken over by a 12-member CBI team on 17th September 2009. The CBI concluded that the two women had died of drowning in the local Rambiar Nallah rivulet and ruled out the possibility of rape or murder. But Majlis-e-Mushawarat, the body that was spearheading the agitation for justice in the case, called for a complete Kashmir bandh on 15th December 2009 to protest against what it called the hushing up of the case by the CBI. Whatever may be the facts of the case, the unnatural death of two young women is an irreparable loss to their families.

A 17-year-old girl was gang-raped by three youths on 12th June 2009 at Surat in Gujarat. According to the police, the rape of the girl was captured on a mobile camera. One of the accused–Abu Bakr, owned a mobile shop where he allegedly sold pornographic clippings. Both the other two accused–saeed saved and Tariq Sayed are sons of policemen. Their involvement in the incident had caused so much anger that the accused were beaten up by an irate group. Various organizations called for a Surat Bandh in protest against the incident, although the offenders were arrested. Many incidents of rape are suppressed by the affected people fearing about the future of girls or possible retaliation for making complaint to the police.

H.M.: What are the other crimes you are dealing with?

Balaji: Petty crimes such as theft, burglary, robbery, group clash, defiance of law and order, etc., are handled by local police stations. Prohibition offences and traffic rules violations are taken up by the respective wings of the police. Our crime branch deals only with serious crimes. As crimes are committed every day, it is not feasible to pursue each case. However, I shall recount a few more cases. A woman soothsayer Perumayee aged 35 at Palaya Udayampatti village in Salem district of Tamil Nadu, used to 'predict' the deaths of children, all the eldest ones in their families, at a village temple. A victim's mother had said that whenever Perumayee claimed that a boy or a girl at a particular house would die, the same would occur within the next six to seven hours. Six healthy children aged between three and seven years, had died from January 2008 to August 2009. The deaths created panic in the village and many villagers migrated to other places. Those who remained in the village grew suspicious about the soothsayer particularly after the death of three-year-old girl Priyadarshini in April 2009. She had succumbed to severe stomach pain. Before dying, she had told her mother that she was forcefully fed sweet rice by Perumayee and her husband. The police sent the bodies of the two children–Priyadarshini and Vinodh for postmortem and their viscera to the Forensic Laboratory at Coimbatore. The reports stated that the children appeared to have died of a poisonous insecticide. Then the police seized 250 gms of rat poison from the house of the soothsayer couple and arrested them on 28th August 2009. The duo attributed their crime to their hope of gaining mystical powers by virtue of such sacrifices. People must give up their superstition to get rid of deceptive prophets.

Sixteen people were shot dead by a group over what appeared to be a land dispute at Amausi village in Bihar state on 1st October 2009. As six of the victims were between 13 and 18 years, the massacre was shocking. In a freak incident, Mrs. Jharna who was pursuing her postgraduate course at Gauhati University in Assam State, was murdered, and her body lying in a pool of blood was recovered from the quarters of Mr. Birlang Narzary, a Reader in the Modern Indian Language Department, on 24th January 2010. Mr. Birlang was admitted to a hospital and undergoing treatment. According to the police, he admitted that he had tried to commit suicide by consuming pesticide after murdering the student. The victim was married to a doctor a short period before the tragedy as stated by her family. Such incident involving a university teacher and his student is very agonizing.

At times, the actions of the police are controversial. Nineteen-year-old girl Ishrat Jahan and three men were killed at Ahmedabad in June 2004. The police claimed that an 'encounter' took place in the morning of 15th June 2004 near Kotarpur Water Works on the outskirts of Ahmedabad. But Ahmedabad metropolitan magistrate S.P. Tamang has ruled that Ishrat and three others were killed in 'fake encounter' by police officers for their personal interests, to get promotions and gain appreciation from the Chief Minister. Mr.Tamang named the then 'encounter specialist' of the Gujarat Police, D.G.Vanzara and others as accused in the 'cold-blooded murder'. He also unveiled a long list of top police officers including N.K.Amin - Mr.Vanzara's then deputy in the crime branch police, the then Ahmedabad Police Commissioner K.R. Kaushik, the then chief of the crime branch P.P. Pandey, another alleged encounter specialist Tarun Barot and many other senior police officers. According to Mr. Tamang's report, the crime branch police had kidnapped Ishrat and three others from Mumbai on 12th June 2004 and took them to Ahmedabad. All the four were killed on 14th night in police custody. The police apparently pumped bullets into Ishrat's body to substantiate their encounter theory. The report added that the explosives, rifles and other weapons allegedly found in their car were all 'planted' by the police after the 'fake encounter'. During the five years from 2004 to 2009, Ishrat's family was in the doldrums. Her mother Shamina reportedly said, "The careers of my children are finished. They all wanted to study. They have no one to support their education. Today my children can move ahead". Ishrat's younger sister Musarrat said, "These five years was the worst period of our lives. It was difficult for us to prove. We were disheartened".

One Dinesh Kumar had boarded a train along with his pregnant wife Kavita and their three-year-old daughter. He had an altercation with two Railway Police constables, namely Ram Singh and Sudhir Singh who allegedly demanded money from him as he was reportedly carrying a cycle in the train. The constables later allegedly threw Kavita and the child out of the running train. The pregnant lady died and the child was badly injured. This incident happened in Uttar Pradesh State of India on 18th June 2009. The two constables were arrested. Instead of taking action as per rule against the passenger if he was found guilty, the constables had behaved in a brutal manner like terrorists.

The police sometimes commit atrocities against common people. In a gruesome incident, a composite force of Adivasi special police officers and security force regulars allegedly killed nine Adivasi villagers including a family of four and two visitors at Gompad village in Dantewada district of Chhattisgarh State on 1st October 2009. Two houses were also burnt. The police crackdown on the villagers happened, missing their target of naxalites. A writ petition filed in the

Supreme Court by 12 villagers accused the security forces of killing the nine people at Gompad and two others from the neighbouring villages, namely Velpocha and Nalkathong. The petition also held them responsible for the deaths of six villagers at Gachanpalli on 17th September 2009. A few petitioners who were picked up by the police on 6th January 2010 did not return to Gompad up to February 2010.

Causing custodial death is a crime committed in some police stations. Police excesses are common. For instance, a Dalit woman in custody was allegedly thrashed by Kailash Nath Dwivedi, station-in-charge of the Musafirkhana police station in Sultanpur district of Uttar Pradesh in February 2010. Vinod Kumar Dubey, station house officer and constables Hari Prakash Rai and Anil Kumar Singh of the Ghoorpur police station in Allahabad were charged with causing custodial deaths of two youths in the same month.The State Government of Uttar Pradesh initially placed all the four policeman under suspension and later terminated their services.

H.M.: What is the cause of increase in crimes?

Balaji: The present education has failed to inculcate morals in the learners. So, they cultivate some sort of vice. They also develop intolerance and a craze for wealth, power and ostentation. They nurse an ardent desire for basking in comforts and others' flattery. Some youths therefore, use their sagacity gained by virtue of education in the wrong direction. Their foibles goad them into committing crimes. Their infatuation for a luxurious life makes them unscrupulous. The advancement of science and technology has added new dimension to their evil thoughts and intrigues. Modern cinema also guides such persons through the methods to commit crimes. So, they are emboldened to commit all kinds of crimes in an intelligent manner. This could be easily understood from bank robberies at gunpoint and cybercrimes that happened in India and elsewhere.

Crimes are committed not only in India but worldwide. Some of the crimes are heartbreaking. For instance, after a tip-off, Turkish police found in December 2009, the body of a 16-year-old girl in a sitting position with her hands tied, in a two-metre hole dug outside her home in Kahta. A post-mortem examination detected large amount of soil in her lungs and stomach, indicating that she was alive and conscious while being buried. The crime was termed as "honour" killing allegedly carried out by the girl's family members and relatives after a "council" meeting, as retribution for her talking to boys and befriending them. Her father and grandfather were reportedly arrested and held in custody for trial. According to official figures, more than 200 "honour" killings take place each year in Turkey.

H.M.: These days, pirates are the bane of merchant ships on the high seas. Though this problem is outside the purview of your organization, I should like to hear your views about this crime.

Balaji: Piracy is a crime on the high seas. In spite of maritime powers' vigilant functioning, piracy has not been eliminated or even contained. It has grown as a threat to navigation, putting exports and imports at risk which has an adverse impact on global economy. Armed pirates gain access to any merchant or fishing ship using a fast vessel. They board the targeted ship even by using ropes with hooks and take control of it, leaving the crew with no chance of resistance. For centuries, piracy has been prevalent off Indonesia, in the Malacca Strait, in the South China Sea and the Caribbean Sea. But the crime in the Gulf of Aden has surpassed the crimes in those seas, since it is a busy shipping route that has provided an ideal situation for Somali pirates. They feel comfortable as their country has been in the grip of anarchy for two decades. Up to 20,000 vessels sail through that Gulf per year. So, pirates have ample scope for their misdeeds. There are many gangs in Somalia who demand a ransom of $ 1.5 million to $ 2 million to release a hijacked ship and its crew. The pirates use simple arms like assault rifles and grenade launchers. They pose threat similar to that of terrorists.

The merchant vessel 'Stolt valor' with 22 crew members was hijacked on 15th September 2008 in the Gulf of Aden and held hostages at gunpoint till 15th November 2008 by Somali pirates for ransom. Besides negotiations by the ship's Japanese owner, there were manifold efforts by trade unions, the Government and the media for the safe release of the ship and its crew. Barely two weeks after their release, heavily armed Somali pirates seized the Liberian-registered cargo ship 'MT Biscaglia' with 31 crew including 25 Indians in the Gulf of Aden on 28th November 2008. The vessel was a chemical tanker that was sailing between Indonesia and Europe. A pirates' ship was sunk by an Indian Frigate in the same month. The Indian Navy foiled a piracy bid in the same gulf on 13th December 2008 and arrested 23 pirates. Twelve of them were from Somalia and the other eleven were from Yemen. Pirates had hijacked over 30 merchant ships in the year 2008 alone. The navies of many countries were alerted against this crime. But the trouble did not come to an end. Priates continued their activities as usual. They began to attack an Italian cruise ship when it was 960 km off the Somali coast on 26th April 2009. According to the captain of the ship, 'the pirates had started firing like crazy at the ship," and tried to put up a ladder with hooks to climb up. At that moment, the vessel's security staff started firing at the pirates and sprayed them with water using fire hose. The attackers abandoned their bid and fled. The ship was slightly damaged in the attack.

A NATO warship foiled an attack on a Norwegian tanker in the Gulf of Aden and briefly detained 19 pirates armed with powerful explosives in the first week of May 2009. In the same period, Somali pirates hijacked a Greek and a Ukrainian ship. A pirate told reuters on the phone that they were taking the Ukrainian ship hijacked in the Indian Ocean with cargo including the United Nations' vehicles and industrial equipment to the Somali coastal town of Haradheere. A group of pirates attempted to board a Liberian-registered merchant vessel with Indian crew on the high seas in the Gulf of Aden on 28th May 2009. According to a spokesman of the Indian Navy, a Chetak helicopter that took off from an Indian warship launched a preventive action and foiled the bid for piracy. A naval search team later took over the skiff, arrested six pirates and seized huge cache of arms, mobile phones and rockets with launchers. A Singapore-flagged bulk container was seized by pirates on 15th October 2009 and a Chinese cargo ship was targeted on 19th of the same month, off the coast of Somalia. After that incident, pirates attacked a Panamanian-flagged ship 'M.V. Al Khaliq' with automatic weapons on 22nd October 2009 and seized it 180 nautical miles west of Seychelles islands. Twenty-four Indians and two Burmese crew members were taken hostage. The ship was released with the hostages on 9th February 2010 after payment of ransom. This attack took the number of piracy incidents in the Gulf of Aden to 47 in the first ten months of 2009. On 1st January 2010, a chemical tanker was on its way from Genoa in Italy to Kandla in India. While it was traversing the Gulf of Aden, it was hijacked by pirates. A British-flagged vehicle carrier was also hijacked off Somali coast on the same day. According to the International Maritime Bureau's global piracy report, as many as 53 ships were hijacked at sea, 1181 sailors taken hostage and eight killed in 2010. The waters off somalia accounted for 92 per cent of all ship seizures in that year.

H.M.: What are the possible steps to counter piracy?

Balaji: The growing piracy off Somalia often endangers the lives of sailors and passengers. Despite patrolling by foreign navies off Somali coast, piracy has been on the rise. Cruise ships were targeted many times. Due to propitious weather, piracy incidents nearly doubled in the year 2009. Pirates earned millions of dollars from seizing ships and taking crews hostage. Having weapons on a passenger or merchant ship to counter the attacking pirates is viewed as dangerous. Effective alternative means need to be provided to ships. Naval and aerial patrolling using advanced information technology must be intensified. Piracy has become a persistent crime in the Gulf of Aden which is ideal for law-breakers. Though navy ships patrol that gulf, they do not attack pirates unless they make an attempt to seize a commercial vessel. When it is necessary, patrol ships and helicopters open fire at pirates. Nevertheless, piracy is growing as a profitable business. Coordinated efforts of all countries with naval powers are necessary to eliminate piracy from the Gulf of Aden and elsewhere.

H.M.: By the way, politicians' crimes are at the forefront of all white-collar crimes. It is a known fact that there are many criminals among politicians. But some of them become the elected representatives of people. Is it not a matter of great concern?

Balaji: The various kinds of crimes committed by politicians are common nowadays. Generally, dominant sections of the society are enjoying high social and economic status in India. People from such sections possess a convenient and comfortable situation to do whatever they want. Many among such people are imperious, and have a malign disposition towards acts of crime. They never hesitate to commit any crime either out of self-interest or against their adversaries because they are not at all scrupulous. Many such people occupy high positions in various political parties or the Government by pushing aside the deserving persons, who along with the disadvantaged sections, continue as party workers until they die. Countless criminals have achieved political power with their subtlety, social and economic status, since educational status gets scant regard in the Indian polity. This power provides them with wide avenues to boost their wealth. Emboldened by this power and wealth, they not only commit crimes of all sorts, but also strive to defend themselves from prosecution or escape from the clutches of the law. Such criminals are successful in politics mainly because of two factors, namely the people's lack of political awareness and favouritism shown to them by the respective party leaders and their aides for selfish gains. As for the people, most of them fall prey to politicians' rhetoric and their freebies. Innocent people do not think about the wealth of elected representatives before and after their election, and so the difference is not evaluated. On the eve of next elections, people either forget or condone their misdeeds and crimes. The people are so gullible that they are pleased to vote in favour of a candidate just for some cheap clothes with no sense of revulsion at their crimes. Such ignorance and attitude of voters encourage those politicians indulging in criminal acts. They are confident that voters could easily be purchased or deceived. On the other hand, party leaders select their candidates on the basis of their caste and money power that could ensure their victory, and their loyalty to the leadership. The leaders feel no concern about the candidates' qualities or criminal background. They choose some persons who would work hand in glove with them, as candidates, in order to make them ministers later and get as much advantage as possible through them. Such a mindset of political party leaders give room for growth of crimes among party Ministers, MPs and MLAs. Regarding the police, they usually wink at the crimes of politicians. All these factors have contributed to criminalisation of politics in India.

In the Lok Sabha (the lower house of Indian Parliament) formed after the general elections held in 2004, there were 128 MPs, with criminal cases and 55 of them had serious criminal records as found in the analysis of National Election Watch (NEW). Compared to these figures, the number of MPs with criminal records in the 15th Lok Sabha constituted after the general elections held in April/May 2009 has gone up. As stated by NEW, there are 150 new MPs with criminal cases pending against them. 73 of them are facing serious charges. The findings show an increase of about 17.2 per cent in MPs with criminal records and 32.7 per cent increase in the number of MPs with serious criminal charges. The Bharatiya Janata Party (BJP) has 42 MPs having criminal cases against them. It has the maximum number among the parties that were successful in getting one or more MPs elected to the Lok Sabha. 17 of its MPs are facing serious criminal cases. The leader of the ruling combine–the Congress having 41 MPs with criminal cases is almost equal to the BJP in this respect. Twelve of them are facing serious charges. The Samajwadi Party which is dominant in Uttar Pradesh has 8 MPs with criminal cases and 7 of them are facing serious charges. The analysis of NEW on the financial status of the MPs in the new Lok Sabha has revealed that there are

300 crorepati (a person in possession of crores of rupees) MPs, showing a quantum leap from the strength of 154 MPs is the last Lok Sabha. It is now clear that political parties do not consider the traits or criminal records of those who seek party nomination to contest elections. Party Leaders have no inclination to probe into the past activities of electoral aspirants for obvious reasons. They give party tickets to contest elections at their own desire and with the sole aim of capturing power. They make aberrations while choosing candidates, neglecting the fact that wrong choice would cost the nation dearly. Such attitude fosters crimes among politicians. If this state of affairs continues, criminal politicians will lead India to ruins. Can any true patriot tolerate this scenario?

H.M.: Thank you very much for your vociferous explanations. Charli...

Charli: Sir... Are you ready to go home?

H.M.: Oh, yes. Shall we start?

Charli: You may please proceed. I shall come later.

H.M.: Why? What is amiss?

Charli: There is nothing like that. I have some engagement with Kumar's father.

H.M.: Is there anything confidential?

Charli: No, sir. I just need some help from him.

Balaji: By all means; what can I do for you?

Charli: I want a list of criminals with their addresses. I request you to give it either from your memory or by taking down the particulars from your records.

Balaji: Do you wish to deal with them?

Charli: I am not a police officer to act like that.

H.M.: He may desire to join them and share their booty.

Charli: I won't join dacoits or robbers because I can't withstand the torture in police lock-up.

Balaji: If so, do you like to convene a meeting of criminals and reform them?

Charli: It will be similar to a meeting of lions to discuss vegetarianism.

H M.: You are right in rejecting criminals.

Charli: You are not right in your judgement about my thought.

H.M.: Let us not be bewildered any more. What is your intention?

Charli: I desire to work under some criminal politician.

Balaji: Why do you prefer that kind of job?

Charli: It is far better to be the PA to a criminal politician than to a headmaster who is always expecting his pay day.

Balaji: In that case, you may also be arrested one day along with your criminal boss.

Charli: If it so happens, my future boss will arrange to acquit me of any charge.

Balaji: It will not be possible to bail you out of trouble. Your boss himself will be behind bars. Further, he will turn the charges that may be levelled against him towards you and make you a scapegoat.

Charli: No. I will never become a fall guy.

H.M.: How are you so confident of your safety?

Charli: I can defend myself and get absolved from any charge.

Balaji: It will entail expenses for legal struggle. Will it not be a problem for you?

Charli: No. By that time, I will have huge amount of money stashed in Switzerland.

All those present are laughing at him. As requested by Mr. Balaji, the headmaster and Charli have their dinner with him and then return home.

14
THE PLIGHT OF SENIOR CITIZENS

The headmaster and Charli arrive at Margaret's home.

Margaret : Good evening, sir.

H.M.: Good evening. Are you staying here alone?

Margaret : No, sir; I am staying in this quarters with my mother Luisa. She is now in the adjoining 'home'. I'll be back with her in a moment. Please be seated.

H.M. : She may come at her convenience. I shall wait.

Margaret hurries out and returns with her mother in a little while.

Margaret : (Towards Ms. Luisa) This is our headmaster, Mum.

Luisa : Hello, sir. I am very glad to meet you.

H.M.: Thank you, madam. Where is Margaret's father?

Luisa : He is no more on the Earth. He passed away in a train accident when Margaret was just two years old. After that tragedy, my in-laws had a growing antipathy towards me. Their aversion to me eventually pushed me out of home. In my bid to secure some livelihood, I was driven from pillar to post for three months. Ultimately, I joined as a 'helper' in this 'Mercy Home'–a home for the aged and the destitute. After five years, following the sudden demise of the then warden, I was posted to her place. Since then this quarters is in my possession. However, I almost remain at the 'home' and relish the service to the inmates.

H.M. : I am extremely sorry to hear about your woes. Time is the cure for all the ills of human life. I wish you to come to terms with the loss of your husband and the consequent hardships.

Luisa : Thank you, sir.

Margaret provides tea for the headmaster and Charli.

H.M. : I like to get from you, some information regarding the aged and the homes that care for them. Could you please oblige?

Luisa : Okay, sir. I shall tell you as far as I know about the matters that you expect from me.

H.M. : You are certainly engaged in a noble service. The homes for the old are gathering momentum nowadays. What are the reasons for this trend?

Luisa : The age-old joint family system has almost disintegrated in India and many other countries. A desire to go abroad seeking lucrative jobs, developed among the Indian Youths in the 1970s. Migration of young people was increasing slowly but steadily since then. Employment opportunities in major cities with in the country and abroad rose to a high level in recent years, especially due to the boom in the Information Technology (IT) sector. This situation has caused the mass exodus of youths from India and other developing countries to foreign destinations. Besides, many young people have moved away from their native places to work in cities within the motherland. These are the basic factors that have led to the necessity and growth of the 'homes for the aged'.

H.M.: Could you please expound on the present state of senior citizens in India?

Luisa : The aged whose children are employed in faraway places, automatically face loss of care and protection that are essential in old age. They are always pining for their loved ones. A few employees fail to extend any monetary support to their parents, usually being prevented from helping them by their spouses. Such parents suffer destitution, and lead a miserable life until death. Many employees send money to their parents regularly. But those parents also struggle hard to live. Their inevitable failing health tops the list of their problems. They have to seek medical aid either often or at regular intervals. Even to get treatment as outpatients, they need somebody's assistance to take them to the clinic and then purchase the prescribed drugs. If both the parents are sick as it so happens frequently, their hearth remains idle. As they are deprived of homely food, they are in desperate need to find someone to fetch food from hotel. If it is not possible, they have to starve. Even if they succeed in getting food from hotel, it is not only below the standards but also in contrast to the diet prescribed for them. Their deviation from diet restrictions usually leads to harmful complications that exacerbate their affected health conditions. Medicines alone cannot cure their illness. The supportive nursing care which is essential is not available to them. When the elders in such a situation need admission to hospital, they become helpless. If fortunately a neighbour or known person offers to take the patient to hospital for admission, the latter and his/her spouse fumble around in their house for articles to take with them for stay. Money has become the prerequisite for getting treatment in hospitals. But the sick elders are practically unable to withdraw money from bank. Even if they possess money on hand or arrange for it through some source, they fail to handle the cash properly. They are forced to depend on someone who deceives them into spending exorbitantly with no real concern for them. While lying in bed as inpatients, they feel starved of assistance and care since nobody is prepared to stay with and look after them although some visitors may call on them. The pathetic parents who were constantly dreaming in the past of their children's prosperity, could have never predicted that they would be left alone in the evening of their lives. The hapless senior citizens, with no possibility of assistance from their sons or daughters at a time when they need their help most, are impelled to live at the mercy of some persons outside their families. Though their children living in faraway places are affectionate towards them, their love is futile. A senior citizen has to lead a lonely life in despair after the death of his/her spouse, with insecure feeling. The non-availability of children within a short distance adds to the elderly lone parent's woes and results in psychological problems, rapid deterioration of health and early death.

Even septuagenarians have to stand in the queue irrespective of its length at the moment and wait for their turn in order to avail themselves of public services provided by fair price shop, post office, bank, reservation counter, etc. In the wake of rapid increase in traffic, senior citizens are at high risk while crossing roads or even walking along them for various purposes. They are at times knocked down by vehicles, even fatally. They are easily targeted by miscreants and robbers. Many instances of murder of elders for money and valuables have been reported. They are slain not only by robbers but also by some known persons or relatives. The aged who are wealthy and living alone are vulnerable to crimes. While they are not able to look after themselves, they are subjected to several external problems. The wealth in their possession not only fails to serve their needs, but also creates threat to their safety. This category of senior citizens therefore, need care with protection and not money only. Although money is vital for living, it cannot be or do everything in life. That's why even well-to-do elders undergo the ordeal of passing the rest of their lives. They are rich in assets but poor in their spirits, hope and confidence. This category includes pensioners who retired from high posts. Apart from monthly pension, they may have income from fixed deposits of money and immovable properties, namely agricultural lands and rented buildings. Some of them own apartments, bungalows, vacant house sites, plantations, estates, etc., which they are not able to manage. All such assets become a burden to them for want of health as well as the escalating costs of maintenance. But they are reluctant to dispose of any property mainly due to their sentimental attachment to assets. Besides, they are imagining the possible increase in the value of their assets after a period of time. They are alas, reckoning the profits from something which they are likely to leave behind at any moment and depart on their last journey.

There is another category of senior citizens whose children are living separately in the same place or nearby areas. Though the youngsters are engaged in and earning money from agriculture, business, government/private job or some other occupation, they do not extend any help or care to their parents while they are in a hole. Modern sons and their wives pick holes in the past activities of their elders and reproach them even for trifles and thus rub salt into their wounds. The senior citizens subjected to such harassment are in the doldrums. They don't have enough money to spend even for their basic needs. As the soaring prices of food and essential commodities have hit hard event the elders with some income or assistance from their loved ones, the situation of other elders is worse. They are not at all able to cope with the rising prices. They are living high and dry. Generally, senior citizens face neglect from relatives, officials, business people, etc., as they are of no use to them. But their greatest affliction is, the neglect from their own children. Ever since their children were born, parents had been paying utmost regard to all their needs. They had given top priority to their children's requirements and toiled for about two and a half decades to make them settled in life. They had taken extreme care to safeguard their children's health against ailments. They were rattled by even minor injuries sustained by their children. They had sacrificed their own needs and comforts for the welfare of their children. Notwithstanding financial problems and other difficulties, they had acted with gusto to provide education for their children apart from the basic needs such as nourishing food, clothes, medical aid, etc. They had also striven for their children's employment/ occupation after education. Then they had taken enthusiastic efforts to get their sons and daughters married. When a marriage was solemnized, parents had heaved a sigh of relief. In order to reach that stage, they had experienced a lot of problems and many of them had become debtors. Unmindful of several hardships, they had played their role at various stages for about a quarter of a century with a feeling that their children would be the only hope for their security and peace of mind in their old age. Having delivered the goods, they were complacent about themselves and optimistic that their children would shoulder all their responsibilities and give them relief, protection and happiness. Until rejoicing of their children's matrimony, parents never perceived it as a turning point that would push them into loneliness and lifelong melancholy. Since their parental obligations to their children were already fulfilled, they are seen as unwanted creatures and marginalized. Under Indian traditions, daughters are married off and sent to their husbands' homes. As for sons, only a very few are affectionate towards their parents and look after them. Others do not think about what their parents have done for their life and prosperity. If anybody draws their attention to their parents' past efforts, they simply retort, "It is only their duty and they have not done anything that is special. We are also doing the same for our children". The boys, when they become grown-ups, are not conscious of their obligation to provide care and attention for their old parents. They detach themselves from their parents and leave them alone, having no concern for them. When both a mother and father become old and sick, they are in a precarious position. The senior citizens therefore, face plenty of problems, irrespective of their financial status. 'Every cloud has a silver lining', but the elders leading a solitary life are always in despair. They therefore, are forced to take shelter in the 'homes for the aged', regardless of their financial conditions. Such homes, though necessary for destitutes, cannot satisfy those having children. Becuase they are deprived of moving with and enjoying the company and care of their kin, which they were dreaming of. But unfortunately, the number of 'homes for the aged' and the inmates have increased constantly, mainly due to the callous attitude of sons and their spouses towards their elders, that gives them no option but to stay in such homes.

H.M.: Do you hope for any improvement in the situation?

Luisa: The plight of the aged at present is not likely to change and it may worsen further in the context of the rapidly changing civilization, culture and lifestyle of youngsters. Ms. Indrani, Director of 'Help Age India', a national level Non-Government Organization (NGO) working for the welfare of disadvantaged elders, said in August 2009 that the number of people at 'old age homes' was expected to reach 10 crore in 2013. By the time the present generation grows old, the population of neglected elders would alarmingly touch 30 crore, she added. The NGO had obtained inputs from school heads at meetings and planned to gather more from the principals' meetings and consolidate the content on 'Caring for Elders'. It intended to approach the Education Department with its request to include a component on 'care of the aged' in the school syllabi at the 5th or 6th level and also to lobby the Central and State Governments to achieve it.

H.M.: What are your suggestions to mitigate the woes of senior citizens?

Luisa: Old age involves medical expenses for elders in addition to their cost of living. When they are forced to live alone without monetary support by their children, they are in desperate need of huge money from their own resources since medical bills are soaring high nowadays. As most of the senior citizens have already exhausted their income in spending for their children, regarding them as their future guardians, they are now in trouble. Their failure to preserve money for their own needs because of their improvident trait, has driven them to flounder at old age. In such a dreary situation, the senior citizens in possession of immovable properties must shed their sentimental attachment to them. They should not hesitate to sell off their assets like land or house with high value. They could move to a comfortable flat that may be purchased or rented. That won't cost much. The balance of proceeds from sale of assets could be invested in fixed deposits in banks or post offices that will yield regular interest. The elders can improve their financial position thus. Those who have done so in the past have gained financical security. If the sellers have surplus money from sale of properties, they can give it to their sons or daughters if they are really deserving of help. Otherwise, the elders may spend it for anyone who extend assistance to them. They may secure proper accommodation if they do not like flats. Housing complexes with such facilities as medical aid, food, entertainment, reading room, security and other services that are ideal for senior citizens, are coming up in many places across India. The elders who can afford to pay normal cost may prefer to stay in such complexes.

Wherever elderly people are staying alone, we find many problems with them. With their failing health, they are unable to tackle any emergency. At present, India has the largest number of the aged. It is time for us to ensure safe and dignified life for them. It is everyone's duty to provide their needs and look after them carefully. A humane approach to the problems faced by elders is necessary to keep them peaceful and happy. There must be a change of mindset among youngsters to bring forth a change to the present dismal state of senior citizens. The youths of today will be the elders of tomorrow. In order to enable children understand this law of Nature, lessons on 'care of the aged' need to be included in the school syllabi as sought by the NGO 'Help Age India'. Every senior citizen must be ethically enabled to spend the rest of his/her life in own home and not in the 'home for the aged'. Elderly people need worthy help and even physical assistance when they are unable to move about. The best way to solve their problems and make society healthy, is a revival of the age-old joint family system for which sincere efforts at all levels are required. It is now absolutely necessary to inculcate in the minds of children, the virtue of preserving the health, respect, freedom and happiness of their elders. The younger generation must be made to realize their responsibilities to keep an eye on senior citizens.

H.M.: Some of the elders suffering from certain painful diseases desire to end their lives and want medical assistance to fulfil their wish. Some doctors and thinkers speak in favour of mercy killing. Are you an exponent of this idea?

Luisa: Ms. Linda Fleming, aged 66, who was living in Washington was reportedly diagnosed with terminal cancer and feared that her last days would be filled with pain and ever-stronger doses of medication that would erode her mind. With late-stage pancreatic cancer, she wanted to be clear-headed at the time of her death. So, she became the first person to kill herself under Washington State's new assisted suicide law, known as 'death with dignity'. With family members, her physician and her dog at her side, Ms. Fleming took a lethal dose of barbiturate in May 2009 and died at her home. A person's intense suffering with unbearable pain outweighs his/her desire to live, especially when the hope of survival is lost. On the part of medical experts, the scope of his/her survival is assessed based on prognosis.

If they decide that the patient is terminally ill and cannot be cured, what is wrong in allowing such patient to prefer an earlier death to a torture, and assisting him/her medically to fulfil his/her last wish? A logical thinking would justify this action. Although euthanasia is considered as illegal in many countries, Holland has legalised it in 2002. The State of Northern Territory of Australia enacted the 'Right of Terminally Ill Act' in 1995 to permit terminally ill patients to opt for mercy killing. But the Act was held unconstitutional by the court, and repealed by the Australian National Senate in March 1997. The 'Death with Dignity Act' was passed in the State of Oregon in the US in 1997 which enabled physician-assisted euthanasia. England and Wales initiated steps in November 2010 to consider passing a law on assisted dying. Belgium, Switzerland, Luxemburg and Thailand are also in favour of euthanasia. Some thinkers held a meet in Mumbai to campaign in support of this practice. A few doctors in the United States, Australia, etc., were found to be assisting terminally ill patients to die. They were prosecuted for defiance of the law. In India, Kerala's Law Reforms Commission headed by former judge of the Supreme Court Hon V.R. Krishna Iyer, recommended legalising one's decision to die and decriminalising suicide attempts and drafted a bill for enactment. It is a laudable and sensible move, rejecting the age-old sentiments.

Ms. Aruna Ramachandra Shanbaug, who was working as staff nurse in Mumbai, was assaulted and strangled by a sweeper with a dog chain to immobilise her in November 1973. Her brain cells got damaged and since then she was in a vegetative state, lying in bed for 36 years up to 2009. Mashed food was administered to keep her alive at a private hospital in Mumbai. There was no possibility of any improvement in her condition. In a pathetic state, Ms. Pinki Virani, a journalist and a friend of Aruna filed a writ petition requesting the Supreme Court to issue instructions "forthwith to ensure that no food is fed to Aruna". Ms. Virani took such effort to find an early end to the life of her beloved. Following this petition, the Supreme Court of India on 24th January 2011, decided to examine whether euthanasia would come within the ambit of Article 21(right to life and liberty) of the Constitution. A case was filed in the Supreme Court of India by an organization - 'Common Cause', to recognize terminally ill patients' right to die with dignity, subjecting themselves to voluntary euthanasia. The petitioner assailed that the natural life span of those at terminal stages were prolonged artificially depriving them of their right to refuse cruel and unwanted treatment like feeding through hydration tubes, being kept on ventilator and other life-supporting machines. A Bench of the Apex Court, later in February 2009, allowed the 'Society for the Right to Die with Dignity' to implead itself in the petition to be taken up for hearing. The court rejected the petition for mercy killing of Aruna Shanbaug, while laying down guidelines on 7th March 2011 for passive euthanasia in exceptional circumstances till Parliament formulates a law.

Sir Terry Pratchett, novelist, while delivering the annual BBC lecture on 1st February 2010, called for euthanasia tribunals consisting of a legal expert in family matters and a doctor with experience of serious long term illness. He said, "The time is really coming for legalising assisted death". His views were backed by 73 per cent of more than 1000 people interviewed for a BBC programme and 80 per cent of 2,053 people who participated in a poll for the London-based 'Telegraph'. The object of voluntary euthanasia is to relieve the irrecoverable patients from their constant suffering with severe pain and ensure their dignity in peaceful death. It may therefore, be regarded as a humane action. Life is of paramount importance in the mind of everyone. If anybody decides to end such life, there should be a strong reason for the decision. But an attempt for suicide is an illegal offence as per the law enacted by the Government and enforced by court by punishing the guilty. However, both the authorities do not act to probe into the cause of such attempt nor do they take steps to address the grievance of the person in distress. The interest shown in prosecuting the offender, is totally absent in finding suitable remedy for his/her problem. Anyone's decision not to live, may be viewed as an individual right. Suicide attempts therefore, need not be treated as a crime. Kerala's Law Reforms Commission's contention in this regard displays sobriety. If euthanasia is legalised with protection against misuse of the law, the number of suicides could be brought down as some suffering patients also take this extreme step. Those who attempt to commit suicide on some other grounds must be provided with counselling for building up self-confidence, instead of being prosecuted.

H.M.: Thank you very much for giving so much information about an important category of people.

Luisa: Not at all, sir.

H.M.: Charli.........

Charli: Present, sir.

H.M.: This is not a school.

Charli: Of course; but we can make it a school for the aged.

H.M.: It is an absurd idea. Who will arrange for a teacher and pay the salary?

Charli: Will you accept if I make someone teach the inmates of this 'home' without any salary but for only food and a room to live in?

H.M.: The warden has to take a decision on this matter.

Luisa: I welcome this move. He may do it.

Charli: (Towards Luisa) Okay, madam. It will be done after the retirement of the headmaster next month. By the by, may I know about the schedule of diet for the inmates of this 'home'?

Luisa: By all means. We serve breakfast by 8.30, tea by 11 O'clock, lunch by 1 O'clock, coffee by 4.30 and dinner by 8 O'clock.

Charli: Is there no brunch?

Luisa: Since there is no omission of breakfast or lunch, the necessity for brunch does not arise. The schedule of diet is followed strictly.

Charli: Do you give extra items like sweets, snacks, chocolates, etc.?

Luisa: We provide such items to the inmates during festivals and other ceremonies. Biscuit packets are given on Sundays.

Charli: Okay, that's fine.

Luisa: Why are you interested to know about our system of food supplies?

Charli: It is just to decide whether the diet schedule followed here will be suitable for your would-be teacher.

Luisa: You are very clever.

H.M.: He is adept in assessing cuisine.

Charli: Thank you, madam. By the way, is there any age limit to admit a person here?

Luisa: No. A few deserted wives below 45 years of age and abandoned children are also living here along with many old people.

Charli: What are the norms for admission to this home?

Luisa: There are no hard and fast rules about admission procedures.

Charli: Do you mean that anybody can be admitted to this home?

Lui a: No. The person who seeks admission should not have any livel hood or anybody to support.

Charli: I may also satisfy your conditions.......

Luisa: No. Being young and healthy, you can earn money and live without anybody's assistance.

Charli: Do you admit educated persons?

Luisa: Education is not a disqualification to stay in this home.

Charli: I mean that an inmate of this 'Mercy Home' must be either a destitute person or an elderly person having nobody to help. Am I right?

Luisa: Your understanding is perfect.

Charli: I have a male senior citizen who is very suitable to live here. I need your help to admit him into this 'home'.

Luisa: When will you bring him here?

Charli: I shall bring him after two months by the same time when the proposed teacher takes up the job. As both of them are closely linked, they can live here together though in different positions.

Luisa: It is a wise decision.

H.M.: Whom do you propose to employ as teacher here?

Charli: It is none but only I.

Luisa: Who is that senior citizen to be admitted here?

Charli: It is none but the headmaster!

The headmaster, Luisa and Margaret are all startled by Charli's denouement, and after a little while, burst into laughter. After having some refreshment, the headmaster and Charli return home.

15

EDUCATION IN PRIVATE SECTOR

The headmaster attained the retirement age before three months. However, he has continued to work up to the end of the academic year as per the existing rules. He is relieved from government service on the last working day of the year. On this day of his retirement, a grand farewell party has been arranged to honour him by the 'parent-teacher association (PTA)'. In the evening, the school auditorium wears a festive look since it has been decked out in colour papers, balloons and flowers, and illuminated. It is packed by the students, their parents, teachers and staff. As the retired headmaster enters the venue of the function, all those present break into ecstatic applause. Biscuits and tea are served to all the participants in the function. Then the Asst. headmaster-cum-secretary of the PTA comes to the podium and begins to address the gathering.

Asst. headmaster: Ladies and gentlemen!

I welcome the headmaster-cum-chief guest to this function with a heavy heart. I am glad to welcome the parents, teachers, staff and students to this farewell party accorded to our beloved headmaster. But on this occasion, we are all filled with nostalgia for the period of his service at this school. Though he has served here only for a year, he is leaving many indelible feats for us. During his tenure, he has expanded the science laboratory and its facilities. He has also set up an English lab. to enable our students develop their communication skills in the global language. He has arranged for indoor games. He has taken initiatives to construct additional buildings for our school. He has arranged for the daily service of a health worker for sanitary maintenance of our premises and toilets. With his efforts, hundreds of saplings have been planted within the school precincts for green environment. He has motivated all the students to participate in sports and games with focus on their physical fitness. Keeping close contact with medical authorities, he arranged to screen all the students, teachers and staff for visual and other health problems. Some disorders with a few could be detected early and timely medical aid was provided for them. The outgoing headmaster involved all the teachers in holding special classes in their respective subjects on holidays to improve the performance of weak students. Though he extracted maximum possible work from the teachers, he has aimed to produce more State level rank-holders from our school. All he did was in the interest of the school. So, every teacher has sincerely obliged his wishes. Besides, he moved with all the teachers in a friendly manner giving no room for rival factions within them as it often happens in many schools. Such factionalism wreaks havoc not only on the good reputation and performance of the educational institutions but also on the future of the students. But in our school, we all stand together in all our endeavours to promote the standards of our school. The retired headmaster has been very kind and helpful even to solve personal problems of teachers. So, we are indebted to him for his guidance and help. We feel sad at his leaving this school but retirement is inevitable in government service. On behalf of all the teachers, I wish him to enjoy a long, peaceful and healthy life. The President of the PTA Mr. Jesuraj will now greet our chief guest.

Jesuraj: Ladies and gentlemen!

As the President of the PTA, I am delighted at the mass attendance of parents, teachers and students at this farewell party to honour our memorable headmaster. His activities have been quite distinct from those of his predecessors. Headmasters generally confine themselves to their duties inside the school. But our respected Mr. Mohan Das unusually involved himself in various outdoor activities. The zeal for social reforms and service has been innate in him. This has impelled him to undertake public welfare activities. He has organized many awareness campaigns in selected large villages against untouchability, child marriage, child labour, HIV/AIDS, climate change and illiteracy. In coordination with the officer-in-charge of the National Cadet Corps (NCC), he has conducted several NCC camps in different places. He has guided the cadets in the formation of link roads between a few villages which badly needed them. He has also utilized the services of the NCC cadets for clearance of rubbish and installation of spittoons in places where people gather, in order to throw light on environmental pollution. Besides, several thousands of saplings have been planted on road-margins and vacant government lands by the cadets as planned and arranged by him.

(Mr. Jesuraj takes a sip of soda and continues his speech.)

Education has become very dear now. Up to the 1960s, education covering all branches and subjects including professional courses, was provided mostly by the Government. Only kindergartens were run by some private persons in towns and cities. In the private sector, schools were only a few and Arts and Science colleges were still less, whereas Engineering and Medical Colleges were seldom found. They too were generally service-minded Christian institutions that were renowned for their devotion to quality education. Education was mainly under the control and management of every State Government in India. The quality of education was so high that several intellectuals, scientists, Nobel Laureates and eminent personalities had studied in government schools and colleges. In the 1970s, the State Governments began to accord sanction liberally to start schools and colleges in the private sector. Privatization of education gathered momentum within a decade. Rich people and politicians were attracted by the educational arena. Having power or huge money, they found no difficulty in getting government sanction to start schools or colleges. It was not a problem for them to get technical approval of the All India Council for Technical Education (AICTE) or the Medical Council of India (MCI) as the case may be. As for politicians, they can fulfil their desires effortlessly with their power and money that come in handy. So, they can establish any college whenever they like, without any impediment. Besides, those who embark on starting schools and colleges acquire vast area of lands.

The Revenue Minister of Tamil Nadu told the Assembly on 22nd April 2010 that 4,000 acres of Poramboke land (unused government land) were encroached upon by private educational institutions across the State.

They buy even hundreds of acres at market values but only the Government values which are always lower, are entered in the sale deeds. The cost of lands, paid over and above the recorded rates, is met from unaccounted money. Similarly, the estimates for buildings are prepared for an amount that is less than the actual expenditure. The cost in excess of the estimates is met from unaccounted money. In other words starting a new school or preferably a college, provides the best avenue for safe and lucrative investment of black money as well as illegal income. So, there have been enormous demands for schools and colleges, especially Engineering Colleges, leading to a rapid increase in their number all over India. Still, there is no let-up in fresh sanctions for educational institutions. Besides other schools and colleges, about one hundred Engineering colleges are coming up every year at national level in the private sector. This trend has let the private schools and notably colleges to mushroom. But after getting degrees, only a few find jobs while all others remain unemployed. In the context of globalisation and growth of multi-national companies, the candidates seeking jobs need to be talented. But most of the graduates are not employable, as viewed by experts. This dismal situation can be ascribed to the absence or lack of activity-based learning, proper infrastructure in many colleges and communication skills. In some institutions, students themselves have clamoured for adequate teachers and facilities to get practical training. But the authorities are apathetic to upgrade the standards of their institutions because they have not been started with the noble objective of providing quality education to students and preparing them for decent careers. Private schools and colleges have been established in order to generate huge profit. The managements therefore, charge exorbitant fees, neglecting the rates fixed by the State Governments. Time and again they collect high rates of charges towards various services and facilities connected with studies as well as stay in the hostel. The managements make every effort to boost their income by fleecing their students. But distressingly, their teachers and staff are poor in salaries. There is a certificate in the Government salary bills as - "Certified that the pay is in accordance with the qualifications prescribed for the post by the Government". But in private educational institutions, this concept of fair play does not exist. Taking advantage of the growing unemployment situation in India, the teachers and staff in the private schools and colleges are always exploited. Even lecturers are getting a monthly salary that is less than the total monthly wages of a mason. But the students have to pay abnormal charges. Thus, education in private schools and colleges entails huge expenditure. So, even middle class people struggle to cope with this situation and the parents with low income are at sea with the same. If this state of affairs continues, education will be beyond the reach of the common people and accessible only to the elite. If it so happens, can anyone be proud of having passed a legislation in the Indian Parliament making education a basic right of all children? There are some private educational institutions in towns and cities that are achieving a hundred per cent pass rate and producing some rank holders. They make wide publicity about their performance and draw students to throng their offices for admission. Having created a situation that is conducive to filling their coffers, they demand and collect sheer amount of donations. Some students and parents crave admission in such institutions at all cost. They are not conscious of the fact that such institutions had admitted only the students with high marks in their previous institutions, and it is the secret behind their performance. For every admission in the I standard at the age of five, these particular managements make an assessment of not only the children's talent but also their parents' financial and educational status to ensure their ability to pay huge amount of money to their schools. There are many parents who accept any conditions and do anything to get an admission to the desired school for their children. The reality is so abominable that some parents reportedly arrange to determine the sex of the growing foetus, name the would-be child, pay a donation to the school of their choice and reserve a seat for the child to be admitted after 5 years. Is it advisable for any democratic Government to allow the authorities of the private schools and colleges to scale the heights of commercialization of education, as it is happening now? The remedy to this problem is to enact stringent laws against malpractices in the vital sector of Education and to rein back private educational institutions, forcing them to comply with the laws. The standards of Government schools and colleges must be raised high by providing necessary infrastructure and imparting quality education to students. The teachers in Government service need to be given refresher course every year. The department must update them on their subjects. They must be given decent salary and encouraged to exercise their talent in teaching their students. Above all, the teachers must be fully devoted to their profession rather than taking it as a means of side income as many of them are doing now. They must be made to realize that theirs is the only profession that can shape the generation for the future. With the sincere cooperation of teachers and the active functioning of the Education Department, the State Governments can surely make their educational institutions transcend the performance of those in the private sector. The Governments must desist from giving the nod to start new schools and colleges in the private sector. As education is pivotal to the development of a nation, the Central and State Governments should give top priority to this sector and shoulder the responsibility for providing education for all children. The Governments need to strengthen their finances to succeed in this task. If they come forward to do so and mull over the advantages, the control and domination of private persons over education could be phased out in the course of time. Only if these measures are taken, quality education will be available to all the sections of society. In such circumstances, our Government school has been achieving a hundred per cent pass rate in + 2 examinations for 10 years in succession, although students with high, medium and poor standards had been admitted, for which I take my hat off to all the teachers here. The Asst. headmaster has given an account of the functions undertaken by the retired headmaster. When he joined duty here a year ago, I thought that being an official on the verge of retirement, he would not play any active role in the affairs of the school. But now, I am ironically taken a'back by his ineffable qualities and achievements within just a little over a year. Apart from his subject, he has taught virtues. A student who is weak in his studies but strong in moral standards can secure some occupation and live happily. But a brilliant student who is lacking in moral values will harm society and make his own life miserable. Hence, to grow virtuous and be a good human being is paramount. The outgoing headmaster has been swaying the students of this school to grow as good human beings. He is the epitome of a versatile teacher. I am aware that he has visited some homes of + 2 students and interacted with the head of each family. As far as I know, it is an unprecedented trait found in a teacher. It is a gesture of public interest. He has not visited my home probably because my daughter Hillary is not a + 2 student but studying only X standard. Besides, I had many occasions to meet him here as he convened the quarterly meetings of the parent-teacher association's executive committee regularly. However, I request him to pay a visit to my home at his convenience. I wish him a long life with sound health and peace of mind as all the parents here like him to possess. Now, I wish to ask the students' leader Prabakar to greet the chief guest on behalf of the school students. Thank you all.

Prabakar : Ladies and gentlemen!

We have had a rare kind of headmaster from every aspect. The Asst. headmaster and the President of the PTA have expounded on what are all the headmaster has done for our school. I therefore, do not have much to say about him. At our students' level, we were surprised at his approach to us on the very first day of his service here. Within a month, we could realize his heart-warming kindness to us. He has displayed care and concern for the students. Apart from our subjects, we were involved in programmes to develop our general knowledge. He has conducted 'Spoken English Classes' on holidays for students from X standard onwards. He has tried to edify students by teaching human values. He has encouraged us to take part in sports and games. Whenever we brought some problem to his notice, he would take necessary steps to solve it. He has balanced our learning and freedom. Unfortunately, his tenure at our school has been short. However, he is leaving with us many hauntingly pleasant memories. He is a versatile illuminator not only for the students but also for the society at large. I am not old enough to greet him. Still, on behalf of all the students, I wish him fine health and eternal bliss. Thank you.

(At this moment, Charli hurries to the podium.)

Charli : Ladies, gentlemen and future ladies and gentlemen!

I address you like this so that my address wili be listened by students too and I need not address the problem of their criticism that may force me to change my address. Now, my position is analogous to that of an uninvited guest since nobody asked me to address you. Mine is a spontaneous speech. All of you know that any voluntary role is far superior to any obligatory role. Who can be conceited of this quality?

One among the audience : It is none but only you!

(The audience breaks into joyous applause.)

Charli : I have hundreds of people here to applaud but nobody to think about my parched throat.

(A student gives soda to Charli.)

Charli : Take it away. It is now obsolete.

(The student hurries back and brings a cool drink. Charli thanks him and imbibes half of the drink. Then he continues his speech.)

Charli : A sense of gratitude is always noble. Hence I have taken up the role of vote of thanks. Let me set aside the custom of taking on this role at the end of the function for certain problems. You are all eagerly awaiting the address of the chief guest. If I come to speak after him, all of you will disperse quickly, leaving only the walls of this hall to hear me. There is another reason about which I shall tell you later. Now, irrespective of whether you perceive my words as banter, cause of your ennui or my ramblings, you have no option but to sit here and listen to me. First, I thank all the teachers for not wincing at my frequent visits to the school to meet my boss, i.e. the headmaster. On some occasions, 3 particular students joined me in swiping mangoes from an enclosed garden. One day, one of the stones that I threw at a mango tree inadvertently fell on a hound. As my act provoked the chase of the quadruped, the students helped me to climb up the compound wall and flinch away from it. I therefore, thank the trio for their help. Some students accompanied me to view the late-night cinema many times. Though I slunk away leaving the headmaster alone at home while he was asleep, the students never divulged my act to him. So, I thank them for being trustworthy. In the 16th century, a young boy who joined some wild young fellows in breaking into, and poaching deer from Sir Thomas Lucy's park at Charlecote near Stratford in England, later became the great dramatist and poet Mr. William Shakespeare. In order to follow in his footsteps, I went along with four students to the nearby hill forest for hunting rabbits. While we were scouring a part of the forest for rabbit holes, we noticed a forest guard at our heels. In our desperate bid to flee from him, I slipped from a boulder. At that moment, two students grasped me by the wrist and prevented me from falling down into a deep ravine. It was a close call in my life. So, I thank them heartily. Fireworks is an important part of Diwali festival celebrations. On the day of last Diwali, a few students met me in the bazaar. After a two-hour search, we secured a donkey. We fastened a packet of firecrackers to its tail and lit the wick at a corner of the packet. With rumblings and excitement, it frisked and ran amok. We and the people around were amused to see that spectacle. But the owner of the animal which lost its tail, later identified the offenders save Charli, and threatened them with legal action. Then the students paid some money to the owner as compensation and settled the issue themselves without exposing my involvement in the incident. So, I thank them very much. As the students joined me in all these playful activities and beguiled only the holidays, they did not play truant. Further, they decently suppressed such matters so that my boss was quite ignorant of them. To be decent on my part, I won't reveal their identity. As for this school, the students at large treated me as their senior although I didn't study here. So, I thank all the students. The 'parent-teacher association' has arranged this farewell party. I therefore, thank all the parents and teachers, being the members of the association. I accompanied my boss when he visited a few homes of +2 students. Then we were treated with affection and hospitality. So, I thank the heads of those families for providing us with drinks and dinner or lunch. They have vindicated a philosopher's notion that "the best way to a man's heart is through his stomach". With the same sense, I hope that the chef and his team engaged today might be ready to serve palatable dishes to all of us.

So, I thank them very much. I do not want to spend my valuable time any more in speech. Hence I take leave of you now. Thank you.

Asst. Headmaster : As much time has passed, many of you may feel hungry. Moreover, Charli's words have reminded us about our dinner and increased our appetite. Let us therefore, have our dinner now before hearing the address you are eagerly waiting for. Our chief guest will deliver his valedictory speech after the dinner is over.

Charli : I already expected the dinner to be served before the address of the chief guest. As I told you, this is the another reason for advancing my vote of thanks. Because I will be unable to speak after devouring my dinner.

(The audience laugh and clap their hands.)

All are savouring their dinner in a happy mood. They relish every dish as the standard of preparation is higher than that expected by Charli. After the dinner is finished, the audience is ready to hear the chief guest's address. The retired headmaster begins his valedictory speech. He is garlanded by Mr. Jesuraj amid applause from the audience.

Headmaster : Brothers, sisters and my dear children!
(retired)

I feel exhilarated to see this clan together on this occasion. All those who spoke here eulogized me as a man of achievements. But I think that I have not performed much to deserve your praise. I have been hailed as a rare teacher out of your overwhelming affection for me. At the time of joining duty here, I was on cloud nine to hear about the hundred per cent pass rate maintained by this school. However, I was anxious about the possibility of at least sustaining the pass rate. But the active cooperation of all the teachers and the students' enthusiasm for learning have reinforced my hope to improve our standards further. We therefore, expect the X standard and +2 students who have taken the Government examinations this year to show better performance in terms of scoring high marks, when the results are published. So, the parents of students studying here need not worry about their success. I request all of you to keep up the health of your children. They need to be in high spirits always. You may encourage them to study well, but at the same time any exertion of force must be avoided. It is better to give them enough freedom and let them play whenever they like. They need not always immerse themselves in studies. They may draw up their own schedule of studies and adhere to it. All parents have their own aspirations for their children's particular career. But at times their wishes are different from those of their children. Students have desires for diverse realms, namely Information Technology, Engineering, Medical, Agricultural, Police, Defence, Transport, Administrative and other services, teaching, business, banking, contract works, politics, arts, music and so on. Let the students choose anything they like after passing +2. Anyone can be efficient and successful in his/her career only if it suits the individual's taste. So, please don't thrust any branch of study on students against their interest.

The President of the PTA has been very helpful to us in discharging our responsibilities. In his lively discourse on today's education in India, we heard his outpourings of grave concern from his heart about deterioration in standards. He has highlighted the adverse impact of privatisation of education on the poor and middle class people, and underscored the need for the Governments to provide education to all and gradually eliminate the private sector education. I do agree with all his views in this regard. But in a democracy, only the people's power could pervail upon the Governments to usher in any reforms, especially radical changes in education that are essential for the welfare of the people. So, the people must be woken up to the seriousness of growing privatisation and commercialisation of education, and motivated to influence upon the Governments to take remedial measures. Students and educationists need to extend their support to achieve success in this endeavour. The President has asked me to visit his home. I shall soon visit his home as well as those of some +2 students whom I had assured to visit, but could not fulfil that for want of time. I find a strong unity among, and robust performance by the teachers of this school. I hope you will continue the same trend. Whenever students commit mistakes in studies or behaviour, I would like you to deal with them smoothly and put them on right track so that the same mistakes will not recur. Please don't rattle them for anything but try to deter them from making mistakes. The best approach to their affairs is to act like a guide and a senior friend. I hope that the teachers would agree with my points of view.

As for students, I have conveyed a plethora of views on many occasions at this school. Still, I like to tell you a little more now. Your cardinal principle must be to realize the difficulties, struggles and sacrifices of your parents to bring you up, provide education and all your needs, and make you settled in life. You must be grateful and loyal to them always and never betray their trust in you at any cost. I expect you to fulfil your obligation to cherish your parents, especially when they are in their twilight years. You should not relegate them to the back of your mind in the wake of any event or situation such as employment, marriage, foreign job or business, prosperity, joy, wealth, etc. You must be conscious that your parents are not only the cause of your advent on the Earth but also the basis of every aspect of your life. Everyone must strive to be a good human being in all respects as pointed out by the President. You should also respect your teachers and abide by their advice. I would like you not to cultivate any foible since it will be a stain on your character. If you study your books consistently form day one, the pressure of studies and consequent loss of sleep and health on the eve of examinations can be averted. The jitters before examinations could also be avoided by self-confidence and interest which gradually develop during consistent learning. You need to hone your communication skills in English, following the guidance provided for you in the classes arranged for this purpopse. In this effort, you should not be addicted to slang as now found among many college students. I like to advise you to take part in declamation contests which will enable you shed your diffidence and bashfulness. The Government library is at present functioning in a rented building away from our school. We have secured 0.5 acre of donated land for construction of own building for the library. Since it is round the corner, you will find it very convenient and useful when the public library is shifted to the new building and enlarged. The use of Information Technology has become a part of all kinds of activities. We therefore, have taken necessary steps to get adequate provision of computers for our needs. Our proposal is in the pipeline. You can make optimum use of them and gain advantage after they are supplied probably in the coming year. We have been doing some social services hitherto. I would like you to continue them during vacations. You can make foray into some new activities. For instance, you may collect information on illiterate elders and teach them the three Rs on holidays. I have also decided to devote myself to social service in tandem with Anand's father Mr. Nagesh who is a social activist besides being an agent for the LIC. Are you puzzled? I have determined to settle and spend the rest of my life in Madapuri itself. (There is a thunderous applause from the audience as a token of their acclamation.) I will be a part of you in any public welfare activities. I am always prepared to serve the people of this area. Some of the students know about my only younger brother Ram who is working at a company in Bangalore. In view of my liking for this place, Ram has decided to establish a small scale industrial unit here and shift his family from Bangalore to Madapuri. Charli will be employed in the new unit and he will continue to stay with me. So, we will be in your midst. I wish the students and teachers success in all their endeavours. I wish the parents to enjoy good health and happiness. I thank all of you for honouring me with this party and your affection for me. Finally, there is one more thing that I like to tell you now. I had asked the +2 students to write a short poem on any topic of their choice. It was neither a compulsion nor a competition but just some encouragement to them to develop their literary spirit. Thirteen students have written poems and given to me. All of them have made sincere attempts to become budding poets and I wish to pat them on the back. Among their poems, the one written by Kaviya has inspired me. So, I desire to give her a personal prize. I request the girl to come to the podium now.

(Kaviya hurries towards the retired headmaster. He gives her a cup made of pure silver and congratulates her on her poetic skill. She kneels down before him and gets his blessing. She is all smiles and walks back.)

I am confident that anyone who is conscious of realities and truth will not take exception to the theme of this poem, and will surely accept it. I shall now read the poem as a food for your thought.

"Thou art the Almighty, Nature!

Bow all we with high rapture

For thy grace in bounty

Showered on every country!

We implore thee, our path

Be laid on pure truth,

Devoid of any evils-and

Avoid all possible perils.

We pray thee, please enjoin

Compassion that can join

The elite having inane hearts

And the poor having inert hearths.

We beg thee, preach love

That makes man learn how

He should his brethren love

And all that on the globe live.

Oh, Lord! We are panting

For virtues and values haunting

To eliminate immense woes many

And celebrate communal harmony.

We beseech thee, kindly bestow

Boundless reason and gusto

Upon mankind to enjoy health

That transcends all wealth."

Charli is ringing the school bell which is symbolic of closing the function.

* * * * *

INDEX

J

S